# Motivational Interviewing

Children and Young People II:
Issues and Further Applications

**Edited by Dr Eddie McNamara**

**Positive Behaviour Management**

**PBM**
7 Quinton Close
Ainsdale
Merseyside PR8 2TD

www.positivebehaviourmanagement.co.uk

First published 2014 by Positive Behaviour Management (PBM)
7 Quinton Close
Ainsdale
Merseyside
PR8 2TD

Tel: 01704 575441
Email: gmcnam7929@aol.com

© Dr Eddie McNamara

All rights reserved. No part of this book may be reprinted or reproduced or utilised in any form or by any electronic mechanical or other means now known or hereafter invented including photocopying and recording, or in any information storage or retrieval system, without permission in writing from the publishers.

ISBN 978-0-9562918-1-3

## Acknowledgements

This book is dedicated to my wife Joan for her unconditional support and encouragement: my children George and his wife-to-be Emma, Edward Jnr., his wife Jo and Christine - for being there - and grandson Matthew Joseph for the joy he brings to all of us.

# Contents

| | | |
|---|---|---|
| *Acknowledgements* | | *iii* |
| *List of Contributors* | | *vii* |
| *Preface* | | *xi* |

**Part 1** — 1

**Issues**

| Chapter 1 | **Motivational Interviewing and Professional Practice**<br>Garry Squires | 3 |
|---|---|---|
| Chapter 2 | **Motivational Interviewing and the Transtheoretical Model**<br>Cathy Atkinson | 17 |
| Chapter 3 | **Motivational Interviewing and Evidence-Based Practice**<br>Kevin Woods, Patrick McArdle and Nadia Tabassum | 33 |

**Part 2** — 47

**Further Applications**

| Chapter 4 | **Motivational Interviewing with Children and Young People: an Overview**<br>Sebastian G Kaplan | 49 |
|---|---|---|

**Section 1** — 59

**Motivational Interviewing in Educational Settings**

| Chapter 5 | **Motivational Interviewing and Group Work**<br>Craig Bridge | 61 |
|---|---|---|
| Chapter 6 | **Motivational Interviewing and Promoting Self-Esteem**<br>Claudia Moss | 73 |
| Chapter 7 | **Motivational Interviewing in Support of Teacher Behaviour Change**<br>Jon Lee, Andy Frey, Jason Small, Hill Walker, Annemieke Golly, Edward Feil, Pam Ratcliffe and Allyson Rutledge | 83 |
| Chapter 8 | **Motivational Interviewing and Training School Student Services**<br>Scott Caldwell and Susan Kaye | 103 |

*vi*

## Section 2         121

### Motivational Interviewing in Clinical Settings

| Chapter 9 | **Motivational Interviewing and Anxiety Management** <br> Roger Lakin | 123 |
|---|---|---|
| Chapter 10 | **Motivational Interviewing and Diabetes Mellitus** <br> John Roberts | 143 |

## Section 3         165

### Motivational Interviewing in the Community

| Chapter 11 | **Motivational Interviewing and Looked After children (LAC)** <br> Eleanor Thomas | 167 |
|---|---|---|

## Section 4         193

### Integrating Motivational Interviewing and Therapeutic Interventions

| Chapter 12 | **Motivational Interviewing and Cognitive-Behavioural Interventions** <br> Garry Squires | 195 |
|---|---|---|
| Chapter 13 | **Motivational Interviewing and Choice Theory** <br> Geraldine Rowe | 209 |
| Chapter 14 | **Motivational Interviewing and Solution Focused Approaches** <br> Mawuli Amesu | 225 |
| Chapter 15 | **Concluding Observations** <br> Eddie McNamara | 239 |

# Contributors

**Eddie McNamara** works as an Independent Educational Psychologist. He has written extensively in the areas of the prevention and management of problem behaviour, changing behaviour through changing how young people think about their behaviour and eliciting motivation to change from children and young people. Eddie has written books, chapters and articles of a very practical nature in these areas.

**Kevin Woods, Garry Squires** and **Cathy Atkinson** are registered practitioner educational psychologists working at the University of Manchester Institute of Education (UMIE). All three are involved in training psychologists and in research that explores how therapeutic approaches can be used in educational settings. They all have an interest in motivational interviewing and have taken different slants based on their other work. Kevin's related work has focused upon narrative therapy, solution focused brief therapy, and child protection; Garry has expertise in cognitive behavioural therapy. Cathy has looked at ways to develop motivational interviewing practices for non-specialists working with children and young people.

**Patrick McArdle** and **Nadia Tabassum** are Educational Psychologists who were following a Doctoral Training Programme at the time of contributing to chapter 3.

**Sebastian G. Kaplan,** Ph.D., is a clinical psychologist and Assistant Professor in the Department of Psychiatry and Behavioral Medicine, Child and Adolescent Psychiatry Section, Wake Forest University School of Medicine. He is also a member of the Motivational Interviewing Network of Trainers (MINT), providing training in MI for mental health providers, health care practitioners, and school-based professionals. His clinical and research interests include the application of MI for adolescents and families.

**Craig Bridge** has been working for Lincolnshire County Council as an Educational Psychologist for 9 years. He is currently working within the Specialist Teacher and Applied Psychology Service and has been working using MI for 6 years. This work has included individual application of MI with Key Stage 2 to Key Stage 4 pupils, with adults via peer support, in groups and organisationally with Head Teachers, Teaching Assistants and whole staff. Craig has also been developing systemic approaches in psychology and the application of CBT with all client groups through his routine Educational Psychology practice.

**Claudia Moss** works for Leeds City Council Psychology Service. Claudia has a particular interest in the use of MI as an intervention to elicit motivational change, supporting young person themselves to be actively involved in exploring their behaviour and initiating change. Her doctoral thesis [2010] focused on the impact of a group based MI approach on pupil self-esteem.

Chapter 7 was written by an interdisciplinary team of researchers and practitioners from the University of Cincinnati (**Jon Lee**), the University of Louisville (**Andy Frey, Pam Ratcliffe,** and **Ally Rutledge**), the Oregon Research Institute (**John Seeley, Jason Small,** and **Ed Feil**), and the University of Oregon (**Hill Walker** and **Annemeike Golly**).

*viii*

Hill Walker is the senior author of the First Step to Success early intervention program, and served as the Principal Investigator, along with Dr. Frey on the Department of Education, Institute for Education Sciences grant that supported this work. John Seeley, Annemeike Golly and Ed Feil served as co-investigators. Jason Small conducted the data analysis, and Ally Rutledge, Pam Ratcliff, and Dr. Lee served as coaches, and were also instrumental in developing the procedural manual for the First Step Classroom Check-Up.

**Scott Caldwell,** M.A., Is a member of the Motivational Interviewing Network of Trainers and coordinates SBIRT (Screening, Brief Intervention and Referral to Treatment) at the Wisconsin Department of Health Services.

**Suzanne Kaye,** MSSW, is a member of the Motivational Interviewing Network of Trainers and since 1993 has worked as a certified K-12 School Social Worker in Wisconsin.

**Roger Lakin** is a Consultant and Honorary Senior Lecturer in Child and Adolescent Psychiatry. He works in East Leeds CAMHS (Child and Adolescent Mental Health Services) and has an MSc in Clinical Psychiatry and a Post Graduate Diploma in Cognitive Therapy. Areas of interest include cognitive behavioural therapy, motivational interviewing, mood and anxiety disorders and the mental health of young offenders. Roger is a trainer of Specialist Trainees in Psychiatry and teaches medical students from Leeds University on Child Mental Health as part of their Paediatric training.

**John Roberts** is an Independent Cognitive Behavioural Therapist specialising in chronic health conditions with young people. Latterly John worked at Plymouth University lecturing on the Improving Access in Psychological Therapies (IAPT) programme. He trains health and social care professionals nationally and internationally in mood disorders, motivational interviewing and the psychological management of chronic healthcare conditions.

**Eleanor Thomas** is a Chartered Clinical Psychologist currently employed by The Together Trust, which is a children's charity. Her specialty is working with looked after children and the staff that provide their care in residential and foster settings. Her focus is upon specialist training, consultation and supervision to these staff and specialised therapeutic work with young people. She also works independently providing therapy to children and adults.

**Geraldine Rowe** is an Educational Psychologist who specialises in the application of Glasser's Choice Theory to improve motivation, behaviour and engagement in schools. Having worked in Local Authorities as a Senior Educational Psychologist and Manager of a multi disciplinary Behaviour and Attendance Team, Geraldine now works as an EP as part of the Senior Leadership Team of The Jubilee Academy an alternative provision free school in Harrow, London. Geraldine is a Faculty Member of the William Glasser Institute.

**Mawuli Amesu** is a qualified Social Work Manager, Trainer and an experienced practitioner using the solution focused brief therapy Motivational Interviewing approach. He regularly works in Education providing training in behaviour management and group work to improve behaviour and attainment.

# Preface

## Eddie McNamara

MI practice continues to expand both with regard to client groups engaged with and the number and nature of the therapeutic interventions it has been integrated with.

The previous publication (McNamara 2009) described the theory and practice of MI with children and young people and applications which were predominantly delivered in educational settings.

The subsequent and ongoing wide spread permeation of motivational interviewing into educational and therapeutic practice is well illustrated by the range of backgrounds of the contributors to this publication.

For example, Claudia Moss carried out her research as part of her Doctoral Training Programme to become an Educational Psychologist: Craig Bridge's contribution is a piece of Action Research based on his work as a consultant Educational Psychologist to a High School: Roger Lakin and John Roberts described MI practice in the context of community Clinical Psychology service delivery while chapter 7 consists of a rigorous evaluation of the effectiveness of MI in an applied setting carried out by researchers in Higher Education and Research settings.

For six of the contributors the publication is their first – and their tolerance of editorial feedback is much appreciated.

This current publication is in a sense a continuation of McNamara (2009) in that the applications of MI with children and young people is reviewed and the contributing authors illustrate i) how MI has been integrated with a number of different therapeutic interventions ii) the wide range of problems that have been addressed using MI as part of the intervention package in clinical, school and community settings and iii) the professional, theoretical and applied issues that continue to be addressed.

The relationship of MI to the TTM (Transtheoretical Model) is a continuing subject for debate – and Cathy Atkinson's chapter is a timely contribution to this ongoing debate. Garry Squires, in a balanced fashion, looks at the issues surrounding professional competency and MI practice while Kevin Wood, Patrick McArdle and Nadia Tabassum address the issue of MI and evidenced based practise.

The first and second sections of Part 2 of this book consists of descriptions of the applications of MI in both educational and clinical settings. The contributions in the education section are split evenly between applications of MI with students and the application of MI with teachers and support professionals.

All therapeutic interventions are of optimal effectiveness when the client is disposed to achieve the change aimed for by the therapeutic intervention. Section 4 describes the integration of MI with a number of therapeutic interventions which aim to achieve this.

*x*

# Part 1

# The Theory and Practice of MI: Issues

*2*

# Chapter 1

# Motivational Interviewing and Professional Practice

## Garry Squires
### *University of Manchester*

Children and young people tend to be referred to counsellors, therapists and psychologists because someone else, a parent or a teacher, has some concerns or worries about them. The child or young person may share these concerns, but this is not always the case. The extent to which the child is ready to change can be assessed using the Transtheoretical Model and the stages of change (Prochaska and DiClemente, 1982). If the child is ambivalent, then the professional working with them might decide to use Motivational Interviewing (Miller and Rollnick, 1991, 2002; Rollnick, Heather, and Bell, 1992; Rollnick and Miller, 1995) as an intervention to increase their motivation for change (Britton, Patrick, Wenzel, and Williams, 2011; Burke, 2011; Watson, 2011). This short summary makes everything seem really straightforward, but is it? Or, to put it another way, what are the professional issues underlying such an approach? This chapter starts to address this question and I am hoping that it will provoke some thought, debate and a degree of argument. The discussion outlined will cover professional competency, knowledge and skills; power relationships and ethical practice; individual versus systemic work; evaluating efficacy of professional practice; and the role of clinical supervision.

### Professional competency

There is a need to protect the public from poor practice, or even harmful practice (British Psychological Society - BPS - 2006), and this has led to the idea that professionals working within a particular field such as Motivational Interviewing should be able to demonstrate a certain level of skill or competence in that field. Part of my work involves meeting with other teams of psychologists to train them in therapeutic approaches such as CBT, and the question of competency often arises in comparison to non-psychologists who have undertaken more extensive therapeutic training or who practice solely within a clinical setting. For example, the degree of competence may be recognised through the award of a particular qualification awarded by a professional body. To practice as a therapist, the practitioner might need to meet the British Association for Behavioural and Cognitive Psychotherapies (BABCP) criteria for accreditation (Dunsmuir and Iyadurai, 2007). A lot of work is needed to achieve BABCP accreditation; currently this involves at least 450 hours formal training and over 200 hours of supervised practice (Holland, 2006). This may be a good standard for someone starting from scratch, but is this the case for all practitioners? A second related question is, while this might be appropriate for a professional working only in a narrowly defined area, the question has to be asked as to whether a professional working in a broader area with a high level of generic training also needs to have a collection of additional qualifications.

Motivational Interviewing has not developed in a knowledge vacuum. Like many other approaches it has evolved from existing psychological and psychotherapeutic approaches, despite its founders' claims that it was not systematically developed from theory but arose out of clinical practice (Miller and Rollnick, 2012). This means that people who already have a good training in psychology or psychotherapy are well on the way to understanding the background to Motivational Interviewing (Squires, 2010). This is not to say that they already know everything that there is to know about Motivational Interviewing, but they do have some understanding and insights into how people think, perceive the world around them and emotionally react and behave. To help think about what competencies are needed in order to be able to apply Motivational Interviewing is useful to consider a distinction made by Roth and Pilling (2007; 2007) between general competencies and specific competencies. General competencies are those that are found in other psychological or psychotherapeutic work while specific competencies are those related only to Motivational Interviewing.

Therapists with training in other psychotherapeutic approaches or with post graduate professional qualifications in applied psychology are likely to have transferrable knowledge, skills and general competencies. In Motivational Interviewing, the therapist is required to display warmth, accurate empathy, genuineness, and to be accepting of the client. There must be a basic trust between the client and the therapist and a well-developed rapport. Therapists must be able to work collaboratively with clients and help them make informed choices and action plans. There are also administrative competencies such as turning up on time, and keeping written records of the sessions and interventions. Socratic questioning is common in many therapeutic approaches, such as cognitive behavioural therapy, but not all approaches and there is a skill to structuring questions in a way that avoids the client feeling as if they are subjected to the 'Spanish Inquisition'. A good starting point to deciding to undertake extensive therapeutic training would be to undertake a personal audit against the list of general competencies proposed by Roth and Pilling (2007).

Many professionals who want to utilise Motivational Interviewing are already working with some therapeutic background knowledge and experience They are then concerned with the specific knowledge that marks Motivational Interviewing out from other approaches with which therapists are already familiar. Much of the writing on Motivational Interviewing refers to the Transtheoretical Model as if this is the core knowledge that is necessary in order to practice Motivational Interviewing. However, purist Motivational Interviewing theorists remind us that motivational interviewing and the Transtheoretical Model are not part of the same theory but they fit well together and evolved at the same time (Rollnick and Miller, 1995). Having said that, the Transtheoretical Model is useful for establishing whether a child is ready for change, and it forms a useful step in the work undertaken. There have been some innovative ways of implementing this with children using questionnaires (Wood, 2009) or Q card sorting exercises (Hughes and Booth, 2009).

Motivational Interviewing has been defined as:

> "A directive, client-centred counselling style for eliciting behaviour change by helping clients to explore and resolve ambivalence."
>
> (Rollnick and Miller, 1995, p. 326)

The underlying assumption is that clients do not change because of their state of ambivalence. Motivational Interviewing involves a discussion with the client that promotes their reflection on both arguments for change and arguments against change so that they can express their ambivalence and in doing so, start to resolve their impasse and come to a decision to change, or not to change. The therapist encourages the client to become autonomous so that the ability to bring about change falls entirely under the client's control. There are an increasing number of conversational techniques that can be employed in Motivational Interviewing to achieve these ends (for examples see McNamara, 1998; 2009b).

It is worth the professional who is engaging in Motivational Interviewing considering the question of how to establish what competencies, skills and knowledge they already possess and what they need to develop in order to draw up an action plan to inform Continuing Professional Development (CPD). Eight key stages for learning and becoming competent in Motivational Interviewing have been identified (Miller and Moyers, 2006):

- Understand the philosophy and ideology of Motivational Interviewing.

- Development of client centred counselling skills. As well as drawing upon approaches such as the Skilled Helper Model (Egan, 2010), Miller and Moyers use the acronym OARS to remind us that in Motivational Interviewing we need to use Open ended questions, to be Affirming, Reflecting and make use of Summarising.

- Recognising and reinforcing change talk. The idea is that the therapist encourages talk that emphasises change and minimises attentional reinforcement of comments that suggest maintaining the status quo.

- Eliciting and strengthening change talk. Open ended questions that encourage thought about change are asked, e.g. "In what ways might change be good for you at this point in your schooling?"

6                                    *Chapter 1*

- Rolling with resistance rather than opposing it. Techniques include over-amplification - exaggerating one side of the argument, and double-sided reflection - presenting both sides of the argument as a reflective comment. For more on these techniques and others such as shifting focus, reflection with a twist, reframing, and coming alongside, see McNamara (2009a).

- Developing a change plan. There is a temptation to develop a plan for the child. However, the child then has limited ownership of the plan and commitment to the plan. The skill is to help guide the child to a plan that they can develop for themselves, prepare for change, and then commit to change.

  This may involve the child wanting to elicit help from key people in their support network, such as teachers, friends, or parents.

- Consolidating client commitment. This involves listening out for phrases that indicate that the client will do something, rather than simply hope they will do something.

- Integrating Motivational Interviewing with other approaches.

There are many ways that therapists can develop competencies (Squires, 2010):

- Undertaking Continuous Professional Development, go on courses, read books like this one and receive training in Motivational Interviewing. Specific training workshops have been shown to be an effective way of increasing therapist competence in the application of Motivational Interviewing (Moyers et al., 2008).

- Evaluation of on-going work e.g. pre-post measures used in Individual Education Plan development, casework discussions within professional teams, peer observation and shadowing, reflective logs, client feedback and follow-up.

- Using models to guide the thought processes around a case and sharing problem formulations with peers.

- Reading and keeping abreast of new developments and research.

- Presenting at conferences, running workshops and publishing examples of work.

## Power Relationships and Ethical Practice

Motivational Interviewing, like other person centred counselling approaches, sees the client and the therapist in a co-worker relationship or as co-scientists trying to explore the client's understanding (Kelly, 1955). This implies an equality of power within the relationship with the more experienced therapist guiding the client in reflecting about the choices that are open to them. However, children differ in a fundamental way from adult clients; the child is referred to the professional rather than referring himself or herself as an adult would. There is an inherent power dynamic in this referral, in which the child initially has no power over whether the referral takes place.

Once with the therapist, this imbalance can be changed or at least reduced. The therapist has the potential to empower the child in decision making about whether to proceed or not. Initially this may involve obtaining the child's informed assent to continue. Some shared understanding of why the adults have referred the child and why the child is sitting in front of the therapist at that particular moment in time. If the child does not want to engage with the therapist or does not want to change then the therapist may feel an ethical dilemma – on the one hand, they can empower the child but things continue as they are with the potential negative consequences associated with this decision; on the other hand, they act in favour of the adults that referred and try to use the therapeutic sessions as a way of moving the child towards readiness for change with the aim of resolving difficulties and reducing the impact and negative consequences of the continuing situation. When the decision is made to press on with an intervention with the child without their commitment then this is not seen as being in the 'spirit of motivational interviewing' (Rollnick and Miller, 1995). The purpose of Motivational Interviewing is not to force the child to want to change through coercion, persuasion, or manipulation. For some professional groups this dilemma can be resolved more easily than for other groups, simply because there is more scope for alternative types of work. An educational psychologist for instance, might go with the child's decision to not engage and be supportive of this decision and then work with the referring adults to look at alternative solutions such as making environmental changes, providing more adult support, or changing adult behaviours or perceptions. If the child wants to work with the therapist then the Transtheoretical Model is useful as a follow on assessment tool for evaluating whether the child is ready to change, or wants to continue as they are, or are in a state of ambivalence about change. If ambivalence exists and the child wants to explore this, then Motivational Interviewing is an appropriate approach to use.

A second related issue it that of confidentiality. Referring adults are concerned about the child and are naturally curious about how sessions are going and whether there are any indications of how they can help the child further. This may lead to them asking questions of the therapist, and the child may see the adults asking the questions. There is a potential threat to trust and therefore to the extent that the child will discuss important issues with the therapist. This can be approached by discussing with the referring adults that what is discussed in the session remains confidential to the therapist and child. The main exception would be disclosures that fall under the Child Protection procedures (HMSO, 2004) or if there is a disclosure of significant harm to the client or to another person. Other exceptions are those required in law, e.g. involvement in terrorist activities, or a court case in which a Judge has power to subpoena any session notes. A similar discussion can then be held with the child and the wording might be something like this:

> *We will be talking together to try to find things that might be helpful to you. As we talk there may be some things that you would not like me to say to anyone else – that's okay. The only things that I will have to pass on to someone else will be if you tell me that someone is hurting you or making you do things that you don't want to or if you are doing something that is not safe.*

8 *Chapter 1*

*As we talk, we may come up with some ideas of things that might be useful and we might need to ask other people if they can help. I won't do that unless you agree.*

The last sentence reminds us as to how confidentiality can be source of frustration when the child comes up with some really great ideas of how others might be able to help, but then tells the therapist that they cannot tell anyone these ideas. All that can be done under these circumstances is to make a note of the ideas and then discuss them again in a future session.

## Individual versus Systemic Work

There is a temptation to think that when a child is referred to a professional, then there must be a problem with the child. However, the child's behavioural responses occur within a social network or interacting system. It is possible to work with the system to produce change so that there is a better fit between the child and their social environment. For instance, whole school development could be achieved through the application of Motivational Interviewing principles in the delivery of staff training (Duckworth, 2009) and the development of consultation models (Duffy and Davison, 2009). Motivational Interviewing could be used as a means of helping teachers consider whether they are ready to change some of their approaches to working with children.

## Evaluating Efficacy of Professional Practice

The benefits of using motivational interviewing as an adjunct to other therapeutic approaches, needs to be carefully evaluated in each piece of casework. In some studies looking at the prevention of osteoporosis, heart disease and diabetes, no beneficial effect has been found (Berkowitz and Johansen, 2012). Yet there have also been many randomised control trials that have found positive but inconsistent effects (Miller and Rollnick, 2012; Vansteenkiste, Williams, and Resnicow, 2012). One of the potential difficulties of using randomised control trials is that they encourage manualised approaches and the flexibility to respond to individual needs and circumstances is lost. The second difficulty with a manualised approach is the need to split clients before establishing whether there is a need to use Motivational Interviewing, i.e. without establishing which clients are ambivalent to change and engaging with the intervention offered. These difficulties are less apparent at the individual casework level where the clinician is free to make more flexible decisions and pace can be matched to individual client needs. This means that efficacy of professional practice is more about what an individual therapist does with an individual client.

One question to be addressed through evaluating the efficacy of professional practice with children in schools is whether pupil motivation is enhanced. Simple measures would include whether more participants complete the therapeutic work and whether there is a lower dropout rate. Slightly more sophisticated measures would encourage clients to rate their willingness to continue with sessions or to look at homework compliance. The most effective evidence of clinical competence is evidence of progress as a result of the intervention being used. This is built into the Code of Practice for SEN (Department for Education and Skills, 2001) as part of the plan-do-review cycle of the IEP (Individual Educational Programme). The use of checklists, observation schedules and self-report questionnaires can enable comparisons to be made between pre- and post-intervention behaviours. The measures do not have to be complex and could involve simple rating scales to detect a change in feelings as an indicator of progress or otherwise.

A second issue regarding the efficacy of professional practice is the ability of the practitioner to carry out the different techniques/skills and attitudes consistent with the underlying philosophy of Motivational Interviewing. In other words, where are they in terms of developing their Motivational Interviewing practice on Miller and Moyer's eight stages? Have they developed the necessary general competencies needed in therapeutic approaches such as those identified by Roth and Pilling? The practitioner could be encouraged to self-audit against the eight stages or general competencies and to seek out further training opportunities or to develop skills further through supervision.

## The Role of Clinical Supervision

Clinical supervision is a common feature of many professionals' working life which promotes more effective professional practice (Squires and Williams, 2003) and improves the way in which practitioners engage and practice their profession (Bégat, Berggren, Ellefsen and Severinsson, 2003). Supervision has been shown to positively predict levels of job satisfaction amongst school counsellors (Baggerly & Osborn, 2006; Crutchfield and Borders, 1997). Small gains over a short time period of introducing clinical supervision have also been shown for self-efficacy and perceived intervention effectiveness (Crutchfield and Borders, 1997; Day, Thurlow and Wolliscroft, 2003). Peer supervision has been shown to contribute to individual supervisee development, improved management and development of supervisee leadership (Hyrkäs, Koivula, Lehti and Paunonen-Ilmonen, 2003). These pieces of research from other professional groups suggest that the use of supervision in Motivational Interviewing practice would have a beneficial effect on the quality of service delivery, efficacy of application of Motivational Interviewing and protect the therapist's own emotional health.

Like any other form of learning, the development of skills in Motivational Interviewing should be considered as on-going as practitioners increase their level of skill from novice to expert, with increasing fluidity of application and generalisation and increasing creativity in approach and the use of therapeutic metaphor. This combined learning process is encapsulated in the Lancaster cycle shown below (Figure 1). In the initial learning cycle, the therapist receives the wisdom of others through attending courses, reading papers and books and watching colleagues or videos. This starts to build up knowledge, skills and attitudes needed to engage with Motivational Interviewing. Supervision at this stage encourages reflection and thought about how the therapist will implement this in practice. It serves to strengthen the internal representation and may include some role play or modelling. The therapist then considers which aspects of Motivational Interviewing they want to develop through experimental practice – discovering which approaches can be incorporated into existing practice. The feedback, e.g. from the client, from monitoring, from recording sessions, from case notes, enables further reflection during supervision.

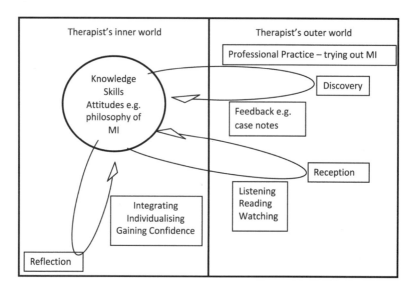

*Figure 1:* Adapted Lancaster Cycle (Burgoyne, 1992)

In one study pursued, I was interested in how easily newly trained psychologists could implement therapeutic skills in professional practice. Most of the difficulties reported were of a general casework nature and only a minority of supervision comments were related specifically to the implementation of the therapeutic model (Squires and Dunsmuir, 2008, 2011). This suggests that most of the supervision needs of therapists are likely to be around generic competencies and could be dealt with through non-Motivational Interviewing based supervision. This would leave specific competencies to be dealt with through Motivational Interviewing focussed supervision. This distinction is important for professionals who wish to practice Motivational Interviewing but work in services or teams were there is limited capacity for Motivational Interviewing supervision or where expertise in Motivational Interviewing does not exist. There are several solutions for receiving specific supervision in Motivational Interviewing when in-house specialist supervision is not available and these are summarised in Box 1.

Motivational Interviewing is not a set of techniques, but is better described as a communication style, that is simple but not easy. That is, it is often subtle and requires considerable practice over time (Miller and Rollnick, 2009). This makes it an ideal candidate for supervision, in which the therapist can reflect on the words used and the impact upon the client with the supervisor. Supervision is also a place where tricky ethical dilemmas can be discussed and decisions made. For example,

> - *Buying in supervision*
> - *Group supervision*
> - *Pairing of neighbouring Services to provide peer support*
> - *Peer supervision, particularly where colleagues have accessed similar CPD*
> - *Setting up networks and support groups for Motivational Interviewing therapists*
> - *Specialist supervision from multiagency partners e.g. Children and Adolescent Mental Health Services (CAMHS)*
> - *Virtual supervision e.g. email contact or Skype with a specialist*

***Box 1:*** Methods of facilitating supervision for therapeutic intervention (Squires and Atkinson, 2011)

the teacher thinks that this child really needs to change or the school will exclude him; but, the child is quite happy as they are. Questions that may arise are: What should I do? Is Motivational Interviewing a useful approach to take and, if so with whom, the teacher or the child?

## Conclusions

In this chapter, I have started to raise some of the professional issues that relate to the application of Motivational Interviewing in schools. The distinction between the Transtheoretical Model and the application of Motivational Interviewing has been made, seeing the two approaches as complimentary. This led to a discussion of the philosophy and skills that underpin Motivational Interviewing with both generic counselling competencies and specific Motivational Interviewing competencies. Eight stages of development of competency were covered. The ethical considerations of the power relationships around referral and the dilemma about whether to engage in motivational interviewing or do something else led into a brief discussion of using Motivational Interviewing at the systemic level rather than at the individual level. Confidentiality and the development of trust were set alongside the need to protect children. I ended by considering how clinical supervision might be used to improve professional efficacy by bringing together reception of learning experiences, internalisation through reflection and discussion and the opportunity to try out skills in professional practice.

In presenting these issues, I am hoping that the reader will reflect on them and think about their own circumstances. Do you agree with the points raised? If you disagree, what is your reasoning, and how is this related to your professional role or personal ideology? Are you going to change or consolidate your practice? What are the practical considerations that you need to think about next?

## References

Baggerly, J., & Osborn, D. (2006). School counselors' career satisfaction and commitment: Correlates and predictors. [Original]. *Professional School Counseling,* 9(3), 197-205.

Bégat, I., Berggren, I., Ellefsen, B., & Severinsson, E. (2003). Australian nurse supervisors' styles and their perceptions of ethical dilemmas within health care. *Journal of Nursing Management,* 11(1), 6-14.

Berkowitz, S. A., & Johansen, K. L. (2012). Does Motivational Interviewing Improve Outcomes? *Archives of Internal Medicine,* 172(6), 463-464.

BPS. (2006). *Code of Ethics and Conduct.* Leicester: The British Psychological Society.

Britton, P. C., Patrick, H., Wenzel, A., & Williams, G. C. (2011). Integrating motivational interviewing and self-determination theory with cognitive behavioral therapy to prevent suicide. *Cognitive and Behavioral Practice,* 18(1), 16-27.

Burke, B. L. (2011). What can motivational interviewing do for you? *Cognitive and Behavioral Practice,* 18(1), 74-81.

Crutchfield, L. B., & Borders, D. (1997). Impact of two clinical peer supervision models on practicing school counselors. *Journal of Counseling & Development,* 75(3), 219-230.

Day, A., Thurlow, K., & Wolliscroft, J. (2003). Working with childhood sexual abuse: A survey of mental health professionals. *Child Abuse & Neglect,* 27(2), 191-198.

Department for Education and Skills (2001). *Special Educational Needs Code of Practice.* Nottingham: DfES Publications.

Duckworth, S. (2009). Using the Stages of Change Model to Facilate Change at a Whole School Level. In E. McNamara (Ed.), *Motivational Interviewing: Theory, Practice and Applications with Children and Young People* (pp. 165-180). Ainsdale: www.positivebehaviourmanagement.co.uk

Duffy, J., & Davison, P. (2009). Incorporating Motivational Interviewing Strategies into a Consultation Model for Use Within School Based Behaviour Management Teams. In E. McNamara (Ed.), *Motivational Interviewing: Theory, Practice and Applications with Children and Young People* (pp. 182-205). Ainsdale: www.positivebehaviourmanagement.co.uk

Dunsmuir, S., & Iyadurai, S. (2007). Cognitive Behavioural Therapy: Effectiveness, expertise and ethics. *Division of Educational and Child Psychology: Debate* (122), 15-19.

*Chapter 1* 13

Egan, G. (2010). *The Skilled Helper: International Edition* (9 ed.). London: Wadsworth.

HMSO. (2004). *Children Act 2004: Chapter 31.* London: The Stationery Office.

Holland, R. (2006). Minimum standards for the practice of CBT. Accrington: *British Association for Behavioural and Cognitive Psychotherapies.*

Hughes, M., & Booth, V. (2009). Assessing Pupil Motivation for Change: Using Card Sorting Methodology. In E. McNamara (Ed.), *Motivational Interviewing: Theory, Practice and Applications with Children and Young People* (pp. 127-144). Ainsdale: www.positivebehaviourmanagement.co.uk

Hyrkäs, K., Koivula, M., Lehti, K., & Paunonen-Ilmonen, M. (2003). Nurse managers' conceptions of quality management as promoted by peer supervision. *Journal of Nursing Management,* 11(1), 48-58.

Kelly, G. A. (1955). *The Psychology of Personal Constructs.* New York: Norton.

McNamara, E. (1998). *The Theory and Practice of Eliciting Pupil Motivation: Motivational Interviewing — a form teacher's manual and guide for students, parents, psychologists, health visitors and counsellors.*
Ainsdale: www.positivebehaviourmanagement.co.uk

McNamara, E. (2009a). Rolling with resistance. In E. McNamara (Ed.), *Motivational Interviewing: Theory, Practice and Applications with Children and Young People* (pp. 43-56). Ainsdale: www.positivebehaviourmanagement.co.uk

McNamara, E. (2009b). The theory and practice of MI. In E. McNamara (Ed.), *Motivational Interviewing: Theory, Practice and Applications with Children and Young People* (pp. 3-42). Ainsdale: www.positivebehaviourmanagement.co.uk

Miller, W. R., & Moyers, T. B. (2006). Eight stages in learning motivational interviewing. *Journal of Teaching in the Addictions,* 5, 3-17.

Miller, W. R., & Rollnick, S. (1991). *Motivational Interviewing: Preparing People for Change.* New York: Guilford Press.

Miller, W. R., & Rollnick, S. (2002). *Motivational Interviewing: Preparing People for Change* (2 ed.). New York: Guilford Press.

Miller, W. R., & Rollnick, S. (2009). Ten Things that Motivational Interviewing is Not. *Behavioural and Cognitive Psychotherapy,* 37, 129-140.

Miller, W. R., & Rollnick, S. (2012). Meeting in the middle: motivational interviewing and self-determination theory. *International Journal of Behavioral Nutrition and Physical Activity,* 9, 25.

Moyers, T. B., Manuel, J. K., Wilson, P. G., Hendrickson, S. M., Talcott, W., & Durand, P. (2008). A randomized trial investigating training in motivational interviewing for behavioral health providers. *Behavioural and Cognitive Psychotherapy,* 36(2), 149-162.

Prochaska, J. O., & DiClemente, C. C. (1982). *The Transtheoretical Approach: Crossing Traditional Boundaries of Therapy.* Homewood: Dowe Jones/irwin.

Rollnick, S., Heather, N., & Bell, A. (1992). Negotiating behaviour change in medical settings: the development of brief motivational interviewing. *Journal of Mental Health,* 1, 22-37.

Rollnick, S., & Miller, W. R. (1995). What is Motivational Interviewing? *Behavioural and Cognitive Psychotherapy,* 23, 325-334.

Roth, A. D., & Pilling, S. (2007). Cognitive and behavioural therapy (CBT) for people with depression and anxiety. What skills can service users expect their therapists to have? London: *Department for Health.*

Roth, A. D., & Pilling, S. (2007). The competences required to deliver effective cognitive and behavioural therapy for people with depression and with anxiety disorders. London: *Department of Health.*

Squires, G. (2010). Countering the argument that educational psychologists need specific training to use cognitive behavioural therapy. *Emotional and Behavioural Difficulties,* 4, 279-294.

Squires, G., & Atkinson, C. (2011). Educational Psychologists and therapeutic intervention. Findings from UK wide research and implications for supervision. Paper presented at the *Supervision in Counselling, Counselling Psychology and Educational Psychology.* Retrieved from https://www.escholar.manchester.ac.uk/uk-ac-man-scw:126789

Squires, G., & Dunsmuir, S. (2008). What is the value in training educational psychologists in cognitive behaviour therapy (CBT)? Paper presented at the *International School Psychology Association 30th Annual Colloquium.*

Squires, G., & Dunsmuir, S. (2011). Embedding Cognitive Behavioural Therapy Training in Practice: Facilitators and barriers for trainee educational psychologists (TEPs). *Educational Psychology in Practice,* 27(2), 117-132.

Squires, G., & Williams, S. (2003). Peer Supervision for Educational Psychologists as a Means to Quality Service Delivery *SEN Newsletter. Stafford:* Staffordshire County Council.

Vansteenkiste, M., Williams, G. C., & Resnicow, K. (2012). Toward systematic integration between self-determination theory and motivational interviewing as examples of top-down and bottom-up intervention development: autonomy or volition as a fundamental theoretical principle. *International Journal of Behavioral Nutrition and Physical Activity,* 9, 23.

Watson, J. (2011). Resistance is futile? Exploring the potential of motivational interviewing. *Journal of Social Work Practice: Psychotherapeutic Approaches in Health, Welfare and the Community,* 25(4), 465-479.

Wood, V. (2009). Assessing Pupil Motivation for Change: a Questionnaire Approach. In E. McNamara (Ed.), *Motivational Interviewing: Theory, Practice and Applications with Children and Young People* (pp. 119-126). Ainsdale: www.positivebehaviourmanagement.co.uk

16                              Chapter 1

# Chapter 2

# Motivational Interviewing and the Transtheoretical Model

## Cathy Atkinson
### *University of Manchester*

### Background to Motivational Interviewing and the Transtheoretical Model

If you asked most education-based professionals familiar with Motivational Interviewing (MI) the question "What do you think of when you think of MI?" the likelihood is that a significant number would make some reference to "the wheel", or the "cycle of change", or the "model" or the "stages of change". In each instance, they would be referring to the Transtheoretical Model of Change (TTM) developed by Prochaska and DiClemente (1982).

When MI first came to prominence through the publication of Miller and Rollick's seminal text, Motivational Interviewing: Preparing People to Change Addictive Behaviour (Miller and Rollick, 1991) the TTM appeared to be a central concept to the developing theory of MI. Miller and Rollick (1991) acknowledged the usefulness of the model in understanding the behaviour of clients and guiding the actions of therapists. Soon after, McNamara (1992) first proposed ideas about how MI could be used to support pupils in educational settings, suggesting that the TTM could be used to identify pupil readiness for change and to identify appropriate behavioural support mechanisms or interventions. McNamara (1992) had been heavily influenced by the work of Henck van Bilsen, a practitioner using MI techniques with heroin-dependent clients in the Netherlands and author of a chapter in the Miller and Rollnick text (van Bilsen, 1991). As MI approaches using the TTM were gaining prominence internationally, so ideas proposed by McNamara (1992) reached practitioners in UK schools.

The original TTM, based on an analysis of over 300 therapy outcomes (Prochaska, 1979) proposed that during the process of change, a client could be identified as being at various stages of change ranging from precontemplative (where a person may not even realise there is a problem), through to maintenance (where the person is actively maintaining a positive change). The model has appeared in a variety of guises over the years (Miller and Rollnick, 1991; Prochaska and DiClemente, 1982; 1998; Prochaska, Norcross and DiClemente, 1994) with debates reigning over whether certain phases, such as precontemplation and relapse, should be central to the model (Miller and Rollnick, 1991; Prochaska et al, 1994); whether there should be a 'termination' phase for behaviours which have ceased to be problematic for a long period of time (Prochaska et al, 1994), and whether the stage preceding direct action should be entitled 'determinism' or 'preparation' (McNamara and Atkinson, 2010; Prochaska and DiClemente, 1998). In educational literature, the Model of Stages of Change (the version of the TTM described by McNamara (1992; 1998) has typically appeared as a six segment 'wheel' incorporating the phases shown in Figure 1 below.

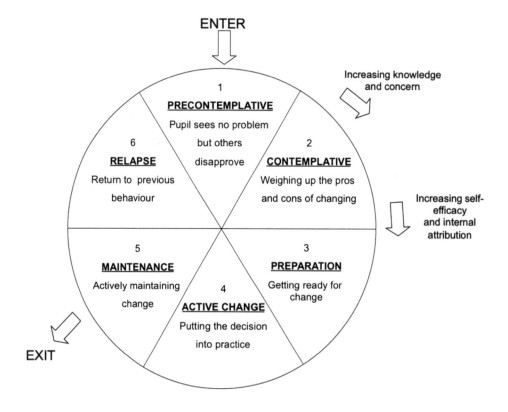

*Figure 1:* The Model of Stages of Change, as presented by Atkinson (2009)[1]

---

[1] Adapted from McNamara (1998) and Prochaska and DiClemente (1998).

*Chapter 2*

Over the years, MI and the TTM have come to be seen as synonymous within educational practice (Atkinson and Amesu, 2007). Indeed, in McNamara's (2009) comprehensive guide to MI and school-based applications, no less than eight of the ten chapters make reference to the TTM, a feature which is directly addressed in the closing chapter. Here McNamara (2009) argues that:

*"...the techniques of Motivational Interviewing have been profoundly influential in helping people change and that the TTM has enabled the practice of Motivational Interviewing to be carried out with a degree of precision which might otherwise have not have been the case"* (p211).

One of the reasons for McNamara's 'defence' is that Miller and Rollnick have increasingly distanced MI from the TTM. In the second edition of Motivational Interviewing (Miller and Rollnick, 2002) references to the TTM are removed from the authored front sections of the book and instead, overlaps between the TTM and MI are explored in a contributed chapter (DiClemente and Velasquez, 2002). Furthermore, in their recent paper Ten Things that Motivational Interviewing Is Not, the number one assertion is that "MI is not based on the transtheoretical model" (Miller and Rollnick, 2009, p130).

Miller and Rollnick (2009) define MI as "a collaborative, person-centred form of guiding to elicit and strengthen motivation for change" (p 137). Central tenets of MI are the 'spirit' and 'principles' (Miller and Rollnick, 2002). These are detailed in Boxes 1 and 2 below:

**Box 1** – The Spirit of MI

---

- Collaboration: *'That the method of motivational interviewing involves exploration more than exhortation, and support rather than persuasion or argument.'* (Miller and Rollnick, 2002).

- Evocation: That MI is not about imparting information, but finding things within the person and drawing them out. It requires finding intrinsic motivation for change from within the person and evoking it.

- Autonomy: Any responsibility for change is left with the client, no matter what the views of professionals. It is the client rather than the counsellor that should ultimately present arguments for change.

---

## Box 2 – The Principles of MI

- **Expressing empathy**

  It is important that adults working with young people seek to understand their feelings in a non-judgemental manner.

- **Developing discrepancy**

  MI aims to help the young person develop a discrepancy between the present state of affairs and how they might like things to be.

- **Rolling with resistance**

  Miller and Rollnick (2002) suggest that resistance can be reframed to create momentum for change.

- **Supporting self-efficacy**

  A young person can be encouraged by the success of others, or by their own previous achievements in changing their behaviour.

A possible reason for the diluting of the link between MI and the TTM within clinical practice may be recent criticisms of the TTM, particularly in relation to the evidence base for its effectiveness as a model of intervention. This chapter will begin by exploring some of the criticisms of the TTM, before considering the relevance of these arguments within educational settings. Some of the possible advantages of using the TTM in school-based practices are then discussed. A re-evaluation of how MI is practised within schools, exploring possible directions for future research and evaluation is then described.

## Criticisms of the TTM

Wilson and Schlam (2004), argue that:

> *"The transtheoretical stages of change model suffers from conceptual and empirical limitations, including problems of stage definition, measurement, and discreteness. Sequential transition across stages has not been established. The model lacks strong predictive utility, and there is little evidence that therapeutic interventions must be matched to stage to facilitate change."* (p 361).

In his article "Putting the TTM (Stages of Change) Model to Rest", West (2005) goes even further, suggesting that *'the problems with the model are so serious that it has held back advances in the field of health promotion"* (p1036). In the face of such stark criticism, one may ask the question why educationalists practising MI are continuing to use such an allegedly out-dated, discredited model for which there is no evidence base. In order to explore this, it is first important to understand why the TTM has attracted such criticism and to examine what the possible advantages of continuing to link MI and TTM might be within school-based practices.

In some domains of clinical practice, the TTM has been used as a framework to develop very clear criteria for what denotes a client's readiness for change. For example, West (2005) refers to smoking cessation models determining, for example, 'precontemplation' to mean 'not thinking about stopping for at least six months'; and 'contemplation' to mean 'an individual planning to stop between 31 days and 6 months'. Similarly, Wilson and Schlam (2004) outline how individuals have been assigned to a stage of change on the basis of questionnaire responses, although responses may not accurately represent their intentions of change (West, 2005).

West (2005) argues that the concept of 'stages' is flawed, and that assigning individuals to arbitrary categories has little useful meaning. Wilson and Schlam (2004) support this, advocating that the stages are not discrete categories and for the TTM to be operable, it should be possible to assign individuals to *"one and only one stage category"* (page 363). Furthermore, they argue that there is little support for the idea that people move sequentially between the stages of the TTM. Wilson and Schlam (2004) criticise the linking of specific interventions to stages of change as advocated by Prochaska et al (1994) and suggested by Atkinson and Amesu (2007) and Atkinson (2009) in relation to school-based practice. They also suggest that it is difficult to predict outcomes based on assessments using the TTM.

Etter (2005) suggests that *"...it has never been convincingly shown that distinct strategies are needed to progress across distinct stages"* (p1041). He argues that the TTM is too rigid and has not evolved significantly since its inception. Etter (2005) also claims that labelling people as 'precontemplators' may be stigmatising and deprive patients of effective treatment. Finally, there is criticism that the evidence base for the derivation and use of the TTM is insufficient (Etter, 2005; West, 2005).

## Using the TTM in MI Practice

DiClemente and Velasquez (2002) report that the TTM has played an integral role in the development of MI, and of brief interventions that use a motivational approach. They note the 'natural fit' of MI and TTM, observing that clinicians and researchers internationally have embraced the two models. Furthermore they describe how MI approaches might be linked to the stages of change from the TTM.

Although the lack of empirical research into the efficacy of MI in educational settings has been acknowledged (Kittles and Atkinson, 2009; Moss, 2010), it should be noted that what has been reported has firstly been positive and secondly has generally centred on the TTM. A number of case-based studies detail the usefulness of MI and the TTM for understanding the needs of and supporting pupils (Atkinson, 2009; Atkinson and Woods, 2003; Kittles and Atkinson, 2009; McNamara, 2001). More recently Moss (2010), in a randomised control trial reported self-esteem gains for pupils accessing a programme based in MI and incorporating aspects of the TTM (Atkinson, 2005).

To date therefore, the evidence relating to the use of MI within school-based practice suggests that considering MI and the TTM simultaneously is useful. It is interesting to note that where MI principles have been disseminated to non-clinical settings, there is also a reliance on the TTM to support the principles of MI. For example, in devising a MI groupwork intervention, Fields (2006) makes frequent reference to the TTM, including asking group members to identify patterns of behaviour in relation to the TTM stages of change. Even within smoking cessation, there is evidence that MI and the TTM continue to be used together to promote and enable change (Erol and Erdogan, 2008).

Perhaps what we are considering, therefore, is the application of MI principles using the TTM as a framework. DiClemente and Velasquez (2002) note that *"...motivational interviewing strategies can be knit together rather seamlessly with the stages of change model"* (page, 213). Both approaches, they propose, are useful in acknowledging that the responsibility for change lies with the individual and that the ultimate goal is to support them in making effective changes to their lifestyle.

The next sections explore different ways in which using the TTM alongside MI can actually enhance the way school-based professionals support children and young people experiencing social, emotional and behavioural difficulties. Specifically the TTM used in conjunction with MI may have benefits in the following areas:

- Training
- Appropriate intervention strategies
- The TTM and young people
- Use of MI alongside other techniques

These will each now be considered in more depth, based on my personal experiences of using the TTM alongside MI.

## Training

In undertaking MI with young people and supporting the staff who work with them, I have always found the TTM to be an accessible, memorable and thought-provoking model. When delivering training, primarily to educational psychologists and pastoral staff in schools, I usually start by presenting the testimony of the former England football captain, Tony Adams, detailed in his autobiography

*Addicted* (Adams and Ridley, 1999) which details his initial ambivalence about his alcohol problems, which later became personally concerning through the increasing impact on his personal and professional life. I then introduce the TTM (as outlined in Figure 1, page 18) and proceed to describe the key aspects of MI. I find the case example (Adams and Ridley, 1999) and the visual framework (TTM) allow professionals to identify with the spirit of MI (collaboration, evocation and autonomy) and the principles (expressing empathy, developing discrepancy, rolling with resistance and supporting self-efficacy) (see Boxes 1 and 2).

Miller and Rollnick (2009) note that *"MI is not easy"* (p135), purporting that MI involves a complex set of skills which cannot be mastered for example via a two-day training course but only through on-going practice with feedback and coaching. Many school-based practitioners of MI however, will not have had access even to this level of input, but instead may have learned about MI through staff training or published resources. They are typically not trained counsellors or therapists and like other practitioners such as nurses, social workers and dieticians who have increasingly begun to use MI, may have previously been trained to provide direct advice about behavioural change. Learning the advanced counselling skills required for MI may require not only considerable time and expenditure in terms of training, but also a significant change to their paradigms of thinking (Resnicow et al, 2002).

Within clinical practice, MI interventions have traditionally been delivered by individuals with training in psychology or counselling. These professionals will often require only a moderate refinement to their skill-base to undertake MI. This is not normally the case with educational practice. In fact, most school-based professionals do not have access to either a significant level of training or to on-going supervision and support in MI. Should this then preclude them from integrating into their practice intervention strategies based on MI principles to support children and young people?

While Miller and Rollnick (2002) position MI as skilled and difficult to master, I have always found that teachers and pupils can readily identify with the TTM. Everyone knows someone who has made (and broken) a New Year's Resolution and as such can use the TTM as a framework to understand that the process of change is not linear, but complex. Providing the TTM as an access point for understanding the spirit and principles of MI is something which appears to be helpful to school-based practitioners.

## Appropriate Intervention Strategies

Miller and Rollnick (2009) argue that *"it is neither essential nor important to explain the TTM stages of change when delivering MI"* (p130) nor to assign individuals to a stage of change in preparation for MI. It should be noted however, that Rollnick, Heather and Bell (1992) strongly cautioned against using certain techniques such as the 'Future and the Present', where the client is invited to explore how they would like things to be different in the future; when undertaking

MI with ambivalent clients they suggest *"This strategy can only be used with clients who are at least concerned to some degree in question"* (p33). This suggests that at the very least, there should be some mechanism for assessing the client's readiness to change. Miller and Rollnick (2009) argue that a skilled MI practitioner would not incorporate an inappropriate strategy of this nature, as it might actually increase the client's resistance to change. However, most school-based practitioners who might want to use MI principles to support children and young people may not have had access to this level of training. Most will not have come from a counselling background and few will have had specific training in MI. Previously McNamara (1998, 2009) has suggested the TTM as a useful model for assessing pupil readiness for change, and this has been my experience when working with young people and school-based practitioners.

DiClemente and Velasquez (2002) propose that the most obvious connection between the TTM and MI is that MI is an excellent approach to use with clients in the early stages of change e.g. precontemplative, because *"Precontemplators do not want to be lectured to or given "action" techniques when they are not ready to change"* (p203). In individual school behavioural management programmes, the key intervention strategy is often to put pupils onto behavioural 'contracts': this involves a series of positive behaviours being identified and then monitored by staff - sometimes with input from the pupil. This strategy is probably most appropriate at the 'action' or even the 'maintenance' stage of change. That is not to say that pupils at other stages of change should not receive a contract, but that other support may be required and that school staff should be open to the possibility that for some young people, it will be an ineffective strategy, particularly when the pupil does not 'own' or is not motivated to achieve the set targets. The TTM provides a visual framework for school-based professionals to discuss, consider and explore approaches which are more likely to help young people explore and challenge behaviours considered by others to be problematic.

## MI and the TTM for Young People

When working with young people using MI, Kittles and Atkinson (2009) found that providing pupils with a 'wheel of change' based on an adapted, pupil-friendly version of the TTM (see Figure 2 for an example) was positively evaluated by the young people. An example of how empowering developing an understanding of change processes can be for a young person can be found in Atkinson (2005). This details the work of a colleague who was able to work with a young person 'Ben', aged 13 on exploring the implications of his behavioural change in relation to 'staying away from the police' using the MI resource pack (Atkinson, 2005). Ben was additionally able to select a shape and an emotion from a selection available in the pack to associate with each stage of change. He was also able to add a statement about how he felt (see Figure 3).

## Chapter 2

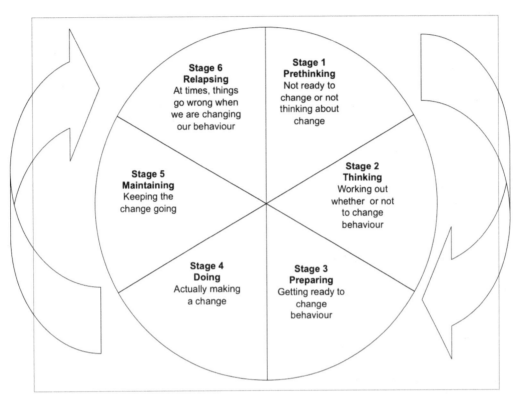

*Figure 2:* TTM adapted for young people

| Stage of Change | Statement | Shape | Emotion |
|---|---|---|---|
| **Stage One** Prethinking | Not bothered. Can't do anything to me. I didn't go to school as well | ■ stuck in a box going nowhere | No control |
| **Stage Two** Thinking | I've been to court and I have realised they can do something to me but I'm thinking about it. | ● things going round in your head 'cos you're thinking | Worried |
| **Stage Three** Preparing | I am going to change because I am on my last legs with the courts | ⊘ no more of the behaviour | Scared |
| **Stage Four** Doing | I am now staying away from the police and going to school | school ▲ home   probation | In control |
| **Stage Five** Maintaining | I now haven't arrested for about 8 months and I have been going to school | ★ I'm a star | I feel I've done well |
| **Stage Six** Relapsing | I could end up in the wrong gang and mess up again | ⚡ this means you're going down | |

*Figure 3:* Ben's (13 years) exploration of his behaviour "Staying away from the police" at the different stages of change

Another possible use of the TTM is to enable the young person to evaluate their behavioural progress using the TTM. During work undertaken as an educational psychologist using MI techniques to help Jessica (14) explore patterns of behaviour, Jessica chose to map onto a wheel of change thoughts she had about anti-social activities she had been engaged in outside school, although referral concerns were school-based. Jessica felt that for the time being she was able to positively maintain changes by staying away from other young people. She was able to talk through these changes and felt that it would be useful to talk to somebody neutral i.e. not with behavioural management responsibility, on a regular basis in school about the progress she was making. At a review meeting held subsequently in school, Jessica reported that she felt able to evaluate her behaviour in school using these techniques.

Hanley, Sefi, Cutts and Pattinson (2013) discuss the importance of collaboration in youth counselling. They advocate that the process of therapy should be co-constructed with the young person, not prescribed by the therapist, suggesting that this is facilitative of *"clients as active self-healing agents, who do not have something done to them in therapy, but rather do something themselves"* (p100). Having a transparent model which young people can relate to may be one way of promoting the 'agency' of young people.

## Use of MI Alongside Other Techniques

Another factor to consider is that many educational-based professionals are not using a single counselling modality in the same way that clinicians and therapists with expert training in MI might. For example, a recent survey of educational psychologists' (EPs') use of therapeutic interventions found that EPs use a wide range of therapeutic interventions, across a range of contexts with a variety of clients, including children and young people, staff and parents (Atkinson, Bragg, Squires, Muscutt and Wasilewski, 2011). In McNamara's (2009) edited book, links are made with a numbers of other therapeutic approaches including Cognitive Behavioural Therapy, Personal Construct Psychology, Positive Psychology and Solution Focused Brief Therapy. If practitioners are already trained in another approach, it makes sense for them to use these skills within a MI-based intervention; or, put another way, to integrate MI into their current practice - that is one which incorporates the spirit and principles of MI. Why then should the TTM also not be integrated into an MI based approach?

## Criticisms of the TTM Considered in the Context of School-Based Practice

Earlier in the chapter, I presented some of the arguments that constitute criticisms of the TTM within the academic literature. I will now explore the relevance of some of these arguments in the context of school based practice.

Firstly, there is the criticism that the 'stages' have been used to identify very specific behaviours. In clinical settings, frequently MI relates to one behaviour e.g. drinking, drug use, smoking. However, in schools, the 'behaviour' causing concern is often multi-faceted. For example, what a concerned adult might define as 'disruptive behaviour' might include talking out of turn, upsetting other pupils, 'backchatting' the teacher and walking out of lessons. Whereas it might be difficult to place each of these behaviours in relation to the TTM, experienced practitioners can often make an accurate judgement of where the pupil is in terms of what might be more broadly termed as 'a positive attitude to school' or the pupil's motivation to respond positively to the demands of school life.

Furthermore, school-based professionals are more likely to have a greater amount of information at their disposal when making a judgement about where the young person might be in relation to the TTM. Unlike non school-based clinicians, who might be meeting the client for the first time and may be reliant on the client's personal testimony via a questionnaire, school-based professionals are likely to have a history of very high level of contact with the young person about whom there is concern.

Additionally, they have the advantages of: i) being able to interact with them in different contexts; ii) observing them at different times of the day in different situations; and iii) accessing information from colleagues who also know the pupil well. Any school-based assessment made about pupil readiness for change in relation to the TTM is likely to be subtle, responsive to on-going information and involve discussion with colleagues. In educational settings this negates Wilson and Schlam's (2004) criticism of clients being assigned to an 'arbitrary' stage of change based perhaps on the results of a questionnaire.

In terms of the TTM, most school-based professionals have understood the model as one which can be used dynamically to assess pupil progress. Because good behavioural management and support programmes are constantly refined and evaluated, there is no need for pre prescribed intervention options which link to specific stages of change. Indeed, where interventions linked to the TTM have been offered (Atkinson, 2009; Atkinson and Amesu, 2007) these are often wide ranging and take into account the child in context. Thus there is a consideration of factors relating to the family, school environment, peer relationships and individual differences in children and young people, all of which may be facilitative or inhibitive of change. In school-based settings, because contact is daily and on-going, predicting outcomes based on assumptions that a pupil is at a particular stage of change is less of an issue. School-based professionals are well-placed to notice changes to motivation or behaviour and support and intervention strategies can be adapted accordingly. The TTM and MI principles can be used dynamically to develop personalised targets and goals and as these are ever evolving, there is not the same concept of a successful or less successful outcome.

The criticism that 'precontemplators' may be deprived of effective treatment is also redundant, as schools have an on-going responsibility to meet the needs of pupils and to seek advice where these are not being addressed. For example, when schools have referred pupils to me in my role as an educational psychologist, it has frequently been those who appear to be at the precontemplative stage of change. The rationale is often that the opportunity for a young person to speak to someone 'external' to the situation can sometimes help to identify opportunities for or barriers to change.

As previously discussed on page 21-22 most of the evidence-base for the use of MI in schools refers to interventions which have incorporated components of the TTM.

## So What is MI in School-Based Settings?

Given the assertion by Miller and Rollnick (2009) that MI is not the TTM and its effectiveness is not dependent on the TTM model, what does MI look like in school-based settings and can we still call it MI? For any intervention to be considered MI, it should reflect the spirit of MI and the principles of MI (Boxes 1 and 2: pages 19 and 20). As an MI practitioner, I am constantly conscious of the need for any MI intervention to reflect these features. However, I do not feel that using the TTM alongside MI, for example in the casework previously described, makes the intervention incongruous with the spirit and principles.

It is also of relevance to note that the spirit and principles are not unique to MI. Miller and Rollnick (2002) acknowledge the profound influence of Rogerian counselling principles (Rogers, 1951) on the development of MI, describing MI as an *"evolution of the client-centred approach that Rogers developed"* (p25). Similarly, Tober and Raistrick (2007) suggest that Rogerian principles of accurate empathy, positive regard and a non-judgemental and non-confrontational manner form the basis for the pragmatic MI approach initially developed by Miller (1983). Links between these elements and features of the spirit and principles, particularly collaboration and expressing empathy, are markedly clear (see Box 2).

Historically, links between MI and the TTM appear to be have been stronger in clinical settings, but it would appear that over time, the rigidity of the TTM's use in interventions such as smoking cessation has appeared to diminish its usefulness and in some cases may have hampered, rather than facilitated client progress. In school-based settings, it is likely that both MI and the TTM are not used in their purest form but instead have become frameworks for thinking about how to support and facilitate pupil change in a positive direction.

On the evidence available, I would argue that at this moment in educational settings, generally MI and the TTM appear to be seen as synonymous. Further research would be useful to ascertain to what extent MI and the TTM are used in parallel and to explore whether school-based MI practice exists which does not hold the TTM as a central framework - and how effective this is in supporting the needs of children and young people. However, from the limited research to date, it would seem that using the TTM alongside MI principles and techniques has been useful to school-based practitioners in considering the needs of young people and in delivering effective interventions.

## References

Adams, T. & Ridley, I. (1999). *Addicted.* Altrincham: Willow.

Atkinson, C. (2005). *Facilitating Change: Using Motivational Interviewing Techniques to Help Young People Explore their Behaviour.* Bath: Sodapop.

Atkinson, C. (2009). *MI in educational settings: Using MI with children and young people.* In McNamara, E. (Ed) Motivational Interviewing: Theory, Practice and Applications with Children and Young People.
Ainsdale: www.positivebehaviourmanagement.co.uk.

Atkinson, C., & Amesu, M. (2007). Using solution-focused approaches in Motivational Interviewing with young people. *Pastoral Care in Education, June,* 31-37.

Atkinson, C., Bragg, J., Squires, G., Muscutt, J. & Wasilewski, D. (2011). Educational Psychologists and therapeutic interventions – preliminary findings from a UK-wide survey. *Debate,* 140, 6-12.

Atkinson, C., & Woods, K. (2003). Motivational Interviewing Strategies for Disaffected Secondary School Students: A case example. *Educational Psychology in Practice* 19, 1, 49-64.

DiClemente, C. C., & Velasquez, M. M. (2002). *Motivational Interviewing and the Model of Stages of Change.* In Miller, W. R., and Rollnick, S. (Eds). Motivational Interviewing: Preparing People for Change. New York: Guildford Press.

Erol, S., & Erdogan, S. (2008). Application of a stage based motivational interviewing approach to adolescent smoking cessation: The Transtheoretical Model based study. *Patient education and counseling,* 72, 1, 42-48.

Etter, J-F. (2005). Theoretical tools for the Industrial Era in smoking cessation counselling: A comment on west. *Addiction,* 100, 1041-1042.

Fields, A. (2006). *Curriculum-Based Motivation Group: A Five Session Motivational Interviewing Group Intervention.* Portland: Hollifield Associates.

Hanley, T., Sefi, A., Cutts, L., & Pattison, S. (2013). *Research into youth counselling: A rationale for research informed pluralistic practice.* In Hanley, T., Humphrey, N., & Lennie, C. (Eds). Adolescent Counselling Psychology: Theory, Research and Practice. London: Routledge.

Kittles, M., & Atkinson, C. (2009). The usefulness of motivational interviewing as a consultation and assessment tool for working with young people. *Pastoral Care in Education,* 27, 3, 241-254.

## 30                                   Chapter 2

McNamara, E. (1992). Motivational Interviewing: The gateway to pupil self-management. *Pastoral Care,* September, 22-28.

McNamara, E. (1998). *The Theory and Practice of Eliciting Pupil Motivation: Motivational Interviewing - A Form Teacher's Manual and Guide for Students, Parents, Psychologists, Health Visitors and Counsellors.* Ainsdale, Merseyside: Positive Behaviour Management: www.positivebehaviourmanagement.co.uk

McNamara, E. (2001). *Motivational interviewing and cognitive intervention.* In Gray, P. (Ed). Working with Emotions: Responding to the Challenge of Difficult Pupil Behaviour in Schools. London: RoutledgeFalmer.

McNamara, E. (2009). *The Theory and Practice of MI.* In McNamara, E. (Ed). Motivational Interviewing. Theory, Practice and Applications with Children and Young People. Ainsdale, Merseyside: Positive Behaviour Management: www.positivebehaviourmanagement.co.uk

McNamara, E., & Atkinson, C. (2010). Engaging the reluctant with Motivational Interviewing. *Counselling Children and Young People,* December, 15-21.

Miller, W. R. (1983) Motivational Interviewing with problem drinkers. *Behavioural Psychotherapy,* 11, 147-172.

Miller, W. R., & Rollnick, S. (1991). *Motivational Interviewing: Preparing People to Change Addictive Behaviour.* New York: Guildford Press.

Miller, W. R., & Rollnick, S. (2002). *Motivational Interviewing: Preparing People for Change.* New York: Guildford Press.

Miller, W. R., & Rollnick, S. (2009). Ten Things that Motivational Interviewing Is Not. *Behavioural and Cognitive Psychotherapy,* 37, 127-129.

Moss, C. (2010). *How Effective is a Group Based Motivational Interviewing Intervention in Promoting Pupil Resilience and Self-Esteem?* University of Nottingham, Unpublished Doctoral Thesis.

Prochaska, J. O. (1979) *Systems in Psychotherapy. A Transtheoretical Analysis.* Homewood, Ill: Dorsey Press.

Prochaska, J. O., & DiClemente, C. C. (1982). Transtheoretical Therapy: Toward a More Integrative Model of Change. *Psychotherapy: Theory Research and Practice,* 19, 3, 276-288.

Prochaska, J. O., & DiClemente, C. C. (1998). *Comments, criteria and creating better models:* In response to Davidson, in Miller, W. and Heather, N. (Eds) Treating Addictive Behaviours, 2nd edition. New York: Plenum Press.

Prochaska, J. O., Norcross, J. C., & DiClemente, C. C. (1994). *Changing for Good: A Revolutionary Six-Stage Program for Overcoming Bad Habits and Moving Your Life Positively Forward.* New York: Quill

Reniscow, K., DiIorio, C., Soet, J. E., Borrell, B., Ernst, D., Hecht, J., & Thevos, A. K. (2002). *Motivational Interviewing in Medical and Public Health Settings.* In Miller, W. R. & Rollnick, S. Motivational Interviewing: Preparing People for Change. New York: Guildford Press.

Rogers, C. (1951). *Client-centred Therapy.* Boston: Houghton-Mifflin.

Rollnick, S., Heather, N., & Bell, A. (1992). Negotiating behaviour change in medical settings: The development of brief motivational interviewing. *Journal of Mental Health,* 1, 25-37.

Tober, G. & Raistrick, D. (Eds) (2005). *Motivational Dialogue: Preparing addiction professionals for motivational interviewing practice.* Hove: Routledge.

van Bilsen, H. (1991). *Motivational Interviewing: Perspectives from the Netherlands.* In Miller, W. R. & Rollnick, S. (Eds). Motivational Interviewing: Preparing People for Change. New York: Guildford Press.

West, R. (2005). Time for a change: Putting the transtheoretical (stages of change) model to rest. *Addiction,* 100, pp. 1036-1039.

Wilson, T., & Schlam, T. R (2004). The transtheoretical model and motivational interviewing in the treatment of eating disorders. *Clinical Psychology Review,* 24, 361-378.

32 *Chapter 2*

# Chapter 3

# Evaluating Motivational Interviewing as Evidence-Based Practice using Systematic Literature Review

## Kevin Woods, Patrick McArdle and Nadia Tabassum

*University of Manchester*

### Introduction

*Evidence-based Practice*

With the aim of providing safe and effective intervention for clients, it is a common requirement for health and social care practitioners to understand and adhere to principles of 'evidence-based practice' (Frederickson, 2002; Roth and Pilling, 2007; Health and Care Professions Council, 2012; Bower and Gilbody, 2010). Accordingly, strategies and databases have been developed to support practitioners to use empirically-validated ('tried and tested') interventions and tools.

The National Institute for Health and Clinical Excellence (NHS, 2011a) provides guidance, sets quality standards and manages a national database ('NHS Evidence') as part of its aim to improve people's health and to prevent and treat ill health. NHS Evidence (NHS, 2011b) was established in 2009 to ensure that everyone working in health and social care has free, quick and easy access to the quality-assured, best-practice information that is required to inform evidence-based decision making. Through NHS Evidence (NHS, 2011b) users can search more than 150 sources simultaneously, including internationally respected evidence-based sources such as the Cochrane Library, British National Formulary and Map of Medicine. The types of resources available include guidelines, primary research and clinical summaries. The National Institute of Health Research (NIHR, 2011) has a supporting role to NHS Evidence through the development of research evidence which can support decision-making by professionals, policy makers and patients, and to make this evidence available.

There is an acknowledgement, however, that the linking of evidence to research is not a simple matter since i) there are different types, sources and qualities of research and ii) research relevant to a particular practice issue may be limited in availability, or indeed absent (Frederickson, 2002; American Psychological Association (APA), 2006). Scott et al. (2001) outline a traditional hierarchy of research evidence for treatment efficacy, with systematic reviews of randomised controlled trials (RCTs) being the 'gold standard', individual opinion being the lowest ranked form of evidence, and quasi-experimental trials and controlled case studies being between the two. Additionally, the APA (2006) identifies the relative merits of different research for evidence-based practice.

For example:

- RCTs as the best approach for drawing causal inferences about the general effects of interventions;

- process-outcome studies as valuable in identifying the mechanisms of change;

- qualitative research as useful to describe the lived experiences of people, including clients in psychotherapy;

- individual case studies as valuable sources of innovation and hypotheses, as well as establishing causal relationships in the context of an individual.

It follows then that the APA (2006) offers a broad definition of evidence-based practice:

*'Evidence-based practice in psychology (EBPP) is the integration of the best available research with clinical expertise in the context of patient characteristics, culture and preferences'* (p.273).

This position is congruent with proponents of 'practice-based evidence' who support the safe trialling of innovative techniques by practitioners, with the aim of building an inclusive, practitioner-led research evidence base (Barkham, Hardy and Mellor-Clark, 2010). Notably, the APA (2006) stresses the importance of not assuming that interventions on which there are no published controlled trials are ineffective.

### Motivational Interviewing and Evidence-Based Practice

Against this background, Motivational Interviewing (MI) practitioners need to be aware of the range of supporting evidence for an MI intervention within a particular context. Woods, Bond, Humphrey, Symes and Green (2011) point out that professional training needs to equip practitioners to become skilled in developing approaches to evidence-based practice, both at individual and organizational levels. A skill set for evidence-based practice will include the skills

*Chapter 3* 35

of finding and critically evaluating evidence from research cf. Munro (2011), as well as specific skills in research design and implementation. This chapter reports upon a practitioner-based enquiry entailing a systematic literature review on the effectiveness of MI with a particular focus for children and young people. As such, the description and evaluation of the review process may be useful to MI practitioners in other contexts, and to practitioners of other similar interventions.

*Background to the Systematic Literature Review*

Research has shown that using MI with adult clients in advance of a standard intervention increases the likelihood of the client staying in treatment and adhering to intervention recommendations, as well as leading to improved outcomes in comparison to the standard intervention without MI (Bien, Miller, and Boroughs, 1993; Brown and Miller, 1993). This is of interest to professionals working with children and young people as it suggests that the use of MI at an early stage of working with pupils might lead to better outcomes for any intervention that is put in place.

A recent United Kingdom (UK) study indicates that MI is the fourth most commonly used therapeutic intervention by educational psychologists after solution focused brief therapy, cognitive behaviour therapy and personal construct psychology (Atkinson, Bragg, Squires, Muscutt and Wasilewski, 2011). Given then the relevance of MI to UK educational psychologists' work, this systematic literature review aimed to answer the following question: what is the research evidence for the effectiveness of individually-based MI with school age pupils in the UK?

### i. *Selection of Research Studies*

In order to identify research relevant to the review question the following databases were searched: Psycinfo, Web of Knowledge, ERIC, and Medline.

The initial search terms used in a search of the Psycinfo database included: 'motivational interviewing', 'school', 'young people' and 'education'. This yielded an unmanageable number of publications (3,104). On the basis of an initial survey of the numerous publications, the search was refined to the above search terms but with the addition of exclusions for 'drug*', "smoke*' or 'alcohol*' in the title or abstract. Searches were then made systematically in each aforementioned database in turn yielding a total of 7 finds. The following inclusion criteria were then applied to the finds:

- MI within an educational/ school-based setting

- MI with child/ young person participants

- MI in the UK

- Recent study, i.e. published between 2001 and 2011

- Study subjected to peer review in an academic journal

36                                    *Chapter 3*

Filtering by the application of these inclusion criteria resulted in two published studies being included – Atkinson and Amesu (2007); Kittles and Atkinson (2009). A third study by Atkinson and Woods (2003) was identified from the reference list of the published study by Atkinson and Amesu (2007).[1]

### ii. Overview

A summary of the sample, intervention, measures and outcomes of each of the three selected studies is provided in Appendix 1.

Following Gough (2007), the three studies were rated by the authors for their methodological quality, appropriateness of research methods, and focus of evidence; these three dimensions were summated to an 'overall weight of evidence' in relation to the review question (see Appendix 2 for rating criteria).

| Study | Methodological Quality | Appropriateness of research method | Focus of evidence for the review method | Overall weight of evidence |
|---|---|---|---|---|
| Atkinson and Woods (2003) | *Medium* | *High* | *High* | *High* |
| Atkinson and Amesu (2007) | *Low* | *Low* | *Medium* | *Low* |
| Kittles and Atkinson (2009) | *High* | *Medium* | *High* | *High* |

### iii. Research Methodology and Quality

All three studies looked at the use of MI to change behavior and motivation when working with pupils of secondary school age who were experiencing 'disaffection' and presenting behavioural concerns. Although MI was the primary intervention approach in each case, Atkinson and Amesu (2007) incorporated the use of Solution-Focused Brief Therapy (SFBT) (De Shazer, 1985; Rhodes and Ajmal, 1995). Atkinson and Amesu (2007) do not detail precisely how they combined SFBT techniques with MI, making it unclear which outcomes might be due to SFBT components, or MI components, or a specific combination of both approaches. Lack of detail in the description of the MI process employed by Atkinson and Amesu (2007) also hinders potential replications by other researchers or practitioners.

All three studies used a case study, or case study series design and so all were evaluated according to an adapted version of the quality evaluation framework for qualitative research from Spencer, Ritchie, Lewis and Dillon (2003) (see Appendix 2) cf. Woods et al. (2011). Both Atkinson and Woods (2003) and Atkinson and Amesu (2007) used one participant in their design, whereas Kittles and Atkinson (2009) used three. Though case studies are not appropriate bases from which to draw statistically generalisable conclusions, a degree of analytic generalisability may be obtained through detailed data which may convincingly illustrate potential

[1] Within systematic literature review, the activity of searching through the reference lists of found research reports is known as 'reference harvesting'.

*Chapter 3*                                                                                    37

causal relationships between observed outcomes and specific aspects of the intervention (Atkinson and Woods, 2003; Atkinson and Amesu, 2007; Kittles and Atkinson, 2009; Yin, 2009). Using case study methodology enables researchers and practitioners to explore, or explain, effectiveness of interventions within the 'real-life' contexts in which children learn and develop and within which practitioners work. In this respect, Atkinson and Woods (2003) provide the most detailed and comprehensive picture about the effectiveness of using MI with a disaffected secondary school pupil.

Drawing from Atkinson and Woods (2003), Kittles and Atkinson (2009) noted that the focus of previous research into the use of MI in educational settings tended to be as an intervention strategy, rather than an assessment tool, which consequently became the focus of their research. Kittles and Atkinson (2009) aimed to evaluate the effectiveness of MI as an assessment tool in initial consultation in relation to its usefulness for informing future involvement and intervention. They also proposed to evaluate the usefulness of the MI menu of strategies (Rollnick et al., 1992), in assessing the social and emotional needs of young people. Furthermore, the authors stated that previous research had evaluated the process of MI by means of outcomes for young people whereas their study would add to this by investigating pupils' views about the MI process. This would be of importance for those practitioners who use MI as it is ethically necessary to consult clients about interventions that are planned in their interest and to give them a voice in relation to these interventions (British Psychological Society, 1997). These aims appear to be well thought out, meet the recommendations of previous research in MI, and by including the views of the young people involved, contribute to a greater understanding of the effectiveness of MI for young people.

With reference to previous research, Atkinson and Woods (2003) clearly justify how their MI intervention is appropriate to work with a disaffected young person at risk of exclusion. Atkinson and Amesu (2007) identify a participant with behavioural and attendance problems though their brief description does not link strongly to the case for an MI intervention, rather than a direct intervention to improve behavioural adjustment. Since MI requires an ability to express thoughts and feelings about events and circumstances (Atkinson and Amesu, 2007), it would have been preferable for all three studies to evaluate language and communication capabilities when identifying potential participants.

Kittles and Atkinson (2009) point out a limitation of their evaluation is that one of the researchers was also the practitioner conducting the MI sessions. They acknowledged that participants might have been more able to be critical of the MI process if they had been interviewed by a non involved interviewer. However, this resource was not available to the researchers and they state that participants were explicitly informed that it was acceptable to be critical of the process of MI.

Whilst Kittles and Atkinson's (2009) qualitative data gathering was sufficiently detailed to allow replication, analyses of qualitative data were limited to the

38                                    *Chapter 3*

researchers' own interpretations i.e. there was no incorporation of validation strategies such as member checking or use of multiple data coders.

Atkinson and Woods (2003) was the only study which administered standardized pre- and post- intervention measures within the case study. They used the 'Myself as a Learner Scale' (MALS) (Burden, 1998) and the 'Pupils' Feelings about School and School Work' (PFSSW) (Entwistle and Kozeki, 1985). Triangulation of findings was supported by teacher completion of an evaluation form. Intervention fidelity was monitored through full audio-taping of MI sessions.

Across the three studies the amount of MI intervention (sometimes known as 'dosage') may have been instrumental, but is not always specified or justified. For example, Atkinson and Woods (2003) provided five one-hour sessions on a weekly basis; Kittles and Atkinson (2009) provided three MI sessions of unspecific duration; and Atkinson and Amesu (2007) do not state how many MI sessions were provided in addition to the initial solution-focused discussion.

### iv.  *Findings*

A general conclusion from all three studies is that the MI intervention was effective when working with disaffected children at secondary school. Atkinson and Amesu (2007) found that although the pupil's attendance increased, the number of behavioural problem incidents also increased. The researchers assert, though without clear justification, that this is a result of the pupil spending longer periods in school. The researchers show that using SFBT measures, such as scaling and goal setting can be used to meet the goals of pupils, whilst also giving an indication of the stage of change the child is at. Atkinson and Amesu (2007) report that an effective strategy for the pupil is to have a link person to talk to when he came into school in the morning, which begs a question as to which MI techniques, if any, were instrumental in effecting positive change.

Atkinson and Woods (2003) use extracts from transcriptions of pupils' MI sessions as evidence that show that the pupil has moved from the 'pre-contemplative' to the 'determinism' stage of change. Discussions with members of staff in relation to attendance and punctuality for the pupil also reported improvements; after the intervention was complete the pupil continued to attend school. Pre- and post- intervention measures from the PFSSW appear to show significant positive change, though the researchers' application of inferential statistical analysis is inappropriate and potentially misleading (Field, 2009). Atkinson and Woods (2003) outline a range of identified 'process' and 'practice' issues within the MI delivery, which meets the broader aim of the study to identify specifically effective MI techniques and applications of MI by practitioner educational psychologists.

In Kittles and Atkinson's (2009) study, two out of the three participants were positive about the process of MI and found the approach useful. One young person - who perceived the MI process in a negative way - was judged to be at

*Chapter 3* 39

the pre-contemplative stage, whereas the other two pupils were judged to be at the contemplative stage. This confirms the authors' proposition that MI may, in different ways, form a useful part of assessment of a young person within an educational context. Kittles and Atkinson (2009) suggest that since 'readiness to change' might affect a young person's response to, and view of, the MI process, a negative view of the MI process might not be problematic in that it may still provide a basis for positive behavioural change. The authors also propose that a young person's 'social communication skills and emotional literacy skills' might be a factor in predicting positive outcomes from MI, although the ways in which this might be evidenced are not elaborated.

Notwithstanding participant feedback, findings from Kittles and Atkinson (2009) do provide evidence for the effectiveness of the MI process in challenging a young person's thinking and enabling them to think about the future. Eleven categories of information were recorded from Kittles and Atkinson's (2009) interpretive phenomenological analysis (IPA) of the first MI sessions, which the researchers posit to show a breadth of useful assessment information. However, it could be argued that in the course of a standard consultation with a young person, many practitioners would be unable to employ IPA as a form of analysis, which is a potential limitation on the ecological validity of the authors' conclusions. Nonetheless, the categories of information which emerged from the initial sessions do undoubtedly provide insight to the lives of the young people concerned, supporting the conclusion that MI could be a useful assessment tool with training and resources in methods of analysis.

Further to the researchers' own analyses of MI first session outcomes, Kittles and Atkinson (2009) evaluated the practical outcomes of the MI sessions with reference to the action plans generated by the young person during their initial session and the subsequent consultation between the MI practitioner and school staff. The researchers identified seven areas in which the influence of the MI assessment information could be seen for one or more of the three young people:

- New information to be shared, e.g. about difficulties/problems experienced

- Appropriate future therapeutic provision

- Behaviour management strategies

- Leisure/vocational opportunities

- Involvement of other agencies

- Academic support

- Relationship building

However, in the absence of follow-up data, the longer term impact of MI and the durability and effectiveness of consequent intervention strategies, remains untested.

## 40                                          *Chapter 3*

*Conclusions and Implications from this Systematic Literature Review*

This systematic literature review revealed that there is a small number of UK research studies evaluating the use of MI with individual children in school. The available studies all employ case study designs, of varying quality, and are reports of practitioner, rather than independently commissioned, research. Nonetheless, the available evidence, though limited in scope and methodological range, provides promising positive indication about the effectiveness of MI with individual school-age children.

In order to consolidate and extend the evidence base for motivational interviewing, it would be useful to undertake:

- Larger scale experimental design research incorporating control or comparison ('treatment as usual') groups, standardized outcome measures, and controlled intervention procedures, to establish the general effectiveness of MI with specified client groups within specified contexts.

- Case study research to explore the use of MI with younger children e.g. of primary school age, and establish its possible effectiveness through age-appropriate adaptations.

In relation to the recommendation for larger scale research it is notable that the research reported within the present review was carried out in each case by practitioners as part of their professional role. The authors would argue that larger scale experimental research is likely to be difficult to incorporate to service delivery models without resourcing or support from an independent commissioner or partner.

*Reflections on Using Literature Review to Support Evidence-Based Practice in MI*

The authors identified two considerations relating to the process of this review which have implications for its utility. First, any review method will contain anomalies, inconsistencies or gaps, which lead to unreliability of findings. For example the paper by Atkinson and Woods (2003) was found through reference harvesting from Kittles and Atkinson (2009) though the latter paper would likely have been publishable without inclusion of the reference to Atkinson and Woods (2003). In this event, the paper by Atkinson and Woods (2003), deemed to be the highest quality study in this review, would have been omitted since it was not, for whatever reason, found using the standard search terms within the main databases. Similarly, with additional resourcing the number of databases searched and/ or search term combinations used, could have been expanded, perhaps yielding one or two additional finds. It is also relevant to the reliability of the review process that ratings of methodological quality may vary between raters, and even high levels of general inter-rater reliability may belie specific inaccuracies or inconsistencies by which some studies are rated unreliably on some occasions. This means that a significant research study could be inaccurately weighted within the emerging evidence base. The authors would recommend that methods to improve study rating reliability should be included in reviews, such as blind reviews, reviewer training and calibration exercises and the use of additional reviewers; reliability co-efficients should be stated and evaluated.

Second, the comprehensiveness of the review analysis depends on what can be and is captured and analysed by the reviewers. The writer of a research study must write within a specified short word limit (usually no more than 5,000 words) and to the requirements of the publication outlet, such as an academic journal. Publication requirements and styles may be influenced by several quality assurance factors, such as nature of the readership, which may affect the balance and content of the finished research report. For example, an academic journal with a high practitioner readership may encourage authors to write more on practical implications of the reported research, reducing the word space for authors to detail methodology, which might in turn affect the judgements about methodological quality by a reviewer who evaluates the work in relation to a specific question about intervention efficacy. In the present review, the study by Atkinson and Amesu (2007) was coded as low methodological quality primarily because the report was clearly serving to provide a generic practitioner readership with background information about MI (and SFBT), relegating the report of the empirical case study to a vignette.

Two further considerations relating to comprehensiveness of the present review are i) the lack of negative case analyses, since practitioner researchers may be less inclined to submit negative findings and ii) the omission, due to lack of available evidence, of any analysis of professional role, training and supervision means that it is not clear whether the MI therapist's background training, rather than the MI itself, was crucial to the effectiveness of MI. Within the present sample all the MI practitioners appeared to be psychologists, trainee psychologists or social workers by professional background, roles which entail considerable experience of individual client work. Findings from the review might not generalize to other practitioners working with school age children who might not have similar levels of training and experience of individual personal development work with children e.g. subject specialist school teachers.

Further to these considerations about the review process, the authors also identify three general considerations which may have implications for the way in which MI practitioners make use of systematic literature reviews in evaluating the relevant research. First, the relevance of the findings is a function of the specific focus of the review question being asked. In the present study, for example, the focus was upon MI delivered to individuals and so relevant high quality research focusing upon MI effectiveness with groups of school-aged children would be completely omitted e.g. Moss, 2011, though the findings may well be relevant if the MI process shows good integrity and the participant sampling is appropriate. Practitioners must therefore be cautious not to generalize conclusions from review findings beyond the scope of the particular review.

42                                    *Chapter 3*

Second, the APA (2006) definition of evidence-based practice indicates use of best available research but this does not suggest criteria by which to decide what research should constitute the 'best available'. For example, in the present review Atkinson and Amesu (2007) received a low overall weighting in relation to the specific research question since the paper was primarily a practitioner information report rather than a research report, yet this study was not excluded from the small pool of 'best available evidence'. Had more relevant research been found, the reviewers might have been able to enhance the potential utility of the review by delimiting the pool of best evidence, perhaps to those studies of at least medium level overall weighting and quality.

Third, though this review's general conclusion that there is promising positive indication about the effectiveness of MI with individual school-age children is justified, there are within the review evidence degrees of such positive finding and indeed some ambivalent finding e.g. that one student in the study by Kittles and Atkinson (2008) did not positively evaluate the MI experience. Practitioners must be cautious not to take simplistic general 'answers' from systematic reviews, instead looking in detail at review findings to identify degrees, or patterns of outcome evidence relating to the specific review question cf. Miller and Frederickson, (2006). Notably, in reviews of quantitative research evidence 'effect size' calculations can be useful in gauging degree of impact of an intervention (Field, 2009). Yet even within an intervention where there is evidence of a general pattern of successful outcomes, that pattern may include some degrees or instances of negative outcome cf. Woods et al. (2011).

In conclusion, the availability of systematic reviews of published evidence is undoubtedly valuable for practitioners working to evidence-based principles since it provides a broader and more controlled context for their learning from practice (Munro, 2011). In essence, practitioners are indeed themselves researchers, with access to data from a series of case studies i.e. their casework. However, since such data are not systematically gathered and analysed for the purpose of generalisation, it is more likely that selective biases, for example due to salience or recency or personal orientation, may influence evaluative judgments. MI practitioners need strategies and access routes for regularly accessing relevant, up-to-date, systematic review information through either specialist databases e.g. PsychInfo, NHS evidence and/ or publicly available search engines e.g. GoogleScholar.

## References

American Psychological Association (APA) (2006). Evidence-based Practice in Psychology, *American Psychologist,* 61(4), 271-286.

Atkinson, C., & Amesu, M. (2007). Using solution-focused approaches in motivational interviewing with young people, *Pastoral Care,* 31-37.

Atkinson, C., & Woods, K. (2003). Motivational interviewing strategies for disaffected secondary school students: a case example, *Educational Psychology in Practice,* 19 (1), 49-64.

Atkinson, C., Bragg, J., Squires, G., Muscutt, J., & Wasilewski, D. (2011). Educational Psychologists and therapeutic interventions: preliminary findings from a UK-wide survey. DECP *Debate, 140,* 6-12.

Barkham, M., Hardy, G. & Mellor-Clark, J. (2010). *Developing and Delivering Practice-Based Evidence: a guide for the psychological therapies.* London: John Wiley & Sons.

Bien, T. H., Miller, W. R, & Boroughs, J. M. (1993). Motivational interviewing with alcohol outpatients, *Behavioral and Cognitive Psychotherapy, 21,* 347-356.

Bower, P. & Gilbody, S. (2010). The Current View of Evidence-Based Practice. In M. Barkham, G. Hardy, & J. Mellor-Clark. (eds). (2010). *Developing and Delivering Practice-Based Evidence: a guide for the psychological therapies.* London: John Wiley & Sons.

British Psychological Society (1997). *Code of Conduct, Ethical principles and Guidelines.* Leicester: British Psychological Society.

Brown, J. M., & Miller, W. R. (1993). Impact of motivational interviewing on participation and outcome in residential alcohol treatment. *Psychology of Addictive Behaviors, 7,* 211-218.

Burden, R.L. (1998). Assessing Children's perceptions of themselves as learners and problem-solvers. *School Psychology International,* 19(4), 291-305.

De Shazer, S. (1985). *Keys to solutions in brief therapy.* New York: W.W. Norton.

Entwistle, N. J., & Kozeki, B. (1985). Relationships between school motivation, approaches to studying a attainment among British and Hungarian adolescents. *British Journal of Educational Psychology,* 55, 124-137.

Field, A. (2009). *Discovering Statistics Using SPSS* (3rd edition). London: Sage Publications.

Frederickson, N. (2002). Evidence-based practice and educational psychology, *Educational and Child Psychology,* 19(3), 96-111.

Gough D (2007). Weight of Evidence: a framework for the appraisal of the quality and relevance of evidence In J. Furlong and A. Oancea (Eds.) Applied and Practice-based Research. Special Edition of *Research Papers in Education,* 22(2), 213-228.

Health and Care Professions Council (HPC). (2012). *Standards of Proficiency: practitioner psychologists.* London: HPC

Kittles, M., & Atkinson, C. (2009). The usefulness of motivational interviewing as a consultation and assessment tool for working with young people. *Pastoral Care in Education,* 27,3, 241-254.

Miller, A. & Frederickson, N. (2006). Generalizable findings and idiographic problems: struggles and successes for educational psychologists as scientist-practitioners. In D. Lane & S. Corrie (eds.). *The Modern Scientist-Practitioner: a guide to practice in psychology.* London: Routledge.

Moss, C. (2011). *How effective is group-based motivational interviewing intervention in promoting pupil resilience and self-esteem?* University of Nottingham: Unpublished doctoral thesis.

Munro, E. (2011). *The Munro Review of Child Protection (Final Report): a child centred system.* Norwich: TSO.

National Institute of Health Research (NIHR). (2011). The National Institute of Health Research. <http://www.nihr.ac.uk/Pages/default.aspx>. [Accessed 12th January 2012].

National Health Service (NHS) (2011a). NICE guidance. <http://guidance.nice.org.uk/>. [Accessed 12th January 2012].

National Health Service (NHS) (2011b). NHS Evidence – about us. <https://www.evidence.nhs.uk/about-us>. [Accessed 12th January 2012].

Rhodes, J. & Ajmal, Y. (1995). *Solution focused thinking in schools: behaviour, reading and organisation.* London: BT Press.

Rollnick, S., Heather, N. & Bell, A. (1992). Negotiating behaviour change in medical settings. The development of brief motivational interviewing, *Journal of Mental Health,* 1, 25-37.

Roth, A.D. & Pilling, S. (2007). *A Competence Framework for the Supervision of Psychological Therapies.* University College London: Research Department of Clinical, Educational and Health Psychology.

Scott, A., Shaw, M., & Joughin, C. (2001). *Finding the Evidence: a gateway to the literature in child and adolescent mental health* (2nd edition). London: Gaskell (Royal College of Psychiatrists).

Spencer, L., Ritchie, J., Lewis, J., & Dillon, L. (2003). Quality in qualitative evaluation: a framework for assessing research evidence: a quality framework. National Centre for Social Research. London: Cabinet Office.

Woods, K., Bond, C., Humphrey, N., Symes, W. & Green, L. (2011). *Research Report 179: Systematic Review of Solution Focused Brief Therapy (SFBT) with Children and Families.* London: HM Government (Department for Education).

Yin, R.K. (2009) *Case Study Research: Design and Methods (4th edition).* London: SAGE Publications.

# Appendix 1

| Study | Sample | Intervention | Target Behaviours | Study Design | Measures | Outcomes |
|---|---|---|---|---|---|---|
| Atkinson & Woods (2003) | Single Yr 10 pupil | 5 one hour MI sessions once a week | - sporadic attendance<br>- poor record of handing homework<br>- 'apathy' towards school<br>- behaviour in class<br>- disaffection | Case study | Myself as a learner scale(MALS)<br>Pupils feelings about school and school work (PFSSW) | - Higher post intervention MALS and PFSSW<br>- Teacher evaluation more positive shift in her attitude and confidence<br>- Quantitative and qualitative analysis shows it's a successful and useful intervention<br>- Improved attendance and punctuality. |
| Atkinson & Amesu (2007) | Single Yr 7 pupil | Combination of using MI and SFBT | Behavioural and attendance issues | Case study | - Scaling<br>- Attendance figures | Improvement in attendance.<br>- Increase in behavioural incidents. |
| Kittles & Atkinson (2009) | 3 pupils aged 13-15 | 3 MI sessions | - Disaffection<br>- At risk of exclusion<br>- Behaviour change | Case study | Evaluation through semi-structured interview | 2 out of 3 were positive about outcomes.<br>7 practical outcomes: info-sharing with staff, therapeutic work, behaviour management, widening leisure/ vocational interest, other agency involvement, academic support,relationship building. |

# Appendix 2 - Rating criteria for MI systematic literature review

## *Methodological Quality*

| | Appropriateness of research design | Sampling Rationale | Data collection well executed | Analysis close to data | Emergent theory relates to problem | Explicit reflexivity | Comprehensive documentation | Negative case analysis | Clear and coherent reporting | Researcher participant negotiation | Transferable conclusions | Attention to ethical issues | **score (/12)** |
|---|---|---|---|---|---|---|---|---|---|---|---|---|---|
| Atkinson & Woods (2003) | Yes | Yes | Yes | Yes | Yes | X | Yes | X | Yes | X | Yes | X | 8/12 |
| Atkinson & Amesu (2007) | Yes | X | X | X | X | Yes | X | X | X | X | X | X | 5/12 |
| Kittles & Atkinson (2009) | Yes | Yes | Yes | Yes | Yes | Yes | Yes | X | Yes | X | Yes | Yes | 10/12 |

Quality rating thresholds: 'Low' = 0-4; 'Medium' = 5-8; 'High' = 9-12; 'data collection well executed' and 'analysis close to data' must both be present for medium or high quality rating.

## _Methodological Appropriateness_

|  | Use of outcome measures | Clear rationale for participant selection | Clear description of MI process |
|---|---|---|---|
| Atkinson & Woods (2003) | Yes | Yes | Yes |
| Atkinson & Amesu (2007) | No | No | Yes |
| Kittles & Atkinson (2009) | No | Yes | Yes |

Appropriateness rating thresholds: 'Low' = 0-1 criterion; 'medium' = 2 criteria met; 'high' = 3 criteria met

## _Focus of Study_

|  | Solely MI used | School age participants | Individually-based MI delivery |
|---|---|---|---|
| Atkinson & Woods (2003) | Yes | Yes | Yes |
| Atkinson & Amesu (2007) | Yes | Yes | Yes |
| Kittles & Atkinson (2009) | Yes | Yes | Yes |

Focus rating thresholds: 'Low' = 0-1 criterion; 'medium' = 2 criteria met; 'high' = 3 criteria met.

# Part 2

# Motivational Interviewing: Further Applications

48

# Chapter 4

# MI for Children and Young People: an Overview

## Sebastian G Kaplan

*Department of Psychiatry and Behavioral Medicine, Child and Adolescent Psychiatry section, Wake Forest University School of Medicine*

William Miller introduced Motivational Interviewing (MI; Miller, 1983) as an approach to help adults reduce problem drinking. Gradually, through creative program development, rigorous research, and professional collaboration, the empirical support for MI as a method to help adults with addictions and other conditions that necessitate behaviour change grew. As is often the case, with the increasingly successful dissemination of MI for adult conditions, clinicians and researchers began to consider whether MI would be an effective method for helping children and young people (CYP) with similar difficulties.

Extending MI to CYP is more than a simple exploration of whether an adult treatment works for youth. Scholars have suggested that MI is particularly well suited to meet the unique developmental needs of adolescents and young adults (Baer and Peterson, 2002). Interactions between adults and youth commonly involve negative or controlling interactions (Ingersoll, Wagner and Gharib, 2002) that frequently results in increased defensiveness on the part of people struggling with complex decisions. On the other hand, major tenets of MI, such as supporting client autonomy, working in collaboration with clients, and honoring client beliefs and values, align well with adolescent developmental processes, including identity formation and striving for independence (Naar-King, 2011).

50                                  *Chapter 4*

Although the rationale for applying MI when working with CYP is strong, it is worth considering how young an individual can be for MI to remain effective? Most of the literature on MI for CYP begins with adolescence due to the aforementioned alignment between normal developmental processes and core elements of MI. While there is limited literature to help guide the question of whether MI works with children 12 years of age and under, it would seem logical that the younger a person is the more difficulty they may have considering how or why they should make complex life changes. Furthermore, the notion of autonomy is also relative when working with younger children whose parents are, and at times need to be, more influential in their children's lives than adolescents.

Despite what appears to be a good fit between MI and the clinical needs of CYP, research on the application of MI with youth is just getting started. Programs have begun to incorporate MI in the treatment of CYP struggling with substance use, chronic medical conditions, and psychiatric difficulties with promising results that encourage further exploration with scientific rigour. What follows is an overview of these diverse applications and commentary on promising future areas.

## MI and Substance Use

Not surprisingly given that MI originated in the treatment of adults with problem drinking, the most widely researched application of MI for CYP has been as a treatment for substance misuse. Consistent with the strong support for MI as a treatment for adults (Hettema, Steele and Miller, 2005), the only meta-analysis on MI for CYP substance use to date found small but significant effect sizes both at post-treatment and at follow-up (Jensen et al., 2011). Jensen et al. examined 21 studies, the majority of which used single-session interventions (62%) delivered by practitioners without advanced graduate degrees (79%). Also noteworthy were the range of substances examined in the studies, which included outcomes for marijuana (57%), alcohol (57%), tobacco (33%), street drugs such as cocaine and methamphetamine (29%), and polysubstances (43%). Therefore MI presents as a flexible and potentially cost-effective intervention strategy.

Jensen et al. (op cit) noted the reliance on community-based samples as a limitation in their meta-analysis. However, it can be argued that delivering MI in community settings may be a particular strength of MI as many youth already receive behavioural interventions in these settings e.g. school, clinics. For example, D'Amico, Miles, Stern and Meredith (2008) designed Project CHAT, a drug and alcohol intervention delivered in an urban community health clinic, which was successful in reducing teens' marijuana use and related behaviours. Kelly and Lapworth (2006) tested a school-based MI intervention for adolescents who smoke tobacco and found short-term effects on reduced smoking compared to standard care. Bailey, Baker, Webster and Lewin (2004) also found promising results from a pilot study using a combined MI and cognitive-behavioural group intervention targeting alcohol use in teens recruited from a community youth center.

Examples of successful MI-based interventions for adolescent substance use occurring in traditional medical settings also exist. Monti et al. (1999) found reductions in alcohol consumption in older adolescents following a single-session MI-based intervention in a hospital emergency department following an alcohol related injury. Colby et al. (1998) found positive short-term results on tobacco behaviour in teens after an MI intervention administered across several hospital settings. Hollis et al. (2005) developed Teen Reach, an MI-based and computer assisted tobacco reduction intervention delivered to teens in pediatric and family practice settings. Hollis et al. (op cit) found long-term reductions in smoking among teens that described themselves as smokers at baseline. These studies demonstrate the flexibility of MI across target substances as well as medical and community settings.

## MI and Chronic Medical Conditions

Research on the application of MI for the management of pediatric medical conditions has shown encouraging preliminary outcomes (Suarez and Mullins, 2008). In two of the earliest studies of MI for the management of diabetes, Channon and colleagues (2003; 2007) conducted a pilot study and subsequent randomized control trial on the use of MI for adolescents with type-1 diabetes. An MI intervention group had significantly lower serum A1C levels than a cohort that received supportive care. In addition to improved glycemic control, differences in psychological variables existed between the two groups, whereby the MI group had greater concerns about their diabetes yet held a stronger belief in their ability to manage the condition.

The application of MI in the management of HIV in youth, both in terms of reducing risky behaviour as well as treatment adherence, has shown promise. The Healthy Choices program, a clinic delivered MI-based intervention, resulted in short-term decreases in viral load (Naar-King et al, 2009), as well as decreases in risky sexual behaviour among predominantly African-American youth living with HIV (Chen, Murphy, Naar-King and Parsons, 2011). Currently, efforts are underway to adapt the Health Choices program for youth living with HIV in Thailand (Koken, et al., 2012).

The treatment and prevention of pediatric obesity is a particularly important area of interest given the elevated rates of the condition worldwide and the enormously problematic impact on health across the lifespan. The effectiveness of MI on weight loss in adults has been demonstrated in a recent meta-analysis (Armstrong et al. 2011). Professional organizations such as the American Academy of Pediatrics have recommended the use of MI in the management of pediatric obesity (Barlow, 2007). The first relevant study found the use of MI increased dietary adherence in adolescents, however, caution should be used in interpreting the results as the study did not use a control group (Berg-Smith et al., 1999). Two subsequent efforts to incorporate MI for pediatric obesity found non-significant results on Body Mass Index (BMI): however, in both studies research participants reported high satisfaction with MI as a treatment modality (Resnicow, Taylor, Baskin and McCarty, 2005; Schwartz et al., 2007).

52                                          *Chapter 4*

More recently, a pilot study investigating the use of MI for overweight African-American teens found reductions in fast food and soda consumption, as well as increased intrinsic motivation for physical activity (MacDonell, Brogan, Naar-King, Ellis and Marshall, 2012). Currently, a number of MI-based programs for pediatric obesity are being tested, including two school-based programs (Glazebrook, et al., 2011; Flattum, Friend, Story and Neumark-Sztainer, 2011) and two primary care programs (Taveras, et al., 2011; Walpole, Dettmer, Morrongiello, McCrindle, and Hamilton, 2011). These projects will likely contribute to the small yet growing literature on MI for pediatric obesity. The promising early research outlined above certainly warrants continued study into the application of MI for the treatment of a variety of chronic pediatric conditions where behavior change is integral to improved outcomes.

**Psychiatric Conditions**

Another area of increasing attention is the use of MI in the treatment of psychiatric conditions, such as anxiety disorders, depression, and eating disorders (Arkowitz, Westra, Miller and Rollnick, 2007). A recent meta-analysis suggested that the use of MI at the outset of treatment approaches can be particularly effective largely due to enhanced engagement in the subsequent intervention (Hettema, Steele and Miller, 2005). In order to capitalize on engagement in a population known for attendance difficulties, efforts to add or integrate MI with Cognitive-Behavioural Therapy (CBT) for adolescents are underway.

For instance, Merlo and colleagues (2010) found preliminary support for the use of MI plus CBT in the treatment of pediatric obsessive-compulsive disorder (OCD). The authors propose that the inclusion of MI increased the participants' belief they could "fight" their OCD. Hoek et al. (2011) tested the combination of a primary care physician delivered MI session with an internet CBT-based program for the prevention of adolescent depression. Improvements were demonstrated in depressive symptoms and depressive episodes for the experimental group after six months when compared with a brief advice/internet program control condition.

Given the frequent co-occurrence of psychiatric and substance use conditions in youth, researchers have also begun investigating how MI fits with relevant treatment designs. Cornelius et al (2010) found improved depression and alcohol use disorder outcomes for youth using a combined treatment of motivational enhancement therapy and CBT. Hides and colleagues (2011) achieved accelerated beneficial outcomes using MI in conjunction with CBT for youth with depression and co-occurring alcohol or marijuana use. These studies reiterate the flexibility of MI as evidenced by the range of delivery modalities and intervention goals.

**Future Directions**

Promising preliminary results exist regarding the application of MI for CYP struggling with substance misuse, chronic medical conditions, and psychiatric disturbances. Given these initial positive outcomes, more research is needed on the application of MI for CYP in the following areas. For instance, a child's school is of particular importance to intellectual, social, and emotional development. Could MI, an approach most often used to enhance intrinsic motivation to change behaviour related to a problematic condition, be used to increase engagement in the classroom or enhance the relationship between teacher and student? How might school officials use MI as an alternative to exclusionary discipline strategies that often lead to student alienation (Skiba and Peterson, 1999)? What kinds of training do teachers and other school officials need (or even want) in order to implement MI as a support for students' intellectual, social, and emotional growth? Initial steps towards exploring MI in schools have already begun (Frey et al., 2011; Reinke, Herman, and Sprick, 2011).

A young person's peer group becomes particularly important during adolescence and as a result, group-based or peer-led interventions are often developed to address problems that arise. D'Amico et al. (2011) contend that MI is an ideal group treatment model for adolescents, as the collaborative nature of MI allows for youth to more freely express their needs and ideas with each other about how to manage their own difficulties. Examples of group-based MI with youth have emerged to address alcohol or drug use (D'Amico, Osilla, and Hunter, 2010). A recent unpublished dissertation examined the use of recent university graduates, trained in MI, serving as peer-mentors for high school students at-risk of school dropout (Daly, 2006). More explorations such as these are needed to better develop MI as a group or peer-involved intervention.

Finally, given the importance of families in the development of CYP the application of MI for use with families is surely another frontier that researchers and clinicians will explore. Similar to the challenge with group-based interventions, how would one adapt MI for use with multiple clients as is the case when working with a family (see Channon and Rubak, 2011). From the pediatric obesity literature, MacDonnell et al. (2012) provide results from their preliminary study, which is part of the FIT Families project at Wayne State University. This project is examining the development of an MI-informed family-based intervention for working with overweight teens. The use of MI when working with families may lead to increased collaboration between family members when working towards challenging goals commonly found in the treatment of pediatric obesity and other conditions.

**Discussion**

Although it would be premature to draw firm conclusions regarding the efficacy of MI for CYP, reason for optimism exists. MI for CYP has been applied in a number of areas already, from substance misuse, chronic illness, to psychiatric conditions. This flexibility in delivery is one of the more important characteristics of MI as an intervention for children and adolescents. The aforementioned studies described programs delivered across a number of treatment settings, including schools, medical facilities and community-based clinics. Furthermore, the Jensen et al. (2011) meta-analysis, as well as the subsequent articles described in the review,

54                                          *Chapter 4*

noted the diversity in practitioners that can deliver MI, such as psychologists, dietitians, physicians, and community-outreach workers. Certainly this flexibility in context and clinician delivery methods will allow researchers and clinicians to continue to adapt MI for the complex needs of youth.

## References

Arkowitz, H., Westra, H.A., Miller, W.R., & Rollnick, S. (2007). *Motivational Interviewing in the Treatment of Psychological Problems.* New York: Guilford Press.

Armstrong, M.J., Mottershead, T.A., Ronksley, P.E., Sigal, R.J., Campbell, T.S., & Hemmelgarn, B.R. (2011). Motivational interviewing to improve weight loss in overweight and/or obese patients: A systematic review and meta-analysis of randomized controlled trials. *Obesity Reviews,* 12, 709–723.

Baer, J.S., & Peterson, P.L. (2002). Motivational interviewing with adolescents and young adults. In W. R. Miller, & S. Rollnick (Eds.), *Motivational interviewing: Preparing people for change* (2nd ed., 320-332). New York: Guilford Press.

Bailey, K.A., Baker, A.L., Webster, R.A., & Lewin, T.J. (2004). Pilot randomized controlled trial of a brief alcohol intervention group for adolescents. *Drug and Alcohol Review,* 23, 157-166.

Barlow, S.E. (2007). Expert committee recommendations regarding the prevention, assessment, and treatment of child and adolescent overweight and obesity: Summary report. *Pediatrics, 120 Suppl 4,* 164-192.

Berg-Smith, S.M., Stevens, V.J., Brown, K.M., Van Horn, L., Gernhofer, N., Peters, E., Greenbers, R., Snetselaar, L., Ahens, L., & Smith, K. (1999). A brief motivational intervention to improve dietary adherence in adolescents. *Health Education: Research, Theory, and Practice,* 14, 399-410.

Channon, S., & Rubak, S. (2011). Family-based intervention. In S. Naar-King, & M. Suarez (Eds.), *Motivational Interviewing with Adolescents and Young Adults* (pp. 165-170). New York: Guilford Press.

Channon, S.J., Huws-Thomas, M.V., Rollnick, S., Hood, K., Cannings-John, R.L., Rogers, C., & Gregory, J.W. (2007). A multicenter randomized controlled trial of motivational interviewing in teenagers with diabetes. *Diabetes Care,* 30, 1390-1395.

Channon, S., Smith, V.J., & Gregory, J.W. (2003). A pilot study of motivational interviewing in adolescents with diabetes. *Archives of Disease in Childhood,* 88, 680-683.

Chen, X., Murphy, D.A., Naar-King, S., & Parsons, J.T. (2011). A clinic-based motivational intervention improves condom use among subgroups of youth living with HIV. *Journal of Adolescent Health,* 49, 193–198.

Colby, S. M., Monti, P. M., Barnett, N.P., Rohsenow, D. J., Weissman, K., Spirito, A., et al. (1998). Brief motivational interviewing in a hospital setting for adolescent smoking: A preliminary study. *Journal of Consulting and Clinical Psychology,* 66, 574-578.

Cornelius, J.R., Douaihy, A., Bukstein, O.G., Daley, D.C., Wood, S.D., Kelly, T.M., & Salloum, I.M. (2011). Evaluation of cognitive behavioral therapy/motivational enhancement therapy (CBT/MET) in a treatment trial of comorbid MDD/AUD adolescents, *Addictive Behaviors,* 36, 843–848.

Daly, M. (2006). Engineering change: The impact of a collaborative training programme for graduate mentors to enhance motivation amongst vocational GCSE pupils. Unpublished doctoral dissertation, University of Liverpool.

D'Amico, E.J., Feldstein-Ewing, S.W., Engle, B., Hunter, S., Osilla, K.C., & Bryan, A. (2011). Group alcohol and drug treatment. In S. Naar-King, & M. Suarez (Eds.), *Motivational Interviewing with Adolescents and Young Adults* (pp. 151-157). New York: Guilford Press.

D'Amico, E.J., Miles, J.N., Stern, S.A., & Meredith, L.S. (2008). Brief motivational interviewing for teens at risk of substance use consequences: a randomized pilot study in a primary care clinic. *Journal of Substance Abuse Treatment,* 35, 53-61.

D'Amico, E.J., Osilla, K.C., & Hunter, S.B. (2010). Developing a group motivational interviewing intervention for first-time adolescent offenders at-risk for an alcohol or drug use disorder. *Alcoholism Treatment Quarterly,* 28, 417-436.

Flattum, C., Friend, S., Story, M., & Neumark-Sztainer, D. (2011). Evaluation of an individualized counseling approach as part of a multicomponent school-based program to prevent weight-related problems among adolescent girls. *Journal of the American Dietetic Association,* 111, 1218-1223.

Frey, A.J., Cloud, R.N., Lee, J., Small, J.W., Seeley, J.R., Feil, E.G., Walker, H.M., & Golly, A. (2011). The promise of motivational interviewing in school mental health. *School Mental Health,* 3, 1–12.

Glazebrook, C., Batty, M.J., Mullan, N., MacDonald, I., Nathan, D., Sayal, K., Smyth, A., Yang, M., Guo, B., & Hollis, C. (2011). Evaluating the effectiveness of a schools-based programme to promote exercise self-efficacy in children and young people with risk factors for obesity: Steps to active kids (STAK). *BMC Public Health, 11,* 830.

Hettema, J., Steele, J., & Miller, W.R. (2005). Motivational interviewing. *Annual Review of Clinical Psychology,* 1, 91-111.

Hides, L.M., Elkins, K.S., Scaffidi, A., Cotton, S.M., Carroll S., & Lubman, D.I. (2011). Does the addition of integrated cognitive behaviour therapy and motivational interviewing improve the outcomes of standard care for young people with comorbid depression and substance misuse? *The Medical Journal of Australia,* 195, 31–37.

# Chapter 4

Hoek, W., Marko, M., Fogel, J., Schuurmans, J., Gladstone, T., Bradford, N., Domanico, R., Fagan, B., Bell, C., Reinecke, M.A., & Van Voorhees, B.W. (2011). Randomized controlled trial of primary care physician motivational interviewing versus brief advice to engage adolescents with an Internet-based depression prevention intervention: 6-month outcomes and predictors of improvement. *Translational Research,* 158, 315-25.

Hollis, J.F., Polen, M.R., Whitlock, E.P., Lichtenstein, E., Mullooly, J., Velicer, W.F., & Redding, C.A. (2005). Teen Reach: Outcomes from a randomized controlled trial of a tobacco reduction program for teens seen in primary medical care. *Pediatrics,* 115, 981- 989.

Ingersoll, K.S., Wagner, C.C., & Gharib, S. (2002). *Motivational Groups for Community Substance Abuse Programs.* Richmond, VA: Mid-Atlantic Addiction Technology Transfer Center.

Jensen, C.D., Cushing, C.C., Aylward, B.S., Craig, J.T., Sorell, D.M., & Steele, R.G. (2011). Effectiveness of motivational interviewing interventions for adolescent substance use behavior change: a meta-analytic review. *Journal of Consulting and Clinincal Psychology,* 79, 433-440.

Kelly, A.B. & Lapworth, K. (2006). The HYP program-targeted motivational interviewing for adolescent violations of school tobacco policy. *Preventative Medicine,* 43, 466-471.

Koken, J.A., Naar-King, S., Umasa, S., Parsons, J.T., Saengcharnchai, P., Phanuphak, P., & Rongkavilit, C. (2012). A Cross-Cultural Three-Step Process Model for Assessing Motivational Interviewing Treatment Fidelity in Thailand. Health Education & Behavior, 1–9. 10.1177/1090198111423679

MacDonell, K., Brogan, K., Naar-King, S., Ellis, D., & Marshall, M. (2012). A Pilot Study of Motivational Interviewing Targeting Weight-Related Behaviors in Overweight or Obese African American Adolescents. *Journal of Adolescent Health,* 50, 201–203.

Merlo, L.J., Storch, E.A., Lehmkuhl, H.D., Jacob, M.L., Murphy, T.K., Goodman, W.K., & Geffken, G.R. (2010). Cognitive behavioral therapy plus motivational interviewing improves outcome for pediatric obsessive–compulsive disorder: A preliminary study. *Cognitive Behaviour Therapy,* 39, 24–27.

Miller, W.R. (1983). Motivational Interviewing with Problem Drinkers. *Behavioural Psychotherapy,* 11, 147-172.

Monti, P.M., Colby, S., Barnett, N., Spirito, A., Rohsenow, D., Myers, M., et al. (1999). Brief intervention for harm reduction with alcohol-positive older adolescents in a hospital emergency department. *Journal of Consulting and Clinical Psychology,* 67, 989-994.

Naar-King, S. (2011). Motivational interviewing in adolescent treatment. *Canadian Journal of Psychiatry,* 56, 651-657.

Naar-King, S., Parsons, J.T., Murphy, D.A., Chen, X., Harris, R., & Belzer, M.E. (2009). Improving health outcomes for youth living with the human immunodeficiency virus: A multisite randomized trial of a motivational intervention targeting multiple risk behaviors. *Archives of Pediatrics and Adolescent Medicine,* 163, 1092-1098.

Reinke, W.M., Herman, K.C., & Sprick, R. (2011). *Motivational Interviewing for Effective Classroom Management: The Classroom Check-up.* New York: Guilford Press.

Resnicow, K., Taylor, R., Baskin, M., & McCarty, F. (2005). Results of Go Girls: A weight control program for overweight African American adolescent females. *Obesity Research,* 13, 1739–1748.

Schwartz, R.P., Hamre, R., Dietz, W.H., Wasserman, R.C., Slora, E.J., Myers, E.F., Sullivan, S., Rockett, H., Thoma, K.A., Dumitru, G., & Resnicow, K.A. (2007). Office based motivational interviewing to prevent childhood obesity: a feasibility study. *Archives of Pediatrics & Adolescent Medicine,* 161, 495–501.

Skiba, R., & Peterson, R. (1999). The dark side of zero tolerance: Can punishment lead to safe schools? *Phi Delta Kappan,* 80, 372-382.

Suarez, M., & Mullins, S. (2008). Motivational interviewing and pediatric health behavior interventions. *Journal of Developmental & Behavioral Pediatrics,* 29, 417-428.

Taveras, E.M., Gortmaker, S.L., Hohman, K.H., Horan, C.M., Kleinman, K.P., Mitchell, K., Price, S., Prosser, L.A., Rifas-Shiman, S.L., & Gillman, M.W. (2011). Randomized controlled trial to improve primary care to prevent and manage childhood obesity: The High Five for Kids study. *Archives of Pediatrics and Adolescent Medicine,* 165, 714-722.

Walpole, B., Dettmer, E., Morrongiello, B., McCrindle, B., & Hamilton, J. (2011). Motivational Interviewing as an intervention to increase adolescent self-efficacy and promote weight loss: Methodology and design. *BMC Public Health,* 11, 459.

58                                    Chapter 4

# Section 1

# Motivational Interviewing in Educational Settings

60

# Chapter 5

# Motivational Interviewing and Group Work

## Craig Bridge
### *Educational Psychologist*
### *Lincolnshire County Council*

This chapter describes how the principles of Motivational Interviewing (MI) were applied to a group of 13-14 year old girls at a secondary school. Prior to this group work the author had used MI successfully with a number of individual school pupils. The idea of using MI as a group intervention came about by chance and seemed like an evolutionary next step in applying MI within school environments. The author wanted to follow the stages and techniques of MI as used with individuals but see how the techniques and methodology could be translated into a group context. Additionally the author was keen to identify the benefits and challenges of using MI with a group.

Motivational Interviewing is an approach that has been used to help people manage change (Miller and Rollnick 1991). Miller and Rollnick (2002) described the approach as:

> '*...a client-centred, directive method for enhancing intrinsic motivation to change by exploring and resolving ambivalence. (p25)*'

The term 'client' used in the above definition can be viewed in a number of ways. The 'client' could be considered by practitioners to be traditionally an individual or perhaps a group or even an organisation. Indeed, the use of MI has evolved and has been used in different ways to facilitate change with different 'clients'. The range of school-based MI includes work with parents (Wood and Rice 2009) and with schools and their staff training (Middleton and Lunt 2009). Its use in schools has been cited as an approach that can help to find solutions (Atkinson and Woods 2003; Atkinson 2009; Atkinson and Amesu 2007).

The approach of MI uses key skills and techniques to help clients to reach a resolution. This resolution can include a decision to do nothing or to do something. These skills or 'general principles' (Miller and Rollnick 2002) include:

- Expressing empathy
- Developing discrepancy
- Rolling with resistance
- Supporting self efficacy

In addition to these core principles MI requires the therapist to be extremely perceptive and mindful of change talk and sustain talk. Sustain talk typically contains comments about maintaining the current behaviour and excusing or explaining reasons for not changing. Sustain talk can also be linked with resistance and a lack of drive to change. In contrast change talk may contain reference to an individual's personal goals and/or ideas around how they might change their current behaviour. It is change talk that is important to reinforce in MI. The dialogue of sustain talk and change talk is also linked to the concepts of importance and confidence associated with wanting to change. Therefore, if a change feels important to do and I feel confident I can do it I may engage more in change talk.

Sustain talk and change talk are associated with differing levels of cognitive dissonance. Cognitive dissonance occurs whenever an individual holds two cognitions which are inconsistent which in turn can lead to dissonance. For example a person may feel that being over-weight is not a healthy state yet they gain pleasure from eating high fat foods for relaxation. This psychological event can lead to psychological tension and stress and this can lead to a motivation to reduce the discomfort and achieve consonance. These cognitions are defined by Festinger (1957) as being 'the things a person knows about himself, about his behaviour and about his surroundings'. Therefore when facts about themselves and/or their current behaviour which do not match their desired goal are reflected back the client may experience cognitive dissonance. This is a major element in MI practice. When there are higher levels of dissonance there may be a higher desire for change and therefore more change talk. Generating more cognitive dissonance can be a powerful tool to promote change.

Methods for evoking change talk and in turn building dissonance have been listed by Miller and Rollnick (2002):

1. Asking Evocative Questions
2. Using the Importance Ruler (a rating scale that explores how important a change is for the client).
3. Exploring the Decisional Balance
4. Elaborating
5. Querying Extremes
6. Looking Back
7. Looking Forward
8. Exploring Goals and Values

*Chapter 5*  63

Where practical, it was planned that each of the 8 principles and methods outlined above would be used to try and work around a target pupil and behaviour but within a group context rather than on an individual basis. At the outset of the intervention it was unclear that the approach could be used in this way, but work in other fields, such as in health (D'Amico et al 2010), suggests that MI can be used in a group setting.

**Group work with Young People**

Geldard and Geldard (2001) described the benefits of group working. These benefits included:

- Groups can promote change;
- A group can parallel the wider social environment;
- A group provides a sense of belonging;
- Common needs can be addressed in a group;
- Groups are cost effective.

The benefits that Geldard and Geldard (op cit) identify about how groups promote change is of particular relevance to MI group working. This relevance is not only associated with the fact that MI is about change but also because if change is achieved in groups then group MI working may have a role to play as an intervention. More specifically there is evidence that groups encourage individual change because of the way the members interact and communicate at a peer level (Rose and Edleson 1987). Change can be facilitated by a group leader using feedback. Such reflection and feedback is a common skill used within MI. In addition to providing feedback through peers, group work also provides an opportunity to develop new behaviours and skills (Berkovitz 1987a,b).

**The MI Group**

Pupil Sam, full name Samantha, was first met at an initial consultation with her mother, school staff and her friend. In this meeting we discussed the concern around Sam's current behaviour as reported by staff in school.

At this point the author had been intrigued by the fact that i) Sam had bought her friend along to this initial consultation and ii) how the two were talking openly and corroboratively about Sam's difficulties. At the closing of the meeting the idea of a MI approach was offered and explained and Sam expressed an interest in engaging with this approach. It was also suggested that Sam might find it useful (or not) to bring along some friends to support her. This suggestion was made based on the observed dynamic that developed in the meeting between Sam and her friend. Additionally the author had developed a hypothesis that Sam may be more comfortable talking within a group of friends rather than just on her own.

The group consisted of four girls: one girl (Sam) was the target pupil. Sam had chosen which peers she wanted as members of the group. Consent was obtained from the parents of the three other pupils and a Teaching Assistant (TA) was asked to attend the group. The TA, who volunteered to join the group, was a member of staff who the group felt comfortable with and felt that they could talk openly in her presence. In fact they seemed very keen to have this particular TA in the group.

The rationale for including a TA in the group was:

1. It allowed the school to be mindful that something was happening and reduce the risk of the group being viewed as being 'dealt with by the EP'.

2. The TA had the opportunity to see what was happening at the process level and to appreciate some of the tasks and thinking behind the approach.

3. The TA was available to the group during the times that the author wasn't in school. This provided the group with a point of contact and support if any problems occurred during the time between sessions.

## How the MI Sessions were Run

The sessions were held fortnightly during the summer term. Each session was approximately 20-30 minutes long and there were 6 sessions. Initially the group were told why they were there and that they were going to support Sam with a possible change of behaviour. Additionally the group were informed that they would learn some psychology around how people change and techniques to help with this. Sam was keen to focus on being less confrontational with staff; she wanted to be better at dealing with adults in a way that didn't create conflict in school.

As the sessions progressed each meeting had an agenda which kept the session focused and purposeful. Items for the agenda were suggested by the group and recorded. There was always a recap on what had happened in the last session.

Next the behaviours that Sam had nominated in previous sessions were revisited. This would then lead into Sam rating how important it was for her to change her behaviour from 0 to 10 (with 0 being not important and 10 being very important). Subsequently Sam would complete the same rating scale with respect to how confident she was about making a change.

The change cycle as suggested by Prochaska and DiClemente (1982) was frequently referred to as a means to assess where Sam was in the change cycle. The cycle also served as a framework for the sessions. By having the model of the change cycle as a guide the group had a visual representation of where Sam was in her change journey. As a group we also looked more generally at what behaviours and discourse might be observed when people were at different points of the cycle. This allowed the group to understand the nature of change and may have helped to normalise some of Sam's choices and steps towards change.

After viewing the agenda, recapping, scaling and reflecting on the change cycle the group started to discuss the main items from the agenda. If there were multiple items then Sam would choose the order for discussion. This kept control with Sam and allowed a simple assessment of what areas were pertinent to Sam and which ones were less so. During the discussion the author would listen to change talk and try to reflect back comments made and reinforce talk that suggested change. Some of the 8 methods mentioned earlier were used. As appropriate, these methods were solely used to support Sam. At the beginning of the sessions the author would ask the questions associated with the 8 methods but as the sessions continued the group also started to try out some of the methods with Sam. This switch allowed Sam to hear different challenging questions from her peers.

At the end of the discussion the main action points, if relevant, were agreed. In later sessions activities were agreed as a form of 'homework' and then the meeting closed.

As Sam and the group moved into different stages of the change cycle the content of the sessions changed. For example, early content would focus on building a case for change but as the sessions continued and Sam moved into the later stages of the change cycle more time was spent looking at action planning for change. Even though other members of the group reflected on their own behaviours and goals the focus of the sessions remained with Sam's chosen behaviours.

## Observations about Group MI

As more discussion and more sessions occurred it became apparent that the four members of the group appeared to have two polarised viewpoints around the target change behaviour that Sam had identified in the early sessions. This naturally led to constructive debates around the positive and negatives of Sam's target behaviour. One benefit of having a group seemed to be that the probability of discrepancy was more likely. The opportunity to explore different perceptions within the group was a real benefit of group-work over individual working.

In a client-therapist, 1:1 model generating discrepancy without third party alternate perceptions is judged by the author harder to achieve. It relies heavily on different questioning styles such as goal based futures and disparity between the clients own view of themselves versus the client's view of how other's may see him/her (Atkinson and Amesu 2007).

Another feature of the group approach as compared with the individual approach was the ratio of therapist talk to client talk. In the early stages of MI it is important to be aware of and avoid certain "traps" (Miller and Rollnik 2002). In particular Miller and Rollnik warn of the Question-Answer trap. In this trap the therapist asks a volley or series of closed questions to which the client responds with short answers. This can lead to the therapist 'hogging the stage' and an increase in client compliance with the therapist's agenda. In the group experience the members had discussions quite freely and their voices were the main commentary in the sessions - even early on. This allowed the author to use

# Chapter 5

66

active listening skills to help emphasise comments made through reflections and summaries. This was especially true when talk around change was mentioned. This meant that the author had to exercise a high degree of vigilance within the session to judge when talk was helpful to the change process and when it was less so. When comments seemed less helpful the author was then able to use questions that allowed the members to consider some other paths or ideas.

As with the individual client method of MI, the group went through similar processes including the use of DiClements and Prochaska's change wheel to frame the process, scaling (importance and confidence), positive and negative analysis, agenda setting, homework and similar processes often associated with the approach of MI

Later in the sessions an action plan was drawn up. This plan is a means of preparing for change (see Figure 1).

**Figure 1.** A Change Plan Worksheet Example (Miller and Rollnick 2002)

The most important reasons why I want to make this change are:

*I want to stop being in trouble*
*I want to make my mum happy*

My main goals for myself in making this change are:

*Stop answering-back the teachers*

I plan to do these things in order to accomplish my goals:

Specific action | When?
--- | ---
*Think before I speak* | *When I'm being told off*
*Listen to my mates* | *I think people are unfair*
*Count to 10* | *I'm feeling stressed*

Other people could help me with change in these ways:

Person | Possible ways to help
--- | ---
*My mates* | *Tell me when to chill-out*
*Teachers* | *Try to see my view*

These are some possible obstacles to change, and how I could handle them:

Possible obstacle to change | How to respond
--- | ---
*When I feel stressed* | *Stop and think before talking*

I will know that my plan is working when I see these results:

*My report card shows that I am trying with my behaviour*
*My mum says she is happier about my attitude*

The plan outlines exactly what the new behaviour is and what might stop the new behaviour from being maintained. The action plan also lets other people know that the person is going to attempt a change.

## What Worked

### *More Content and Discourse to Utilise*

The amount of dialogue in the sessions allowed more opportunities to explore different facets of the behaviours that Sam targeted. The group were able to raise a number of issues to explore and they also generated a great deal of discussion about each one. The rich verbal content also created different perceptions of a problem or behaviour. Sometimes these differences were between the target pupil and one of her friends but sometimes the different perceptions were expressed by two or more of Sam's friends. This provided an opportunity for Sam to observe and hear an 'argument' about two different points of view and so allowed Sam to hear alternate possibilities as opposed to arguing her own current point of view. This led to the development of cognitive dissonance.

Another benefit of the group producing so much content was the reduction in uncomfortable pauses. With so much dialogue the author did not need to try to get Sam to talk by asking numerous questions, thus avoiding any question-answer interactions which may have felt like an interrogation for Sam.

### *More Insight into The Culture of The Pupil*

A major difference between these group sessions and individual sessions was the vocabulary used by the group – they freely used vocabulary which reflected their culture and used their own terminology frequently. The group's cultural dialogue used within the sessions appeared to suggest that the comments the group were making were less likely a response which conformed to the adult-child dynamic. The author did consider to what extent the members of the group conformed to each other. Observing and interacting within their culture was challenging but it also felt much more dynamic, genuine and effective for change.

### *Opportunity for Direct Feedback to the Focus Person*

The group were able to feedback on comments made by Sam in real time. In individual sessions the use of questions around other's perception can be used to generate change talk and cognitive dissonance (Atkinson and Amesu 2007; Amesu 2009): for example;

> *'If I were to ask your support worker what they thought of you, what would they say?'*

68                                  *Chapter 5*

In the group sessions this style of question was used first with Sam to get her thoughts on how she felt she was behaving out of the sessions. Then the actual question was asked of each member of the group one at a time in order to triangulate and verify or contradict Sam's view. The answers were often varied and powerful. This created further discussion between the group members and sometimes led to Sam dismissing answers that appeared difficult to take on-board or Sam thought were 'wrong'. Sometimes these reflections from her peers were never listened to again in the sessions. Sometimes Sam would revisit the difficult answers or make reference to them later in the sessions when she may have felt more comfortable to address them. This may demonstrate the movement around the change cycle; people may not be ready to view different pieces of evidence at certain times.

*More Eyes Looking at the Effort*

As Sam moved on from the Contemplative stage, though the Determinism stage and into the Active Change stage of the change cycle a change plan was devised. One element of entering a commitment to change involves making the intent to change more public. This public commitment helped Sam to try out new behaviours but also moved the problem behaviour/intended new behaviour from within the sessions out into the 'real world'.

Having members of Sam's social network part of the process seemed to provide an element of public audience early on. Having more members in the group meant that they were gathering evidence of any new behaviours Sam was trying. This helped in the action planning stage. The group also helped to highlight any changes that they had seen that Sam had forgotten to raise in the sessions.

## What Didn't Work

*Identifying Change Talk and Sustain Talk*

In the early stages of an MI intervention the therapist attempts to assess the client's readiness, confidence and willingness to change. A key strategy in this process is for the therapist to focus on the language and ideas expressed by the client. In their dialogue the client may show two types of talk; change talk and sustain talk. Change talk often highlights goals different from their current situation, e.g. describing themselves as being 'fed up' with their current situation. Sustain talk is different in that the client will justify their current situation even if they are not having their longer term goals met. Sustain talk may also refer to external reasons why they have not been able to change or why they can't change. Sustain talk can also occur when people feel they are being 'rushed' into a change and/or when they lack belief about being able to change .

Within these two styles of dialogue it is very common for clients to show ambivalence. They may seem like they want to change but will return to a state of no-change. Therefore, the need to assess what is said by the client is an important early step in an MI intervention.

During the sessions the dynamic of a group session as compared with an individual session meant that the sheer amount of content was much greater. This made it quite challenging to differentiate between discussions and communication that reinforced sustain talk and change talk. It was possible that opportunities to reinforce some change talk were missed because of the sheer volume of discussion and the rate of dialogue. When there was little change talk it was hard to direct the discussion into areas that might build cognitive dissonance because the four members of the group would move in and out of topics very fluidly.

*Preventing Negatives of Current Behaviour Becoming Positives*

As the sessions moved forward it became challenging to pin down a thread of discussion and relate it to behaviour that Sam wanted to change. It was hoped that after we had looked at the positives of maintaining the current behaviour we could move on to identifying and considering the negatives of the target behaviour. This was achieved to a degree but trying to minimise the positives of maintaining current behaviour in the group proved difficult. To some extent the social group that Sam had chosen seemed to find discussing the positive consequences entertaining and it gave more attention to the positives of the current behaviour. To some degree even talking about maintaining negative behaviours seemed to give Sam and the behaviour a cult status within the group - it was cool to talk back to staff. We did move on to the negatives of the current behaviour and did build a degree of cognitive dissonance as a group. The use of open questions and summarising also seemed less effective in the session due to the other members occasionally answering the questions with or on behalf of Sam.

*Keeping Focused - Not Always Keeping a Tone of 'We're Here To Do Something'*

The group dynamics lent themselves to more humour than other sessions. The members of the group laughed at behaviours that were disruptive in a classroom environment. This appeared more frequently when the negatives of such behaviour were either discussed for periods of time or when they were amplified. Perhaps the stress that was being generated by the increasing cognitive dissonance led to a coping strategy of joking within the sessions. Much of this behaviour was ignored where possible. If the joking was a coping strategy it could be that Sam had a high level of dissonance and therefore was trying to relieve the psychological tension through humour. This meant that maybe the behaviour that was being laughed at might be relevant for discussion but emotionally and psychologically difficult for Sam to explore. It required a degree of skill and question management to ensure that the group did not slip into joking about the negative behaviour and so end up glorifying a negative behaviour rather than addressing the behaviour in a more objective manner.

To some extent this could be a form of resistance to change and so 'rolling' with it was the strategy. At other times there were opportunities to reflect back what was being observed and said.

70                                          *Chapter 5*

*Keeping Focused - Managing the Possible Distraction Around The Main Concern*

With so much discourse it was challenging to keep the balance between pursuing all the areas of possible concern without being pulled into irrelevant topics. The group seemed to enjoy discussing some topics in detail even if the relevance to the sessions was questionable - and this made it difficult to keep the dialogue relevant to change. For example, when discussing friends outside of the group the members would go on to talk about these people even though their relevance to the target pupil and her "problem" behaviour were negligible. This sometimes felt as if the group were 'having a chat' rather than engaging in a change intervention.

*The Group Breaking Up*

During the latter half of the sessions relationship issues between the members of the group developed out of the sessions. This led to some members not attending the sessions. This created another distraction - the discussion of why someone was not attending the group. In response to this the agenda of each session was reiterated as a means to bring the group back to task. Although this was broadly successful this was something that was not an issue in individual MI sessions.

## Future Considerations for MI Group Work

*The Role for Psycho-Education in a Group*

After this experience of using MI in group sessions I identified some different areas that could be further developed. In the group session there was still a principle problem owner and the members of the group were set the agenda to work on Sam's behaviour. Perhaps a group session could take the issues of all the members and look at these at a lower level of analysis. To some extent the interview sessions would be more about teaching and explaining how people change, what the change cycle is and strategies that can be used to facilitate people to change. This idea of psycho-education would follow some of the principles of Cognitive Behavioural Therapy where people learn how to rethink their ideas.

*Ensure that the Target Behaviour Generates Enough Cognitive Dissonance*

MI has a background within health where changes of behaviour can be linked to clear medical implications and negative risk factors such as alcohol abuse and liver damage. In the educational context it is likely that behaviour change is focused around less 'life threatening' actions. Because drug use, for instance, has significant risk factors associated with it the negative consequences of not altering drug behaviour can be a 'useful' fact for generating dissonance. The same degree of "threat" is unlikely to be the case for behaviours such as classroom disruption or swearing and therefore may not generate such high levels of dissonance and potential for change. It is therefore important to be very clear about a target behaviour or issue. By allowing enough time to visit all the concerns early on in the process and by using summaries and reflection to check that the therapist has a targeted behaviour that generates enough motivation/cognitive dissonance to change is crucial. Additionally, future goals and peer pressure could be areas to explore to help develop greater levels of cognitive dissonance as a driver for change.

## Conclusion

Sam made significant positive changes to her target behaviour. This was evidenced through the eye-witness comments from her peer group, the TA's judgement and from e-mails from the staff who came into contact with Sam. In addition Sam was reported to have sustained the changes six months later. Further, the group are planning to continue meeting with the TA. In these future proposed sessions with the TA the group decided to move away from having Sam as the target pupil alone and allow each of the group to bring an issue for consideration

This project shows that group MI has the potential to generate certain types of dialogue that can aid behaviour change in schools. It could be potentially more time efficient than working with individuals. In addition, the nature of the dialogue generated and the ability to use peers and feedback directly in sessions seems a powerful element of group work MI. Further work with different groups and with different issues is required to explore how successful a group MI approach could be with different pupils addressing different issues.

## References

Amesu, M. (2009) Combining Solution Focussed Approaches with Motivational Interviewing. In E. McNamara *Motivational Interviewing: Theory, Practice and Applications with Children and Young People.* Merseyside, Positive Behaviour Management. positive behaviourmanagement.co.uk

Atkinson, C. and Amesu, M. (2007) Using Solution-Focused Approaches in Motivational Interviewing with Young People. *Pastoral Care.* 31-37.

Atkinson, C. and Woods, K. (2003) Motivational Interviewing Strategies for Disaffected Secondary School Students: a case example. *Educational Psychology in Practice* 19 (1), 49-64.

Atkinson, C. (2009) MI in Educational Settings: Using MI with children and young people. In E. McNamara *Motivational Interviewing: Theory, Practice and Applications with Children and Young People.* Merseyside, Positive Behaviour Management. positive behaviourmanagement.co.uk

Berkowitz, I. H. (1987a) Application of group therapy in secondary schools. In F.J.C. Azima and L.H. Richmond (eds). *Adolescents Group Psychotherapy.* Madison: International Universities Press.

Berkowitz, I. H. (1987b) Value of group counselling in secondary schools. *Adolescent Psychiatry,* 14: 522-45.

D'Amico, E. J., Osilla, K. C. and Hunter, S. B. (2010) Developing a Group Motivational Interviewing Intervention for Adolescents At-Risk for Developing an Alcohol or Drug use Disorder. Alcoholism Treatment Quarterly, 28 (4), 417-436.

Festinger, L. (1957) *A theory of cognitive dissonance.* New York: Harper & Row.

Geldard, K. & Geldard, D. (2001) *Working With Children in Groups.* Hampshire: Palgrave.

Middleton and Lunt (2009) A Short Term Qualitative Evaluation of MI INSET in an EBD School Setting. *In McNamara, E. Motivational Interviewing: Theory, Practice and Applications with Children and Young People.* Merseyside: Positive Behaviour Management.

Miller, W. R. and Rollnick, S. (1991) *Motivational Interviewing: Preparing People to Change Addictive Behaviour.* New York: Guildford Press.

Miller, W. R. and Rollnick, S. (2002) *Motivational Interviewing: Preparing People for Change.* New York: Guildford Press.

Prochaska, J. O. and DiClemente, C. C. (1982) The Transtheoretical Approach Crossing Traditional Boundaries of Therapy Homewood. IL, Dowe Jones/Irwin

Rose, S. D. and Edleson, J. L. (1987) *Working with Children and Adolescents in Groups: a Multi-method Approach.* San Francisco: Jossey-Bass

Wood and Rice (2009) Using MI with 'Hard to Reach' Parents. In E. McNamara *Motivational Interviewing: Theory, Practice and Applications with Children and Young People.* Merseyside: Positive Behaviour Management. positive behaviourmanagement.co.uk

# Chapter 6

# Motivational Interviewing and Self-Esteem

## Claudia Moss
*Educational Psychologist*
*Leeds City Council Complex Needs Service*

### Introduction

This chapter is based on the author's doctoral thesis which explored the impact of a group based MI approach on pupil self esteem.

Motivational Interviewing (MI) is an approach that attempts to engage individuals through using a non-directive, goal-oriented, humanistic approach and one that may well be appropriate in promoting social inclusion. Literature in the field, particularly health, suggests it can have a significant impact on changing individuals' thoughts and behaviour. Successful application of MI in educational settings have been reported (Atkinson 2005, McNamara 2009). However, while MI has been widely researched, with demonstrated success across other domains e.g. Rollnick et al 1992 and Gray, McCambridge and Strang 2005, there is a need for more data and evidence to be collected on its impact in the area of education. Further, as observed by Miller and Rollnick (2002, p. 388) 'There is significant room and need for studies integrating MI with group processes'.

Consequently, the author carried out a randomised control trial evaluating the impact of a group based Motivational Interviewing intervention in an applied setting. Randomised Control Trials are often described as the 'gold standard' of research as they provide evidence for effectiveness (Robson 2002).

Motivational interviewing aims to promote self-esteem, self-efficacy, internal attribution and increase knowledge and concern (McNamara, 2009). MI is different from many other interventions because the assumption is not made that clients are ready to explores their feelings and accept the need for change.

The author considers that through adopting a humanistic, client centred approach MI may facilitate the development of self-esteem. The investigation of this possibility was the goal of this study.

## Self- Esteem and Young People

Self-esteem is a complex human characteristic and theorists have put forward different definitions of the term. Generally it can be defined as 'how we positively or negatively feel about being ourselves. It is the value we place upon ourselves as a unique and valuable human 'being' rather than a human 'doing'. It depends on how well we know ourselves and the extent to which we feel we are accepted, and on our belief that we can exert an influence over other people and the world' (Morris 1997, p.3).

Morris (2002) reported that low self-esteem can have a negative impact upon individuals learning and ability to succeed. McLean (2003) emphasised the importance of considering the role of self-esteem in motivated learning. He believed that exploring self-esteem in relation to the four mindsets of motivation - self-efficacy beliefs, attitudes to achievement, ideas about ability and explanations for progress -will create a deeper knowledge and understanding of the relationship and impact that self-esteem can have upon achievement. Some theorists suggest that group interventions may impact positively upon an individual's self-esteem as they promote confidence and a sense of belonging (Clemes and Bean, 1990). Clemes and Bean further reported that low self-esteem can impact significantly upon pupil's academic learning and create feelings of disaffection within school. This can in turn create loss of interest in school and a lack of motivation. The current chapter is a report of a study which aimed to promote pupil self-esteem through the use of an MI approach.

It has been reported that the ages of 5 to 15 years are vital with regards to the development of self-esteem and self-efficacy as this is the age range in which children first begin and then continue to assess their capabilities and develop feelings of success and failure (Apter, 1997). Apter believes that school is the key arena in which pupils experience challenges that create such feelings and that therefore schools should seek to maximise and support pupils' development in this area. Such findings were considered when selecting the target age group for the current research study. The sample selected were aged 13 -14 years - a critical time with regards to the development of self-esteem (Apter, 1997).

Evidence e.g. Morris (2002) appears to suggest that poor self-esteem can impact significantly upon pupil achievement with some studies reporting critical stages of development in which children begin to assess their own capabilities (Apter, 1997). The school environment plays a vital role in this and targeted interventions aimed at promoting self-esteem and motivation have proved effective. The present study aimed to gather more evidence in this field through adopting a targeted intervention based upon motivational principles to promote pupil self-esteem in the school setting.

The author decided to use a group based approach to MI because

   i) the limited research to date has demonstrated that a supportive group based MI intervention can deliver effective results (Fields, 2004) and

   ii) it could give more pupils the opportunity to access the intervention

Setting up the intervention involved discussions with the Head Teacher and the Pastoral Support Leader. The discussions focused upon the feasibility and pragmatics of implementing an MI intervention within a school setting. The staff consulted felt that an MI intervention would meet the schools needs with regard to further promoting the social inclusion of pupils. They expressed concerns regarding a number of pupils who they felt had a poor self-image and low self-esteem. The staff felt that these pupils could benefit from the intervention, particularly as many appeared unmotivated and reluctant to consider change. MI thus appeared to be most appropriate with regard to working with these pupils.

School personnel were keen to learn about the MI package and its delivery so that, if successful, they could continue to implement the programme across the school once the study had ended.

**Facilitating Change: An Intervention**

The researcher implemented Atkinson's (2005) package 'Facilitating Change', which is based upon the key principles of MI. The materials comprise of a well-structured five session programme that encourages young people to think about, understand and change aspects of their behaviour. The sessions involve activities that aim to i) build rapport with a young person and ii) explore with the pupils how people around them affect their behaviour. The later sessions then explore the importance of motivation in changing behaviour and encourage the young people to evaluate their own conduct in relation to the stages of change model (Atkinson 2005).

The structure of the sessions is as follows:

Part 1 **Thinking Positively** This encourages the young person to identify positive aspects of their life under the broad themes of Things I do well, Good Times and Personal Characteristics. This session stimulates a great deal of discussion and promotes rapport building.

Part 2 **Understanding Yourself** This aims to help the young person understand that the people and environment around them have an impact on their behaviour.

Part 3 **Understanding Change** This introduces the notion that in order to want to change your behaviour you have to be motivated to do something about it. Part 3 also begins to explore the stages of change model.

Part 4 **Stages of Change** This provides young people with an adapted model of the stages of change. The session gives an opportunity for participants to revisit a problem discussed in earlier sessions and explore it further in relation to the model. It also provides opportunities for the young person to try and associate colours, shapes and emotions with the stages of change.

Part 5 **Change and Me** This offers the young person the opportunity to evaluate their own behaviour in relation to the model of stages of change and to identify steps to effect behaviour change.

The programme can be used universally, but has been particularly effective when implemented with vulnerable young people (Atkinson in McNamara 2009).

## The Sample

48 Year 8 pupils, aged 13-14, were selected from the 150 Year 8 pupil cohort in a mainstream secondary school in the Yorkshire and Humber region.

All 150 pupils completed the Self Image Profiles questionnaire (Butler 2001). This provides an overview of an individual's view of themselves. The 48 pupils with the lowest self-image scores (scoring 50 and below) were randomly allocated to the treatment and no treatment groups.

The 24 pupils in the experimental group received a five week motivational interviewing intervention, each session lasting for fifty minutes. The 24 pupils making up the no treatment group constituted the equivalent of a waiting list control group and received the MI intervention once the study had ended.

None of the pupils who participated in the study were on the Special Educational Needs register (SEN), had English as an Additional Language (EAL), were Black Minority Ethnic (BME) or were Looked After Children (LAC). All of the pupils who took part in the study were White British (WB).

## Pre and Post Intervention Measurements

Pupils completed the Self-Image Profiles Scale (Butler 2001) before and after the intervention.

The responses to this self-report measure can be used to generate a visual display of both self-image and self-esteem. Individuals are first asked to rate their actual self by indicating 'How I am' against 25 items using a Likert scale (0 = not at all, 6 = very much) and then are asked to rate their ideal self by indicating 'How I would like to be' against the same 25 items. Statements include concepts such as 'kind', 'helpful' and 'good looking'. The discrepancy scores between the two, i.e. actual self perception as opposed to ideal self perception provides an estimate of the pupils' self-esteem.

*Chapter 6*  77

Four scale scores are calculated for positive self-image (sum of items 1-12), negative self-image (sum of items 14-25), sense of difference (item 13) and self-esteem (sum of discrepancy scores). The positive self-image score was initially used to select the sample i.e. the 48 pupils forming the sample had the lowest positive self-image scores calculated from the sum of items 1-12. It was the self-esteem scores (the sum of discrepancy scores) that were then used in the current study pre and post intervention to measure the impact MI had on pupil self-esteem.

A high self-esteem score on Butler's Self Image Profiles (above 62) reflects a wide discrepancy between participant's perceptions of how they think they are and how they would like to be and this is symptomatic of low self-esteem. This acknowledges the sense of how an individual might wish they were not like they are (Butler 2001).

The scales provide an immediate visual display of an individual's ideal self and actual self – reflected in how pupils coded their responses i.e. a shaded box indicates how they think they are and a star in a box indicates where they would like to be.

**The Intervention**

Participants were allocated to either the MI condition or the waiting list control condition. The researcher delivered the MI intervention for five consecutive weeks with the support of the school's Pastoral Support Leader. Four MI interventions were undertaken between July 2009 and January 2010 with six participants in each group.

Two intervention group pupils left the school during the intervention so the post-intervention measures could not be obtained for these pupils and their data were not utilised. Each session was delivered in exactly the same way by the researcher. The twenty-four pupils who made up the waiting list control condition received no intervention.

The researcher delivered the Motivational Interviewing intervention in the school on Tuesday and Friday mornings using the 'Facilitating Change' materials produced by Atkinson (2005). Each session lasted approximately fifty minutes. The school's Key Stage 3 (KS3) Pastoral Support Leader attended some of the sessions. The Leader's role in the school is to provide support and advice to students and to promote their social care and personal development with respect to learning and health and safety.

Two pupils with challenging behaviours were excluded from the study prior to random allocation. They were at risk of permanent exclusion due to their unacceptable behaviour towards members of staff and peers. It was judged by the school staff that the involvement of these pupils in a group based intervention at the time may have unsettled the dynamics of the group. See Figure 1 for an overview of the Research Design.

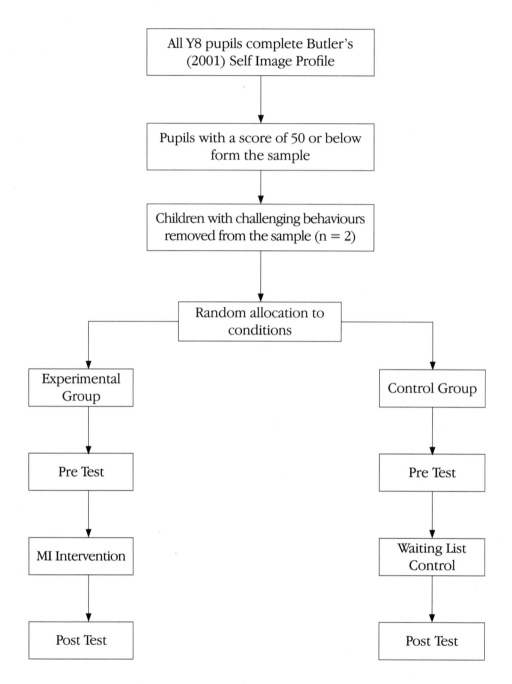

***Figure 1:*** An Overview of the Research Design

*Chapter 6*                                                                              79

## Results

All data were inputted into the software package SPSS version 17 for statistical analysis.

Independent and paired t tests were utilised to explore within and between group differences. These facilitated comparisons between progress made in relation to self-esteem by the groups receiving and not receiving the MI intervention.

Even though the selected pupils were allocated to the experimental and control groups in a random manner, there was nonetheless a significant difference in the pre intervention self-esteem scores between the experimental and control groups. An ANVCOVA was therefore utilised.

The ANCOVA converts the design from a mixed to a single factor design, reduces error variance and makes use of the difference in pre test scores between groups by adjusting the post test scores (Gliner et al 2003).

An ANCOVA is often described as a combination of an ANOVA and multiple regression and is commonly used in pre–post test designs that involve participants being given measures pre and post intervention (Brace, Kemp and Snelgar, 2009).

Furthermore, in order to examine the impact of the intervention on participants' self esteem in more detail, gain score analysis was employed to examine each individual's gain score in both conditions - by subtracting their pre test score from their post test score. This type of analysis further assesses whether or not the means of the gain scores for the two groups are equal (Gliner et al 2003).

By employing this process it was evident that the experimental group demonstrated considerably bigger gains from pre to post testing in comparison to the control group see Figure 2.

Figure 2 highlights the mean pre and post self-esteem scores for both the experimental (MI intervention) and control group. A reduction in the self-esteem score, at post testing, indicates an increase in participants' self-esteem. This is because at post intervention there was a smaller discrepancy between participant's perceptions of how they thought they were and how they would like to be than there was at pre intervention.

The mean score for participants in the experimental condition dropped considerably from pre (M=61.3, SD=15.6) to post testing (M=48.5, SD=19.8), suggesting an increase in their self-esteem. A small decline in the control group scores is also evident from pre (M=34.3, SD=19.3) to post testing (M=32.1, SD=15.7).

The paired t test was used for within group comparisons. There was a significant difference between participants' pre and post self-esteem scores in the experimental group suggesting that the MI intervention had a positive effect on pupil self-esteem.

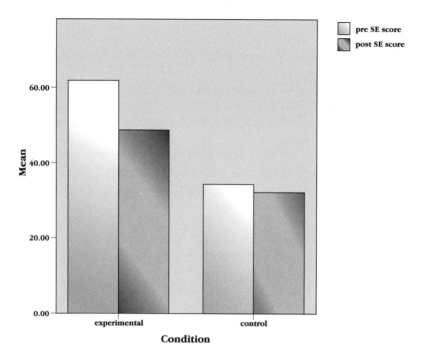

*Figure 2:* The Mean Pre and Post Self - Esteem Scores for the Experimental and Control Group

A paired t test showed that there was no significant difference between participant's pre and post self-esteem scores in the control group.

In summary, there was a significant within group increase in self-esteem for the experimental group, but not for the control group. This outcome supports the researcher's hypothesis that participants in the Motivational Interviewing condition will show significant increases in their self-esteem as measured using the Butler's Self Image Profiles.

## Conclusions and Future Directions

A key goal of MI is to promote individuals' self-esteem (Miller and Rollnick 2002). In the current study, pupils in the experimental group increased their levels of self-esteem considerably following the implementation of the MI intervention.

The present study offers an original contribution in the field of educational research as it is the first randomised control trial design exploring the effectiveness of an MI intervention based in schools. The research literature suggests the need for more interventions in the area of self-esteem and mental well being targeting the secondary age phase e.g. Adi et al (2007), hence the researcher's decision to contribute by carrying out this research.

Miller and Rollnick's more recent definition of MI is 'a collaborative, person-centred form of guiding to elicit and strengthen motivation for change' (McNamara 2009, p.210). They have expressed concerns that more recent work and interpretations have moved away from their understanding of the concept of MI. For MI is now perceived by some to be 'motivational dialogues and/or conversations'. This can create difficulties and mismatches between individuals as to what actually constitutes MI (McNamara 2009). Therefore, future investigations should ensure that the concept of MI that is being adopted by the researcher is made explicit.

Further work is required employing studies across a range of educational contexts. The current study was carried out in a secondary school, but studies examining the impact of MI with other vulnerable groups, such as school refusers and excluded pupils, could also contribute a more wide ranging evidence base (Kittles and Atkinson 2009). The possibility of adapting and breaking down the demands of some of the complex language used in MI interventions would also facilitate the possibility that MI would be appropriate for use in primary settings. This is something that the researcher would consider when undertaking future research in the field of MI as 'the language of MI' arose as a potential issue with some of the pupils involved in the current study.

Literature and research in the field of MI has recorded its successes. More recently, practitioners have demonstrated its value in education when applied in work with children and young people. This evidence base is slowly growing, with the current study being the first randomised control design in this area. Future studies should continue to evaluate the effectiveness of MI approaches when used in educational settings and research exploring how and why it is useful would further develop our understanding and conceptualisation of MI.

## References

Adi, Y., Killoran, A., Janmohammed, K., and Stewart-Brown, S. (2007) *Systematic review of the effectiveness of interventions to promote mental wellbeing in children in primary education: Report 1: Universal Approaches Non-violence related outcomes.* Centre of Public Health Excellence, NICE.

Apter, T. (1997). *The confident child.* New York, NY: W. W. Norton company, Inc.

Atkinson, C. (2005) *Facilitating Change Materials. Using Motivational Interviewing techniques to help young people understand their behaviour,* CD- Rom.

www.facilitatingchange.org.uk

Atkinson, C. and Woods, K. (2003) Motivational Interviewing Strategies for Disaffected Secondary School Students: a case example. *Educational Psychology in Practice,* 19, 1.

Brace, N., Kemp, R. And Snelgar, R. (2009) *SPSS for Psychologists* (4th ed). Hampshire. Palgrave Macmillan.

Butler, R.J. (2001) *The Self Image Profiles For Children & Adolescents.* London: Harcourt Assessment.

Clemes, H. and Bean, R. (1990). *How to raise children's self-esteem.* Los Angeles, CA: Price Stern Sloan, Inc.

Fields, A. (2004) *Curriculum-Based Motivation Group: A Five Session Motivational Interviewing Intervention,* Hollifield Associates: Portland.

Gliner, J.A., Morgan, G.A. and Harmon, R.J. (2003) Pretest-Postest Comparison Group Designs: Analysis and Interpretation. *J. AM. ACAD Child Adolesc Psychiatry.* 42, 4.

Gray, E., McCambridge, J. and Strang, J. (2005) The Effectiveness of Motivational Interviewing Delivered by Youth Workers in Reducing Drinking, Cigarette and Cannabis Smoking Among Young People: Quasi-Experimental Pilot Study. *Alcohol and Alcoholism,* 40, 6, 535-539

Kittles, M. and Atkinson, C. (2009) The usefulness of motivational interviewing as a consultation and assessment tool for working with young people. *Pastoral Care in Education,* 27, 3, 241-254.

McLean, A. (2003) *The Motivated School.* London. Paul Chapman Publishing.

McNamara, E. (2009) Motivational Interviewing Theory, Practice and Applications with Children and Young people. Positive Behaviour Management. Positivebehaviourmanagement.co.uk

Miller, W.R. and Rollnick, S. (2002) *Motivational Interviewing: Preparing People for Change.* Second Edition, London: Guilford Press.

Miller, W.R. and Rollnick, S. (1991) Motivational Interviewing: *Preparing people to change addictive behaviour.* New York: Guilford Press.

Morris, E. (1997) *Building Self-Esteem in Children, Workbook.* Gloucester. Buckholdt Publishing.

Morris, E. (2002) *Insight Secondary: Assessing and Developing Self-Esteem.* London. Nfer Nelson.

Moss, C. (2010) *How Effective is a Group Based Motivational Interviewing Intervention in Promoting Pupil Resilience and Self- Esteem?* Thesis submitted to the University of Nottingham.

Robson, C. (2002) Real World Research, Oxford: Blackwell.

# Chapter 7

# Motivational Interviewing to Support Teacher Behaviour Change

*This chapter was written by an interdisciplinary team of researchers and practitioners from the University of Cincinnati (Jon Lee), the University of Louisville (Andy Frey, Pam Ratcliffe, and Ally Rutledge), the Oregon Research Institute (John Seeley, Jason Small, and Ed Feil), and the University of Oregon (Hill Walker and Annemeike Golly).*

**Acknowledgement:** The research reported here was supported by the Institute of Education Sciences, US Department of Education, through Grant R324A090237 to the University of Louisville. The opinions expressed are those of the authors and do not represent views of the Institute or the US Department of Education.

This chapter is concerned with adapting Motivational Interviewing to an early intervention addressing challenging behavior in classrooms.

Motivational Interviewing (MI) is a powerful vehicle for increasing motivation and changing behaviour in adults, and has been shown to increase participant time in treatment, effort, and adherence to intervention protocols (Aubrey, 1998; Bien, Miller, and Boroughs, 1993; Brown and Miller, 1993; Saunders, Wilkinson and Phillips, 1995). Given that these attributes are transferrable to authentic educational settings, MI reveals itself as a promising intervention with wide ranging application in schools. Although the use of MI as articulated by Miller and Rollnick (2002; 2012) is currently limited in educational settings, a growing literature base demonstrates its relevance to school interventions and best practices. Just as with any adaptation of MI its application requires modification to the characteristics of the population it is applied with, as well as the contextual demands of the setting - in this case educational environments.

84                                   *Chapter 7*

We have previously reported on the promise of MI in the perspective of school mental health and highlighted the potential of MI to improve teacher and parent adoption and implementation of effective interventions, often referred to as treatment adherence (Frey, et al., 2011; Frey, Lee, Small, Seeley, Walker and Feil, 2013). While relevant to both academic and behavioural intervention, increasing treatment adherence may be particularly problematic for teachers of children with challenging behaviours because of the clear advantages to implementing ineffective practices. As suggested by Maag (2001), many negative behaviour management techniques e.g. telling off, removing children from the classroom, and advocating suspensions, are reinforcing to the teacher because they are effective in the short term ie the behaviour is suppressed. Thus, it is not surprising that teachers may resist effective strategies to address challenging behaviour, which are typically less negative, less reactive and require changes in teacher behaviour.

A few researchers have developed procedures to infuse MI into existing school-based practice protocols. Specifically, adaptations of MI have been developed and implemented with parents (Dishion and Stormshak, 2007; Dishion, Stormshak, and Siler, 2010) and teachers (Reinke, Lewis-Palmer, and Martin, 2007; Reinke, Lewis-Palmer, and Merrell, 2008). With parents and teachers, the applications are similar to those in health and substance abuse settings in that they employ individualized assessment, performance feedback, and intervention planning routines. However, the educational environment and teachers vary dramatically from the clinical environment and clientele in and with which MI has traditionally been practiced. These differences can constrain the typical practice of MI, and must be negotiated to transfer the benefits commonly associated with MI to educational settings.

The purpose of this chapter is to describe the process and preliminary outcomes of an adaptation to MI for school settings. Herein, we discuss the constraints associated with the practice of MI in educational contexts, and particularly with teachers. Next, we present the adaptations to MI utilized by our research team to overcome these constraints. Following the adaptations to MI, we describe the *First Step Classroom Check-Up (First Step CCU),* developed for use in educational contexts to address teacher behaviour change within an empirically based intervention for children who exhibit disruptive behaviour in classroom settings – the First Step to Success early intervention program (Walker, et al., 1998). Finally, we present selected results from our feasibility trial of the First Step CCU with a small sample of public primary school teachers.

**Constraints Associated with Educational Settings**

In this section we suggest the identification of i) target behaviours for change ii) expertise of school personnel and iii) time constraints associated with educational settings and teachers that, in our experience, often necessitate the adaptation of typical MI practice.

## Chapter 7

**Target Behaviours for Change.** The identification of target behaviours for change with teachers can be challenging. Often the application of MI in schools is indirect in that the target behaviour for change belongs to the child e.g. improved social skills, reduced disruptive behaviours. However, the evidence suggests that changes in teacher behavior, e.g. improved classroom behaviour management skills, may be the most promising target to achieve pupil behavior change. In other words, problem behavior associated with the child is treated indirectly by changing teacher behavior towards the child.

The identification of teacher behaviours that are influential and demonstrate potential to change child behaviour is critical i.e. "good teaching practice" or "appropriate classroom management" - but this not easily defined or measured. Teachers have unique teaching styles, were trained differently, and have varying approaches to classroom management. Therefore, it is necessary to establish standards, principles or criteria to use in identifying teacher target behaviours and measuring subsequent change. An example of the use of standardized criteria in identifying target behaviours can be found in more common applications of MI in the fields of health management, substance abuse and mental health. In these fields, diagnostic criteria e.g. DSM-IV, or symptoms that serve as indicators of impairment, help to identify target behaviours. A unified system of classification is not yet available in the field of education for the pedagogical concerns we posit here. Thus, the identification and measurement of target behaviours is challenging, and requires the adoption of objective criteria that are specific enough to be measured, yet generalizable across the wide-ranging differences found between schools, classrooms and teachers.

**Expertise of School-Based Personnel.** It is well-established that empathy, client centered counseling skills, and MI-specific skills are all necessary to practice MI proficiently. In our school applications, we have identified two additional foundational skills: i) the desire to develop and maintain a therapeutic working alliance and sustain the requisite spirit of MI and ii) the capacity to engage teachers in productive problem solving. These skill sets are typically not developed in school administration and teacher education programs. The effort necessary to train clinicians to use MI effectively can be rigorous and requires significant initial and ongoing training, performance feedback, and coaching. The amount of coaching and support required to teach school personnel, who frequently lack these skills sets, may prove challenging. A further barrier is that current training systems for the development of MI skills are focused largely on behavioural health applications. The development of MI training systems that are responsive to needs and characteristics of educational settings and the professional skill sets of school administrators and teachers is vital, and will require substantial research and development.

**Time.** Working in an environment with powerful demands on their time, teachers are limited in their opportunity to schedule lengthy or frequent meetings. In the development of the Classroom Check-Up, Reinke and colleagues recognized that performance feedback was commonly associated with frequent consultation meetings that were unrealistic given teachers' schedules. She and her colleagues (Reinke, et al., 2007; Reinke, et al., 2008) evaluated the effects of an alternative approach to lengthy or frequent meetings. In this approach, consultations were fewer and limited to thirty minutes and daily visual representations of objective data-based information were added in place of longer meetings. Brief sessions with teachers are likely a necessity given the demands on their time, and in Reinke and colleagues application they were successful.

## Adapting Motivational Interviewing for Educational Settings

As presented next, two specific adaptations of MI were developed to address the constraints described above: the Motivational Interviewing Navigation Guide (MING) and the Motivational Interviewing Training and Supervision (MITS) module.

**Motivational Interviewing Navigation Guide.** Despite the appeal of MI as an approach for enhancing intervention efficacy in educational settings, few processes, models or frameworks based on this approach were available to inform the integration of MI into the existing First Step program. We relied on the work of Nock and Kazdin (2005), Dishion and Stormshak (2007), and Reinke et al. (2008) in the development of the MING (Frey, et al., 2013a; Frey et al., 2013b), which is also derived from Miller and Moyer's eight strategies for learning MI (2006) and the Motivational Interviewing Navigation Map (Frey et al., 2011). The MING, our first adaption of MI to address the constraints described previously, provided the structure necessary for the development of our intervention process. It has recently been revised to assist researchers interested in developing new interventions or enhancing engagement and implementation of existing interventions using an MI approach (see Herman, Reinke, Frey and Shepard, 2013). The MING is a 5-Step process to increase intrinsic motivation for teacher and parent adoption and implementation of evidence-based practices (Frey, et al., 2013). The five steps of the MING process include: i) engage in discovery of values ii) assess current practices iii) share performance feedback iv) offer extended consultation, education and support and 5) provide closure (see Figure 1).

We believe the MING represents a resource to help address the requisite expertise of school based personnel, as it provides those learning to apply MI the opportunity to locate themselves within a streamlined hierarchy of MI objectives, and may work to reduce the time required to train school personnel.

**Motivational Interviewing Training and Support System (MITS).** Our second adaptation, the MITS, is a supplemental training and support module for school personnel e.g. psychologists, social workers, school counselors, disability liaisons, and resource teachers. It consists of i) fifteen hours of professional development focusing on the knowledge and skills that are critical to implementing MI within educational settings; ii) two 3-hour school-based team trainings that include watching and discussing audio and video-recorded examples of teacher consultations utilizing an MI approach, like the MING, in educational settings;

and iii) three individual supervision sessions with expert consultation. The fifteen hours of MITS professional development consists of five three-hour training sessions arranged around the following topics:

1. Introduction to Motivational Interviewing
2. Skills for Engaging
3. Values Discovery / Focusing
4. Evoking Change Talk and Exchanging Information
5. Change Planning

The MITS is in the process of pilot testing, utilizing the *Video Assessment of Simulated Encounters – School Based Applications* (Lee, Frey, and Small, 2013a) and the *Written Assessment of Simulated Encounters – School Based Applications* (Lee, Frey, and Small, 2013b) to measure MI proficiency. These instruments are adaptations of the Helpful Response Questionnaire (Miller, Hedrick, and Orlofsky, 1991) and the Video Assessment of Simulated Encounters (Rosengren, Baer, Hartzler, Dunn, and Wells, 2005). The measures have been revised to reflect scenarios that school personnel commonly encounter with parents and teachers.

## Tables and Figures

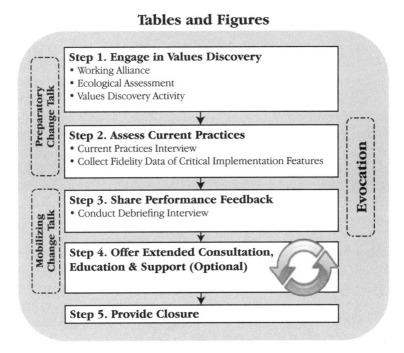

*Figure 1:* The Motivational Interviewing Navigation Guide

### The First Step CCU

Based on the MI adaptations described above, we developed the First Step Classroom Check-Up (FS-CCU) to enhance an existing evidenced based educational practice – the school component of the First Step to Success early intervention program (Walker et al., 1998). The original First Step intervention is briefly described, followed by a more detailed description of the FS-CCU.

88                                  *Chapter 7*

**First Step to Success.** The First Step to Success is an early intervention program designed for at-risk elementary school children in the primary grades. These students show clear signs of emerging externalizing behaviour patterns including aggression toward others, oppositional-defiant behaviour, tantrum throwing, rule infractions, and escalating confrontations with peers and adults (Walker, et al., 1997). The at-risk child is the primary focus of the First Step to Success program. Teachers, peers, parents, and/or caregivers participate in the intervention as implementation agents under the direction and supervision of a trained First Step behaviour coach, who is frequently a related service provider e.g. early interventionist, school counselor, school social worker, school psychologist or behavioural consultant. This trained coach has overall responsibility for coordinating the intervention's school and home components. The school component of First Step is an adapted version of the Contingencies for Learning Academic and Social Skills (CLASS) program, developed by Hops and Walker (1988), for use with conduct disordered students in kindergarten through third grade. CLASS is divided into three successive phases: Coach, Teacher, and Maintenance. The coach phase (program days 1-5) is the responsibility of an adult, trained as a First Step behavioural coach, who coordinates the implementation process. Teachers assume control of the program, after participating in training and the coach phase, for the remainder of the program (program days 6 – 30).

The premise for the program is a game that utilizes a green card, which the teacher shows to the focus child to provide positive feedback for following teacher expectations ie classroom rules and routines. The other side of the card is red, and utilized to provide non-verbal feedback when the student does not comply with teacher expectations. Great emphasis i.e. teacher recognition and encouragement, is placed on "green card behaviour," while very little emphasis is placed on behaviour that does not meet classroom expectations. The CLASS program begins with a twenty-minute daily implementation period, and is gradually extended over the course of the program, to the whole day, while the teacher's use of the green card is faded out in favour of more natural classroom reinforcement such as verbal and non verbal encouragement.

**First Step Classroom Check-Up (FS-CCU).** Our research adopted the work of Reinke et al. (2007; 2008) by taking the core components of the Classroom-Check-Up model (assessment, performance feedback, and intervention planning) and integrating it with the school component of the First Step intervention to support teacher behaviour change. The FS-CCU procedures have been aligned with the five steps of the MING as described below.

***Step 1: Engage in values discovery.*** The Teacher Values Discovery activity provides a structure for learning about the teacher's values, both generically and in relation to the classroom environment. During this activity the teacher's values are identified, validated and affirmed and their vision of what an ideal classroom environment comprises is explored. In general, the teacher is encouraged to sort through a stack of value cards (see Figure 2), identify the values that resonate with her or his teaching style or approach, and elaborate on why she or he chose each value. Coaches are encouraged to consider what is best for each teacher individually and to tailor the Teacher Values Discovery Activity[1] to meet the teacher's needs. For example, some teachers may be more open when the identification of values is approached through an interactive discussion of the topic rather than the use of value cards.

| Acceptance/Tolerance | Cooperation |
|---|---|
| To model and teach acceptance and respect for differences. | To model and teach cooperation and collaborative work with others. |
| **Responsibility** | **Self-esteem and Confidence** |
| To model and teach reliability and responsible decision making | To feel good about myself, to accept myself as I am. |

*Figure 2:* Example of Teacher Value Cards

As identified values are crucial to successfully navigating upcoming steps of the FS-CCU, the coach remains within the spirit of MI, affirming the teacher's values, emphasizing autonomy while remaining neutral, resisting confrontation and the 'selling' of change, education, or judgment. In order to foster a rich discussion of the teacher's values the coach utilizes open-ended questions such as:

- *"I see you value responsibility; what does that mean to you?"*

- *"Thinking about the future, what will children from your class look like when they move to the next grade that tells you you've been successful in instilling cooperation as a value? (How about in 5 years? 10 years?)"*

Further, the coach responds to the teacher's answers with positive regard and complex reflections, and provides summaries to facilitate transitions in the conversation. The coach is encouraged to keep detailed notes to assist during later steps of the FS-CCU in developing discrepancy between the teacher's identified values and his or her current classroom management practices following step 2.

**Step 2: *Assess current practices.*** The identification of a target behaviour for change is critical. To overcome the previously discussed challenges associated with the identification of target behaviours, we included the Five Universal Principles of

1 Adapted from W.R. Miller, J. C'de Baca, D.B. Matthews, and P. L. Wilbourne; University of New Mexico, 2001.

Positive Behaviour Support (Golly, 2006; Sprague and Golly, 2012) in the FS-CCU protocol. These principles establish a set of classroom expectations within which the First Step CLASS component is more likely to have a positive impact on the focus child and the child's peers, and are useful in identifying target behaviours for change: i) Establish clear expectations (classroom rules and routines) ii) Teach the expectations ie reinforce compliance with classroom rules and routines, through positive feedback iii) Minimize attention for minor inappropriate behaviours and iv) establish clear consequences for unacceptable behaviour.

The principles are specific yet generalizable so as to be used across the wide variety of circumstances between schools, classrooms and teachers. The purpose of the assessment of current practices then, is to introduce the Universal Principles, provide the opportunity for the teacher to self identify areas of strength and growth in light of the principles, and gather observational data in relation to the principles – in an effort to narrow the teacher's focus for the identification of possible behaviour change options. To do so, we created two activities to assess current teacher practices i) the Universal Principles Interview and ii) the Teacher Observation of the Universal Principles.

The Universal Principles Interview provides an opportunity for the coach to learn about existing classroom management practices, and encourages teachers to consider their practices in relation to the Universal Principles and to their own values. To do this, we recommend exploring teaching practices by introducing the Universal Principles and facilitating a discussion about each. The teacher is provided with a visual prompt for each principle (see Figure 3), and the coach asks questions such as:

- *"Tell me about your classroom expectations for behaviour, both those that you hold for yourself as a teacher and those that you have posted in the room for the children."*

- *"Can you provide some examples of how you state your expectations positively, teach, and review them periodically e.g. class meetings?"*

- *"In what ways do you use your expectations as pre-corrections for potentially difficult times (transitions, special events)?"*

| Establish Clear Expectations | | | |
|---|---|---|---|
| ✓ Expectations are stated positively. | Rate Yourself: How well do you make use of clear expectations? | | |
| ✓ Expectations are specifically taught. | O Not very well at all | O Could do better | O Well enough |
| ✓ Expectations reviewed periodically. | | | O Very well |

*Figure 3:* Example of Teacher Universal Principles Visual Prompt

After encouraging the teacher to rate their application of any one of the Universal Principles, the coach then solicits their ratings in regard to the extent to which they believe using the principle as a core component of classroom management is important, and how confident they are in their ability to use the principle. Importance (see Figure 4) and confidence rulers are used as a visual prompt to help facilitate this conversation.

| Importance Ruler | | | | | | | | | |
|---|---|---|---|---|---|---|---|---|---|
| 1 | 2 | 3 | 4 | 5 | 6 | 7 | 8 | 9 | 10 |
| Not Important | | | | | | | | | Very Important |

**Figure 4:** Importance Ruler

**Prompt:** "On a scale from 1-10, with 10 being extremely important, how important would you say it is to implement this Universal Principle?"

**Follow-Up:** "I'm interested in why you said ____ [insert the number they gave you] and not 0."

During the Universal Principles Interview, the coach emphasizes and reinforces change talk, through simple or complex reflections, followed by open-ended questions that work to encourage elaboration. Frequent summary reflections are utilized to check for understanding and provide an opportunity to promote autonomy. During this interview coaches must remain keenly aware of sustain talk, and be prepared to differentially respond with common MI counseling strategies. For example, the coach might respond to sustain talk with a neutral reflection that slightly understates the teacher's meaning, or a simple reflection followed by a change of topic. In our experience, any response that could be perceived as confrontational is better left for the next step of the FS-CCU – Share Performance Feedback. Remaining neutral in an information gathering stance is desirable at this point.

The Teacher Observation of the Universal Principles is a measure of teacher interaction that provides an opportunity for coaches to make qualitative notes related to each of the five Universal Principles, and a structure for subjective coding of the two Universal Principles that represent the teacher's use of attention to appropriate and inappropriate behaviour, the latter being the more likely cause of coercive interactions. Our observational system allows for the collection of data related to the teacher's use of attention, and provides a vehicle to engage in a MI consistent performance feedback routine. The observation provides a view of the positive or negative valence within the classroom, and a measure of the specific amount of reinforcement used by the teacher. For this observation, reinforcement is defined as the teacher's verbal or non-verbal attention to the focus student's appropriate and inappropriate behavior. This step includes two 30-minute observations during teacher-directed instruction. The frequency of the teacher's use of reinforcement is recorded across three targets: the focus student, any other peer in the class, or the class as a whole - see coding form example in Figure 4. Tracking the teacher's use of reinforcement across these three targets can reveal discrepancies for which the teacher may be ambivalent, and thus unaware of as a possible target for behaviour change.

| Reinforces Expectations (attention to appropriate behavior) | | | | | |
|---|---|---|---|---|---|
| | | Focus student | Peer | Class | |
| **General** | Verbal | | | | |
| | Non-Verbal | | | | |
| **Specific** | Verbal | | | | |
| | | | | | |

**Figure 5:** Observation of Teacher Behaviour Coding Form

Coding the teacher's use of reinforcement as either behaviour specific or general provides additional information regarding the teacher's use of reinforcement. Behaviour specific reinforcement provides the child a reference to the behaviour in question e.g. "I notice your materials are ready", and has more influence in changing children's behaviour, as opposed to general reinforcement, which does not reference any behaviour e.g. "Good job!"

Data from these observations are used to guide the Teacher Debriefing Interview. In preparation for this process, the coach takes time to coalesce all information gathered to this point; this is a process of professional reflection that we refer to as case conceptualization. Beginning with the initial contact between coach and teacher, case conceptualization is an ongoing process of assimilating key information gleaned from interviews, activities, and observations in the classroom, in order to develop a strategy for the use of directional MI and, when applicable, for extended consultation, education, and support. In addition to considering ecological information, values, ideals, and the teacher's reactions to the Universal Principles and observational data, the coach must also reflect on the frequency and spontaneity of sustain talk and change talk. Autonomy remains central to the MI process, so the coach must resist the urge to approach teacher meetings with a detailed blueprint of how the interaction should unfold. However, the ongoing conceptualization process should allow the coach to enter each meeting with the teacher with a well thought-out approach to effectively i) respond to sustain talk

*Chapter 7* 93

which may be likely to arise around certain issues ii) address barriers to desired change iii) support the teacher's control, autonomy, and choice to freely consider change and make decisions consistent with their values and goals and iv) enhance importance and confidence.

After the case conceptualization process, the coach enters into Step 3 - Share Performance Feedback, and is prepared for the Teacher Debriefing Interview, which is a significant process in gaining a commitment for behaviour change.

**Step 3: Share performance feedback.** The purpose of sharing performance feedback is to obtain the teacher's commitment to improve his or her use of one or more of the Universal Principles. The vehicle utilized during performance feedback is the Teacher Debriefing Interview. During the Teacher Debriefing Interview the coach works to reveal any existing ambivalence in the teacher's perception and use of the Universal Principles, and if necessary to amplify any discrepancies that exist between the teacher's identified values and ideals, and current behaviour. If the teacher perceives the issues to be important and is confident she or he is capable of changing, commitments to change are made, options are discussed, specifics are negotiated, goals are created, and a plan of action is developed and formalized - typically in writing.

The structure and duration of the debriefing interview is highly variable, and dependent upon the teacher's perception of his or her implementation of the Universal Principles as well as motivation to change. The interview begins with the coach soliciting the teacher's impressions of a graphic representation of the Teacher Observation of the Universal Principles (see Figure 6). The coach responds to the teacher's perception of the data after evaluating the teacher's perception of importance and confidence in regards to behaviour change. Attempts to enhance the teacher's confidence in their ability to change are recommended if the teacher's implementation is strong (defined as a ratio of 3:1 attention to appropriate vs. inappropriate behaviour) and self-ratings are high, irrespective of motivation level.

If implementation is weak but teacher motivation to change is high, the coach attempts to enhance the teacher's confidence in their ability to change, and then invites the teacher to move to Step 4. If implementation of the five Universal Principles is weak and teacher motivation is low, we recommend the coach cultivate importance, by emphasizing discrepancies between current conditions and ideals of self, classroom, and values, using data-based feedback and elaborating on the pros of change in present, past and future. Following this, the coach solicits teacher impressions of the data for the second time and moves to enhance confidence in their ability to change. The coach then offers the option of receiving extended coach support or brings the FS-CCU consultation process to a close i.e. Step 5, if motivation to change is insurmountable.

Throughout the debriefing interview the coach attends to change talk, encourages elaboration and requests details - adding significance through complex reflections tied to the teacher's values and ideals.

There are no concrete rules to signify an appropriate time to transition to the final process of Step 3. Nevertheless, teacher ratings of importance and confidence should be considered, but should not be the only indicators used to make this decision. Additional readiness signs include decreased sustain talk, increased frequency and spontaneity of change talk, as well as direct requests to get on with implementation. These readiness signs indicate that the teacher has identified their own strengths and can easily acknowledge the advantages of developing a plan to change their behaviour.

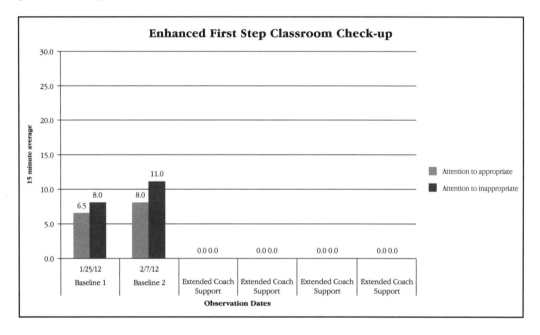

***Figure 6:*** Results of Observation of Teacher Behaviour

During the creation of a change plan, the teacher is encouraged to choose one or two of the Universal Principles to focus on. Next, the coach and teacher negotiate the following components: i) a description of the specific goals of the teacher ii) planning for additional Observations of Teacher Behaviour iii) teacher's perceptions of importance and confidence and iv) specific assistance/support provided by the coach. Many options exist to help teachers implement the Universal Principles more consistently. These options are self-selected and self-monitored by the teacher within the context of focusing on evidenced-based practice, with support from the coach when requested. Utilizing a written change plan can be beneficial in situations with multiple identified barriers and when focusing on multiple Universal Principles.

**Step 4: *Offer extended consultation, education and support.*** Teachers who are motivated to change and negotiate the specifics for and commit to a change plan are offered additional Observations of Teacher Behaviour. Data from each additional observation are added to the original graph. If agreed upon by the coach and teacher during the debriefing interview, for example, the coach might add to the chart indications of the expected amount of attention to appropriate behaviour associated with any goals determined at that time. This presentation of data allows the teacher to review progress and monitor the effectiveness of their self-selected change strategies. These data are provided to the teacher without elaboration, or can be provided with extended consultation, education and support involving the Universal Principles if requested. Extended support typically involves educational strategies like conferencing, modeling, and role-playing, in addition to problem solving barriers to implementation. The process continues as necessary and as agreed upon by the teacher. Additional behaviours may be targeted, observed and discussed, as Step 4 is often iterative. The process ends with a celebration of accomplishments.

***Step 5: Provide Closure.*** Whether a teacher selects closure due to high confidence in their ability to change their behaviour without assistance or due to low motivation, steps should be taken to ensure that the relationship ends on a positive note. This step typically occurs after the Debriefing Interview or any Extended Consultation, Education and Support has been completed. We have found relationships are supported when the coach expresses gratitude for the teacher's engagement in the FS-CCU process; whether the relationship has been challenging or not, the teacher can only stand to benefit from receiving affirmations at the time of closure. Closure need not be lengthy, but should be sincere. Additionally, the coach offers to return to this topic in the future if the teacher changes their mind.

### Feasibility Trial

It was our intention to fully develop an FS-CCU intervention to influence teacher behaviour change with respect to their use of the Universal Principles. Our expectation was that this intervention could be implemented with coaches adhering to the 5-step process and implementing MI proficiently. Further, we expected adherence to the 5-step process and use of high quality MI would result in strong coach-teacher alliance and teacher commitment to establishing a behaviour change goal related to at least one of the Universal Principles. We were particularly interested in teachers' increased attention to appropriate behaviour and/or decreased attention to inappropriate behaviour.

**Participants.** We utilized the Critical Events Index and the Adaptive and Maladaptive Behavior Indices of the Systematic Screening for Behavior Disorders (SSBD) (Walker and Severson, 1990) to screen for the most severe behaviour challenged student in participating classrooms from three different elementary schools. We then garnered parent consent for participation and verified the serious nature of the children's behaviour challenges using the externalizing scale of the Child Behavior Checklist- Parent Report Form (CBCL; Achenbach, 1991). The resulting sample of twelve children consisted primarily of boys (83%), whose average age would place them in the first grade. Sixty-seven percent of the sample was Caucasian while the remaining 33% were African American. Their teachers were predominately Caucasian women (92%) with graduate degrees (84%), with an average of 10.6 years of teaching experience. Three coaches, who had no previous experience with MI and one year of intense training i.e. the MITS, and

# Chapter 7

experience within our project, participated during the 2011-2012 school year. All three coaches had Masters Degrees, one in education (Coach 1), one in social work (Coach 2), and one in school counseling (Coach 3).

**Motivational Interviewing Proficiency.** The coaches' ability to apply MI was measured using a slightly modified version of The Motivational Interviewing Treatment Integrity (MITI) code (Moyers, Martin, Manuel, Miller, and Ernst, 2007). Coach interactions with focus teachers were audio recorded (n = 12) and provided to the Clinical Training Institute (CTI) in Chicago IL. CTI staff randomly selected 20 minutes of each tape to code. As can be seen in Table 1, coaches' mean rating across the five global domains was 4.16 (SD = 0.14), which is considered Competent according to the MITI manual.

**Table 1.** Motivational Interviewing Implementation Quality

| Coach ID ($n$) | Global Spirit Composite $M (SD)$ | Reflections Questions Ratio | Percent Open Questions | Percent Complex Reflections | Percent MI Adherent |
|---|---|---|---|---|---|
| 1 (4) | 4.00 (.56) (C) | .81 | .50 (B) | .46 (B) | .92 (B) |
| 2 (3) | 4.22 (.46) (C) | 1.18 (B) | .45 | .46 (B) | 1. (C) |
| 3 (5) | 4.27 (.65) (C) | .47 | .44 | .29 | 1.(C) |
| $M (12)$ | 4.16 (.14) (C) | .82 | .46 | .40 (B) | .97 (B) |

$n$ = case-load size. MITI Summmary Score Competency Thresholds; C = Competency (highest level); B = Beginning Proficiency.

Mean ratios of reflections to questions ($M$ = .82), and percent open-ended questions ($M$ = .46) were just short of Beginning Proficiency. Participating coaches met the Beginning Proficiency thresholds for percent complex reflections ($M$ = 40%) and percent of MI adherent utterances ($M$ = 97%). Table 1 also reveals differences among the three coaches. All three coaches met the Competency threshold for global spirit ratings; Coach 1 and Coach 2 reached Beginning Proficiency or Competency thresholds for three of the four summary measures; Coach 3 attained the Competency threshold for one of the four summary measures. Our findings suggest it is feasible for school personnel to implement MI proficiently. The strongest evidence we have is that our coaches reached the Beginning Proficiency or Competency threshold for three of the five MITI summary scores. A more detailed description of the process used to adapt the MITI, and a more complete reporting of our coach's proficiency, is reported in Frey, et al., (2013a).

**Coach-Teacher Alliance.** Throughout the FS-CCU process, coaches worked diligently to establish working alliances with teachers. We measured this relationship with the Coach-Teacher Alliance Survey, a survey modified from a core measure disseminated by the National Behavior Research and Coordination Center (SRI International). Coaches and teachers answered the same eight items on a five-point scale ranging from *never* to *always,* measuring the respondent's

*Chapter 7* 97

perception of shared goals, communication, trust, and effectiveness of the partnership with respect to implementation. Teachers' perceptions of the alliance with their coach were higher on average ($M$ = 4.97, $SD$ = 0.09) than were coaches' perception of this alliance ($M$ = 4.39, $SD$ = 0.24). Both coaches and teachers rated their perception of the alliance highly, indicative of a strong working relationship.

Our experience is that the alliances built during the FS-CCU were often sharply concentrated on the focus student and peers from the classroom. Many coach-teacher relationships took on a professional feel, akin to professional development or a cognitive coaching model (Costa and Garmston, 2002), yet at the same time different. These relationships were built on the values and goals of the teacher in the classroom whose autonomy in the change process was complete, allowing the teacher to guide the course of action.

**Teacher Behaviour.** After implementation of the FS-CCU intervention, each teacher in our sample was motivated to set a personal goal, and follow-up observations indicate that each teacher changed their behaviour in positive ways by increasing attention to appropriate behaviour and/or decreasing attention to inappropriate behaviour.

**Table 2.** Within-subjects Analysis; Observation of Teacher Behaviour categories.

| | Baseline M (SD) | Post M (SD) | F | p-value | $\eta_p^2$ |
|---|---|---|---|---|---|
| Total | | | | | |
| Praise | 36.3 (24.3) | 62.3 (23.9) | 10.64 | .008 | .192 |
| Reprimands | 29.5 (26.6) | 19 (11.6) | 2.2 | .166 | .050 |
| Specific | | | | | |
| Praise | 11.3 (9.6) | 24.5 (12.0) | 10.21 | .008 | .220 |

$\eta_p^2$ = partial eta squared, a measure of effect size or practical significance.

Table 2 summarizes means, standard deviations, and effect sizes from a within subjects analysis of the Observation of Teacher Behaviour categories of Total Praise i.e. attention to appropriate behaviour and Reprimand i.e. attention to inappropriate behaviour and Total Specific Praise. The use of the term 'total' indicates that data were collapsed, for both general and specific categories of both praise and reprimands and across focus-student, peer and classroom-directed feedback. The category of specific praise is also displayed. There was a statistically significant increase in the average occurrence of praise ($F$ (1, 11) = 10.64, $p$ = .008) for this sample of teachers, and while the average occurrence of reprimands was reduced, decreases did not reach statistical significance. Overall teacher behaviour change in the category of Specific Praise rose to statistical significance and demonstrated a medium effect size ($\eta_p^2$ = .220)

98                                Chapter 7

**Social Validity.** Coaches and teachers responded to questionnaires designed to measure the overall importance and the acceptability of goals, procedures, and outcomes for the FS-CCU, as it related to their role in and satisfaction with the intervention. Our questionnaire utilized response options along a five point Likert-type response continuum ranging from *strongly disagree to strongly agree.* Overall, teachers' responses to the questionnaire suggested they were slightly more satisfied than coaches, and as a group demonstrated strong satisfaction with the FS-CCU intervention ($M = 4.60, SD = .57$). Coaches' responses to questions in regards to the FS-CCU intervention were as follows; *was the FS-CCU compatible with the needs of the teacher?* ($M = 4.38, SD = .52$), *was the FS-CCU intervention effective in teaching effective strategies to deal with challenging behaviour?* ($M = 3.75, SD = .89$), *did the FS-CCU intervention have a positive effect on teacher-child interactions?* ($M = 3.88, SD = .83$). The coaches reported satisfaction that can be classified as good overall ($M = 3.94, SD = .39$).

Additional evidence that this sample of teachers found the FS-CCU intervention to be socially valid arose from an analysis of focus group interviews completed at post intervention. Teachers provided open and honest responses during focus group interviews that were positive on the whole, and found to be most prevalent within the themes of intervention procedures, outcomes, and the overall purpose and importance of their use positive feedback. A comprehensive review of this analysis is beyond the scope of this chapter.

## Conclusion

This chapter examined the constraints associated with the use of MI in education settings, adaptations in order to navigate those constraints, and results from a feasibility pilot study. The FS-CCU was developed by integrating MI (Miller and Rollnick, 2002; 2012) procedures into the existing First Step to Success early intervention protocol. The resulting intervention, an adaptation of Reinke et al.'s (2008) Classroom Check-Up, focuses on the classroom teacher's use of the Five Universal Principles of Positive Behaviour Support (Golly, 2006; Sprague and Golly, 2012) to address challenging behaviour.

Our study of the resulting intervention provides an example of how MI can be used with teachers, advances existing knowledge, and makes unique contributions in several areas. First, it extends nearly two decades of work examining the original First Step to Success program by examining enhancements designed to influence teacher motivation to decrease problematic behaviour and increase adaptive behaviour of students with more severe problem behaviours (Carter and Horner, 2007, 2009; Diken and Rutherford, 2005; Golly et al., 2000; Golly, Stiller, and Walker, 1998; Nelson et al., 2009; Overton et al., 2002; Sprague and Perkins, 2009; Walker et al., 1998; Walker et al., 2009; Walker et al., 2005; Walker et al., 2013). Second, this study extends the literature base related to the application of MI in school settings. While a number of studies have investigated interventions that infuse MI into their procedures, the extent to which interventionists in school settings actually implement MI with fidelity has only recently been addressed

*Chapter 7*                                                                    99

e.g. Frey, et al., (2013a). The examination of MI fidelity, proficiency, and quality of interventionists within a school-based application is an important step in the further development of MI as it is applied in educational contexts. These preliminary results are important, as they suggest this is a feasible and acceptable approach within the schools and that the training and supervision procedures utilized with coaches were successful. Furthermore, the findings lend support to the possibility that school personnel can learn to implement MI proficiently.

## References

Achenbach, T. (1991). *The Child Behavior Checklist: Manual for the teacher's report form.* Burlington: University of Vermont, Department of Psychiatry.

Aubrey, L. (1998). *Motivational interviewing with adolescents presenting for outpatient substance abuse treatment (Unpublished doctoral dissertation).* University of New Mexico. Albuquerque, NM.

Bien, T., Miller, W., and Boroughs, J. (1993). Motivational interviewing with alcohol outpatients. *Behavioral and Cognitive Psychotherapy,* 21, 347-356.

Brown, J., and Miller, W. (1993). Impact of motivational interviewing on participation and outcome in residential alcoholism treatment. *Psychology of Addictive Behaviors,* 7, 211-218.

Carter, D., and Horner, R. (2007). Adding functional assessment to First Step to Success: A case study. *Journal of Positive Behavioral Interventions,* 9, 229-238.

Costa, A., and Garmston, R. (2002). *Cognitive Coaching: A Foundation for Renaissance Schools (2nd ed.).* Norwood, Mass: Christopher-Gordon Publishers Inc.

Diken, I., and Rutherford, R. (2005). First Step to Success early intervention program: A study of effectiveness with Native-American children. *Education and Treatment of Children,* 28(4), 444-465.

Dishion, T., and Stormshak, E. (Eds.). (2007). *Intervening in children's lives: An ecological, family-centered approach to mental health care.* Washington, DC: American Psychological Association.

Dishion, T., Stormshak, E. and Siler, C. (2010). An ecological approach to interventions with high-risk students in schools: Using the Family Check-Up to motivate parents' positive behavior support. In M. R. Shinn and H. M. Walker (Eds.), *Interventions for achievement and behavior problems in a three-tier model including RTI (pp. 101–124).* Bethesda, MD: National Association of School Psychologists.

Frey, A., Cloud, R., Lee, J., Small, J., Seeley, J., Feil, E., Walker, H., and Golly, A. (2011). The promise of motivational interviewing in school mental health. *School Mental Health,* 3, 1-12.

Frey, A., Lee, J., Small, J., Seeley, J., Walker, H., and Feil, E. (2013a). Transporting motivational interviewing to school settings to improve engagement and fidelity of Tier 2 interventions. *Journal of Applied School Psychology,* 29(2), 183-202.

Frey, A., Lee, J., Small, J., Seeley, J., Walker, H., and Feil, E. (2013b). Motivational Interviewing Navigation Guide: A process for enhancing teacher's motivation to adopt and implement school-based interventions. *Advances in School Mental Health Promotion.* DOI:10.1080/1754730X.2013.804334

Golly, A. (2006). *Five Universal Principles of positive behavior support.* Verona, Wisconsin: Attainment Company, Inc.

Golly, A., Sprague, J., Walker, H., Beard, K., and Gorham, G. (2000). The First Step to Success program: An Analysis of outcomes with identical twins across multiple baselines. *Behavioral Disorders,* 25, 170-182.

Golly, A., Stiller, B., and Walker, H. (1998). First Step to Success: Replication and social validation of and early intervention program for achieving secondary prevention goals. *Journal of Emotional and Behavioral Disorders,* 6, 243-250.

Gresham, F., and Elliott, S. (1990). *The social skills rating system (SSRS).* Circle Pines, MN: American Guidance Service.

Gresham, F., and Elliott, S. (2008). *Social skills improvement system.* Circle Pines, MN: Pearson Assessment.

Herman, K., Reinke, W., Frey, A., & Shepard, S. (2013). *Motivational Interviewing in Schools: Strategies for Engaging Parents, Teachers, and Students.* Springer Publishing Company.

Hops, H., and Walker H. (1988). *CLASS: Contingencies for Learning Academic and Social Skills.* Seattle, WA: Educational Achievement. Systems.

Lee, J., Frey, A.J., & Small, J.W. (2013). *The Video Assessment of Simulated Encounters – School-Based Applications.* University of Cincinnati. Cincinnati, OH.

Lee, J., Small, J.W., & Frey, A.J. (2013). *Written Assessment of Simulated Encounters-School-Based Application.* University of Cincinnati. Cincinnati, OH.

Maag, J., (2001). Rewarded by punishment: Reflections on the disuse of positive reinforcement in schools. *Exceptional Children* 67(2), 173-186.

Miller, W. R., Hedrick, K. E., and Orlofsky, D. (1991). The Helpful Responses Questionnaire: A procedure for measuring therapeutic empathy. *Journal Clinical Psychology,* 47, 444-448

Miller, W., R., and Moyer, T., B. (2006). Eight stages in learning motivational interviewing. *Journal of Teaching in the Addictions,* 5, 3-17.

Miller, W., and Rollnick, S. (2002). *Motivational interviewing: Preparing people for change (2nd ed.).* New York: Guilford Press.

Miller, W., and Rollnick, S. (2012). *Motivational Interviewing: Helping people change (Applications of Motivational Interviewing) (3rd ed.).* New York: Guilford Press.

Moyers, T., Martin, T., Manuel, J., Miller, W., and Ernst, D. (2007). *The Motivational Interviewing Treatment Integrity (MITI) Code 3.0.* Unpublished coding manual. University of New Mexico, Center on Alcoholism, Substance Abuse, and Addictions.

Nelson, J., Hurley, K., Synhorst, L., Epstein, M., Stage, S., and Buckley, J. (2009). The child outcomes of a behavior model. *Exceptional Children,* 76, 7-30.

Nock, M., and Ferriter, C. (2005). Parent management of attendance and adherence in child and adolescent therapy: A conceptual and empirical review. *Clinical Child and Family Psychology Review,* 8, 149–166.

Nock, M., and Kazdin, A. (2005). Randomized controlled trial of a brief intervention for increasing participation in parent management training. *Journal of Consulting and Clinical Psychology,* 73, 872–879.

Nock, M., and Photos, V. (2006). Parent motivation to participate in treatment: Assessment and prediction of subsequent participation. *Journal of Child and Family Studies,* 15, 345–358.

Overton, S., McKenzie, L., King, K., and Osborne, J. (2002). Replication of the First Step to Success model: A multiple case study of implementation effectiveness. *Behavioral Disorders, 28,* 40-56.

Reinke, W., Lewis-Palmer, T. and Martin, E. (2007). The effect of visual performance feedback on teacher use of behavior-specific praise. *Behavior Modification,* 31(3), 247-263.

Reinke, W., Lewis-Palmer, T. and Merrell, K. (2008). The Classroom Check-Up: A class wide teacher consultation model for increasing praise and decreasing disruptive behavior. *School Psychology Review,* 37(3), 315-332.

Rosengren, D. B., Baer, J. S., Hartzler, B., Dunn, C. W., Wells, E. A. (2005). The Video Assessment of Simulated Encounters (VASE): Development and validation of a group-administered method for evaluating clinician skills in motivational interviewing. *Drug and Alcohol Dependence* 79(3), 321-330.

Rosenthal, R., and Rosnow, R. L. (2008). *Essentials of Behavioral Research: Methods and Data Analysis* (3rd ed.). New York: McGraw-Hill.

Saunders, B., Wilkinson, C., and Phillips, M. (1995). The impact of a brief motivational intervention with opiate users attending a methadone programme. *Addiction,* 90, 415–424.

Sprague, J. and Golly, A (2013). BEST Behavior. *Building Positive Behavior Support in Schools.* Second Edition. Longmont, CO. Sopris Learning.

Sprague, J., and Perkins, K. (2009). Direct and Collateral Effects of the First Step to Success Program. *Journal of Positive Behavior Interventions,* 11(4), 208-221.

Walker, H., Kavanagh, K., Stiller, B., Golly, A., Severson, H., and Feil, E. (1998). First Step to Success: An early intervention approach for preventing school antisocial behaviour. *Journal of Emotional and Behavioural Disorders,* 6(2), 66-81.

Walker, H., Seeley, J., Small, J., Severson, H., Graham, B., Feil, E., ... Golly, A. (2009). A randomized controlled trial of the First Step to Success early intervention: Demonstration of program efficacy outcomes in a diverse, urban school district. *Journal of Emotional and Behavioral Disorders,* 17(4): 197-212.

Walker, H., and Severson, H. (1990). *Systematic screening for behavior disorders: User's guide and technical manual.* Longmont, CO: Sopris West.

Walker, H., Severson, H., Seeley, J., Feil, E., Small, J., Golly, A. Frey, A.J., Lee, J., Sumi, C., Woodbridge, M., Wagner, & Forness, S. (2013) The Evidence Base of the First Step to Success Early Intervention for Preventing Emerging Antisocial Behavior Patterns. In H. Walker & F. Gresham (Eds.), *Handbook of Evidence-Based Practices for Students Having Emotional and Behavioral Disorders* New York: Guilford.

Walker, H. M., Sprague, J. R., Perkins-Rowe, K. A., Beard-Jordan, K. Y., Seibert, B. M., Golly, A. M., Severson, H. H., and Feil, E. G. (2005). The First Step to Success program: Achieving secondary prevention outcomes for behaviorally at-risk children through early intervention. In M. H. Epstein, K. Kutash, and A. J. Duchnowski (Eds.), *Outcomes for children and youth with emotional and behavioral disorders and their families: Programs and evaluation best practices* (2nd ed., pp. 501-523). Austin, TX: PRO-ED.

Walker, H., Stiller, B., Golly, A., Kavanagh, K., Severson, H., and Feil, E. (1997). *First Step to Success: Helping children overcome antisocial behavior. Implementation guide.* Longmont, CO: Sopris West.

# Chapter 8

# Training Student Services Staff in Motivational Interviewing

## Scott Caldwell
*Wisconsin Department of Health Services*
*Madison, Wisconsin USA*

## Susan Kaye
*Madison Metropolitan School District*
*Madison, Wisconsin USA*

Motivational Interviewing (MI) is a well-established evidence-based practice (EBP; Lundahl et al., 2010) with potential application within schools (Herman et al., 2014; Kaplan et al., 2011; McNamara, 2009). Recent studies show MI to be a promising approach to address a range of student problems in the school setting, including alcohol, illicit drug, and tobacco use (Barnett et al., 2012; Jensen et al., 2011; Kelly & Lapworth, 2006; Winters et al., 2007, 2012), mental health (Frey et al., 2011), classroom behaviors (Reinke et al., 2011), and academic achievement (Strait et al., 2012). Because of its brevity and apparent flexibility, MI may be a particularly useful approach for a multidisciplinary team of student services staff (social work, psychology, counseling, nursing) who work within schools with the charge of promoting student health and well-being.

As research continues to support the dissemination of MI in school settings, demand for training will likely increase. Although there exists a growing MI training literature (Barwick et al., 2012; de Roten et al., 2013; Madson et al., 2009) and related implementation science (Fixsen et al., 2005; Forman et al., 2013), to our knowledge, only two studies (Burke et al., 2005; Frey et al., 2013) have specifically examined MI training with student services staff.

104                                    *Chapter 8*

The purpose of this chapter is to describe a comprehensive approach to training student services staff in MI. First, we identify key insights of effective training from the emerging literature of MI training. Then, we describe a model for implementing MI as an Evidence Based Practice which has three stages: exploration, adoption, and implementation (Fixsen et al., 2005). Next, we describe MI training goals, key content, methods, processes, duration, and barriers within each implementation stage. Finally, having collectively provided 34 trainings to over 600 student services staff as members of the Motivational Interviewing Network of Trainers, we draw upon our training experiences to identify lessons learned. This chapter will be relevant for MI trainers working with schools, school leaders considering MI training for staff, and student services staff who seek to learn MI as an EBP.

## Insights from MI Training Research

To date, over 40 MI training studies have been conducted (Rosengren and Dunn, 2012) and training reviews are emerging (Barwick et al., 2012; de Roten et al., 2013; Madson et al., 2009). Several insights can be taken from this growing literature. First, there are essential elements of the MI method that must be emphasized in training (Miller and Moyers, 2006; Miller and Rollnick, 2013). These elements include the underlying spirit, that is, a way of being with students (collaboration, evocation, support autonomy, acceptance, compassion); the "OARS" microskills (Open questions, Affirmation, Reflective listening, Summarizing); and recognizing, eliciting, and responding to student change talk i.e. any speech about a particular behavior that is in the direction of change. Because proficiency in each of these practice elements independently predicts positive behavior change outcomes (Miller and Rose, 2009), the importance of incorporating this content into training cannot be overstated. Indeed, in a review of 27 MI training studies (Madson et al., 2009), all trainings addressed at least one of these elements and 17 trainings (63%) addressed all three elements of spirit, skills, and recognizing change talk.

Second, an important outcome of MI training is staff 's own behavior change. The adoption of MI into practice requires a shift in attitude and behavior on the part of staff and that often means letting go of practices that have been shown to be ineffective or counterproductive in promoting behavior change. In our training experiences, student services staff initially show a tendency toward more talking than listening to students as well as "non-adherent" behaviors such as persuasion, denying student choice, or advising and educating without first drawing out the student's ideas for change. This last observation was echoed by Frey and colleagues (2013) who found staff expertise to be a barrier to learning MI and that training could help staff "suspend innate tendencies to fix the problem themselves or act as the authority" (p. 196). Thus, an important goal of MI training is to help staff eliminate or minimize MI non-adherent behaviors (Miller and Mount, 2001).

Third, the design and delivery of training should maximize staff 's involvement in the learning process. Described as "active learning" (Beidas and Kendall, 2010, p. 2), training should utilize multiple methods, including experiential skill building exercises, group discussion, role play, and demonstration or viewing training videos with structured observation. Such an array of teaching methods were identified by Madson and colleagues in a review of MI training (Madson et al., 2009) as well as in a recent survey of MI trainers which found that "integrating experiential exercises is a highly valued component of MI training" (Madson et al., 2012, p. 21).

Fourth, MI is not easy to learn (Miller and Rollnick, 2009). Although MI training can promote favorable learning outcomes for diverse professionals (de Roten et al., 2013; Madson et al., 2009) including school-based personnel (Frey et al., 2013), the traditional "one shot" training format is inadequate for promoting even a basic level of competency in MI (Arkowitz and Miller, 2008) or in any EBP for that matter (Beidas and Kendall, 2010; Fixsen et al., 2005). Amplifying the problem is the tendency for staff to overestimate their skillful use of MI following a single workshop (Miller and Mount, 2001). Yet no correlation exists between self-perceived and independently assessed level of MI skill (Miller and Rollnick, 2009). As Arkowitz and Miller (2008) note, "a workshop is not the means but rather only the *beginning* of learning MI (p. 19, italics in original)."

A final insight from the MI training literature is that learning how to deliver MI with fidelity can be accelerated when training is infused with evidence-informed learning methods. In a landmark training study that randomized practitioners to one of several MI learning conditions, Miller and colleagues (2004) showed that, following a single workshop, proficient MI was best achieved when performance-based feedback on practice was coupled with coaching for skill development. As depicted in Figure 1, these components comprise a robust cycle of learning: 1) direct observation of practice e.g. audio recorded session, using an MI coding instrument because as Miller and Rose (2009) note, there is "no reliable and valid way to measure MI fidelity other than through the direct coding of practice samples" (p. 530); 2) performance-based feedback on the practice with comparison to established MI fidelity standards i.e. basic competency and proficiency; Miller and Rollnick, 2013; 3) opportunities for continued practice and skill building; and 4) staff goal setting and development of an individualized learning plan. This learning cycle repeats commencing with the next direct observation of practice.

These selected insights from the MI training literature can be summarized as follows: training must emphasize the essential elements of MI in a process of learning that promotes staff 's own behavior change; this is likely best achieved through a skills-focused, experiential and active learning process which involves direct observation of practice, feedback, and opportunities for ongoing skill development. Taken together, these insights inform the design and delivery of effective MI training.

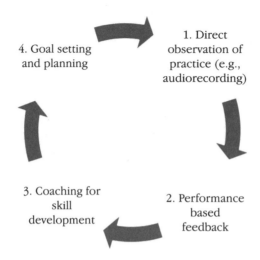

***Figure 1:*** Cycle of Learning Motivational Interviewing.

## Implementation of MI in Schools

Designing and delivering effective MI training with student services staff means that staff work toward delivering the method to fidelity standards so that desirable student outcomes can be achieved. Fidelity is the extent to which an EBP is delivered as intended. Without fidelity of practice, the expected beneficial outcomes will not be achieved. Although MI training is a critical part of helping staff to achieve fidelity, training itself is but one part of a larger implementation process (Barwick et al., 2012). Only when effective training is coupled with quality implementation will the best outcomes be realized (Forman et al., 2013; Fixsen et al., 2005). As depicted in Figure 2, contrasting the extent to which MI is delivered to fidelity (low, high) with the quality of implementation (low, high) yields four possible conditions.

MI implementation quality

|  |  | Low | High |
|---|---|---|---|
| MI fidelity | Low | 1 | 2 |
|  | High | 3 | 4 |

***Figure 2:*** Conditions of Implementation Quality and Fidelity for Outcomes in the Delivery of Motivational Interviewing (adapted from Fixsen et al., 2005).

When MI services are delivered with low fidelity (Conditions 1 and 2), student outcomes will be poor regardless of implementation quality. Moreover, even if training enables staff to deliver MI with fidelity, poor implementation will also lead to poor outcomes (Condition 3), that is, without addressing the processes and factors that drive successful implementation, training will ultimately be a waste of valuable staff time (Forman et al., 2013). Only when staff delivers MI with fidelity and the quality of implementation is high (Condition 4) will effective student outcomes be achieved (Fixsen et al., 2005).

Fortunately, there exists a growing body of literature known as *implementation science* which "focuses on understanding the processes and factors related to successful integration of EBIs (Evidence-Based Interventions) in a specific type of setting, such as a school" (Forman et al., 2013, p. 80). Using a stage-based implementation model developed by Fixsen and colleagues (2005), we draw upon three stages to describe specific goals and methods of MI training. During the *exploration* stage, the goal of training is for school leadership and interested staff to obtain basic information about MI and raise awareness of its potential applications in school settings in order to make an informed decision to either adopt MI into practice, or not. School leadership includes the director of student services, program coordinator, or other key administrator at the district level, as well as principal, assistant principal, or other key administrator at the building level. During the *adoption stage,* a decision has been made by the leadership to pursue learning MI and a strategic plan is formulated for how MI training and implementation will proceed. Adoption training focuses on staff's initial skill acquisition and practice of the method. During the *implementation* stage, training is geared to help staff incorporate MI into routine practice and learn the method to proficiency standards.

In this stage-based model of implementation (a parallel to Prochaska and DiClemente's Stages of Change model; Rogers, 2003), tasks within one stage must be adequately completed before staff can successfully move to the next stage. Moreover, stage-specific roles and responsibilities are implicated for the trainer. To facilitate quality implementation, sometimes the trainer roles and responsibilities must go beyond the confines of a workshop in order to assist school leadership and staff in the MI implementation process.

**MI Training with Student Services**

In this section, we integrate insights of effective MI training with three stages of implementation (exploration, adoption, and implementation) to comprehensively describe MI training with student services staff. For each stage, we identify the goal of training, general methods, processes, and duration of training (see Table 1), as well as barriers to progressing to the next stage and strategies for addressing the barriers.

| Implementation stage and goal | Key content | Training methods and processes | Duration |
|---|---|---|---|
| **Exploration:** leadership and staff gather basic information about MI. | • MI definition and theory<br>• Review of evidence base<br>• Elements of practice<br>• Benefits and limitations of MI<br>• Learning MI | • Didactic lecture<br>• Group discussion<br>• Demonstration<br>• Examine staff motivation for learning; group decisional balance exercise | 1 – 4 hours |
| **Adoption:** decision by leadership to purse MI training; initial skills acquisition by staff. | • Implementation planning<br>• Skills-focused training (OARS; recognizing, eliciting, responding to Change Talk) | • Experiential exercises<br>• Develop initial implementation plan (organization)<br>• Develop individualized learning plan (staff) | 2 days |
| **Implementation:** initial service delivery with students; staff work toward MI proficiency; ascertain practice-based evidence | • Continued recognition of student language cues (Change Talk, Sustain Talk)<br>• Continued OARS skill development<br>• Integration of MI into practice<br>• Set up data collection | • Experiential exercises and case presentations<br>• "Learning to learn" approach<br>• Direct observation of practice, coding, and feedback<br>• Small group and individualized coaching for skill development<br>• Trainer consultation | 2 – 3 days<br><br><br><br>as needed |

**Table 1.** A Comprehensive approach to MI Training with Student services Staff.

Our descriptions here are guided by reviews of EBP implementation within school settings (Forman et al., 2013; Wagner et al., 2004; Winters et al., 2007) as well as by our experiences with training student services staff in MI.

### *Exploration*

During the exploration stage of implementation, leadership and staff are actively considering delivering MI in the school setting. The purpose of training is to convey basic information about the theory, research, practice, and learning of MI. Dissemination of information can take many forms such as written materials, teleconference, webcast, or face to face presentation during a team meeting, conference session, or workshop. Face to face presentations are typically brief (1 to 4 hours) and use didactic lecture as a method to efficiently convey information. However, these presentations can also incorporate large group experiential exercises, demonstration of MI, and discussion to maximize participant engagement.

Information about MI should include what is known about its benefits and limitations of delivery in school settings (see Table 2).

| Benefits | Limitations |
|---|---|
| • Well-established EBP with promising applications in school settings to address multiple student behaviors | • Research is underdeveloped |
| | • Tested down to age 11 (6th grade) |
| • EBP with adolescents | • Not useful for students who have already initiated behavior change |
| • Targets student motivation for change | |
| • Consistent with student-centered, strength-based, and harm reduction approaches | • Inconsistent with "zero tolerance" or abstinence-only approaches |
| | • MI is not easy to learn to proficiency |
| • MI is relatively simple and straight-forward to understand and use | • Takes staff time, efforts, and organizational resources to learn to proficiency |
| • Growing evidence-base for how staff learn the method to proficiency | |

**Table 2.** Some Benefits and Limitations of delivering MI in School Settings.

In general, the benefits of MI include: well-established EBP with promising applications to school settings (Herman et al., 2014); MI is very efficient and can address a wide range of adolescent behavioral health concerns (Naar-King & Suarez, 2011); it can be utilized as an intervention or indicated prevention approach; it targets motivation for change – often the missing piece of the student behavior change puzzle; MI is compatible with student-centered and strength-based student services values and philosophies; and as a relatively straight-forward and simple method to deliver, there is a growing evidence-based for how staff can learn MI to proficiency. It is of note that many of these benefits of MI reflect characteristics of an innovation that is likely to be widely adopted into practice. That is, MI has relative advantage over routine practice for promoting student behavior change, it has compatibility with existing approaches, and it is relatively simple to understand and use (Rogers, 2003). There are also several limitations of MI which include: limited number of studies testing MI in school settings; tested down to age 11 (6th grade); not particularly useful for students who have already initiated behavior change; the harm reduction approach of MI may be inconsistent with a school's "zero tolerance" policies or abstinence-only approaches (Masterman and Kelly, 2003); and training staff to proficiency in MI takes a great deal of time and resources (Frey et al. 2013). During exploration, school leadership and staff must obtain the basics about MI, then carefully weigh the pros and cons of adopting MI into practice.

Barriers to progressing from exploration to the adoption stage may include the following: too many competing school district initiatives; lack of leadership support; lack of interest and buy-in among staff, or the mistaken belief that staff

110                                    *Chapter 8*

"already do MI." It is recommended that during exploration the trainer directly address leadership support and staff motivation for learning MI (Barwick et al., 2012). During exposure training, one useful exercise is to have leadership and staff rate (0-10 scale) their levels of readiness and perceived importance for delivering MI, then discussion proceeds as to how those levels may be increased. Another exercise asks leadership and staff to collectively identify their perceived cons (limitations and barriers) and pros (benefits) of adopting MI into practice, then the trainer summarizes both sides of the argument and asks participants to draw conclusions. These exercises are intended for staff to explore their motivation for learning, to identify real and perceived barriers to adoption, and to resolve ambivalence among leadership while also helping to create buy-in among staff for learning. Ultimately, the goal of exploration is for leadership and staff to make an informed decision as to whether to adopt MI into practice, or not.

**Adoption**

Adoption of MI is based on a decision by school or district leadership to pursue MI, that is, the perceived pros of delivering MI outweigh the cons. This stage involves assisting the leadership with strategic planning and addressing key questions such as:

- What student behavior(s) will be the focus of MI e.g. alcohol/drug involvement, mental health, truancy, academic performance? How does this focus fit with the district's existing priorities or initiatives?

- How will students be determined for receiving MI services and when will services be initiated?

- How will MI be integrated into practice? How will this integration look by student service discipline i.e. social work, psychology, counseling, nursing and will any adaptations of practice need to be made?

- What are the barriers to implementation and how can those be minimized or eliminated?

- What will be the components and expectations of training? Which staff will be selected for training?

- How will fidelity of practice be monitored?

- What supports and resources can be made available for staff to continue learning MI beyond formal training?

These questions encompass the scope of a school or district's implementation project. The trainer can present to the leadership these questions in worksheet form and provide guidance for completion, as needed. Implementation planning ideally involves staff "champions" as well, that is, individuals who are respected opinion leaders among their peers and who express strong desire for learning MI.

Of particular importance during planning is to assist the leadership and champions in connecting how adopting MI into practice will advance the school or district's existing priorities or initiatives. For example, if a district's priority is to address student alcohol or illicit drug involvement, then implementing MI as a brief intervention would greatly enhance the district's capacity to effectively address that problem (Winters et al., 2007, 2012). If the delivery of MI fits with existing priorities, the practice will be more likely to be implemented and sustained.

Once an implementation plan is formulated and staff are selected, initial training begins. The first author (S. C.) developed a 2-day (14 hour) adoption training for student services staff with the following components: 1) completion of a pre-training initial implementation plan by leadership and selected staff prior to on-site training; 2) initial 1-day skills-focused workshop with submission of an audio recorded practice sample at its conclusion; 3) 1-month trial delivery of MI with students; reviews of recorded practice samples by the trainer; and 4) follow-up 1-day workshop with individualized written feedback to each staff participant, continued skill building, and refinement of the implementation plan.

For this adoption training, a protocol was developed to guide staff's delivery of MI as a brief intervention. Manualizing an intervention comes highly recommended for the successful implementation of EBP in school settings (Forman et al., 2013; Wagner et al., 2004; Winters et al., 2007). Although manualizing MI may not yield optimal outcomes (Hettema et al., 2005), our experiences with student services staff is consistent with that of Frey and colleagues (2013) who found that having a protocol to guide delivery of MI greatly promoted staff fidelity of practice and enhanced implementation quality. The protocol developed for this adoption training integrated well-established MI strategies (opening strategies, agenda setting, importance ruler, decisional balance, change planning, confidence ruler) into the fundamental processes of MI (engaging, focusing, evoking, and planning; Miller and Rollnick, 2013) to guide intervention on a range of possible target behaviors. The single-page protocol provided open questions and other MI-adherent prompts which guided staff to draw out student change talk on the target behavior. Training emphasized recognition of student change talk cues, directive use of OARS skills to proactively elicit and respond to student change talk, and practice delivering the protocol. This was accomplished through use of experiential skill building exercises, group discussion, demonstration with structured observation, and other teaching methods (MINT, 2008).

Student services staff MI practice samples were obtained during five adoption trainings delivered by the first author (Caldwell, 2013). At the conclusion of the 1-day initial training, each staff participant (N = 84) submitted an audio recorded sample of MI practice (utilizing the protocol described above) based on a structured student role play. Audio recordings were reviewed and coded by the trainer using the skill behavior count system of the Motivational Interviewing Treatment Integrity instrument (MITI; Moyers et al., 2009). The MITI allows the coder to count and categorize (mutually exclusive) practitioner utterances based on the following behaviors: open question, closed question, simple reflection, complex reflection, MI adherent behavior e.g. permission asking, affirmation, emphasis on student choice, or MI non-adherent behavior e.g. advising, warning, confronting, or informing without student permission. Total counts for each category were made for the 84 tape reviews with descriptive statistics calculated for the mean (M), standard deviation (SD), and range: 843 open questions (M = 10.04, SD = 3.57, range = 3-19); 348 closed questions (M = 4.14, SD = 2.93, range = 0-12); 627 simple reflections (M = 7.46, SD = 3.15, range = 0-16); 201 complex reflections (M = 2.39, SD = 1.65, range = 0-9); 190 adherent behaviors (M = 2.26, SD = 1.48, range = 0-8); and 17 non-adherent behaviors (M = 0.2, SD = 0.51, range = 0-3). As shown in Table 3, staff's total behavior counts were used to calculate MI measures of practice, then were compared to the MI fidelity standards advanced by Miller and Rollnick (2013).

**Table 3.** Adoption Training with Student Services Staff (N = 84) and Results of MITI-Coded Practice Samples Compared to Fidelity Standards.

| MI Measure of Practice | Staff Results | Fidelity Standards | |
| --- | --- | --- | --- |
| | | Basic Competency | Proficiency |
| Percentage of Open Questions of total Questions | 70.8% | ≥ 50% | ≥ 70% |
| Percentage of Complex Reflections of total Reflections | 24.3% | ≥ 40% | ≥ 50% |
| Ratio of Reflections to Questions | 0.7 | ≥ 1.0 | ≥ 2.0 |
| Percentage of MI-Adherent | 91.8% | ≥ 90% | ≥ 98% |
| Percentage of MI-Non Adherent | 8.2% | ≤ 10% | ≤ 2% |

Note. MITI is Motivational Interviewing Treatment Integrity instrument. MI fidelity standards taken from Miller and Rollnick (2013, p. 400).

Results showed proficient use of open questions which suggests good use of the protocol by staff. Additionally, staff achieved basic competency in the use of MI adherent behaviors with relatively few non-adherent behaviors (total of 17), suggesting that training helped to minimize staff advising, warning, or confronting. However, staff did not achieve even basic competency for either the frequency (ratio to questions) or depth (percentage of complex reflection) of reflective listening. This finding is not surprising given that reflective listening (accurate empathy) is a complex skill which takes years of dedicated practice to master (Moyers and Miller, 2012). The results here suggest that student services staff can demonstrate limited use of MI skills at the conclusion of an initial 1-day adoption training.

During the follow-up 1-day adoption training approximately one month later, staff discussed their trial delivery of MI with students. The trainer provided written individualized feedback to staff, which included the behavior count results, examples of utterances, and comparison of staff's results to the fidelity standards – similar

*Chapter 8* 113

to the format of Table 3. Skill building continued with emphasis on reflective listening. Staff also continued practicing delivery of the protocol-guided brief intervention with peer-observer feedback. Time was allotted for staff to review and refine their implementation plan. In sum, this adoption training appeared to be a good start for preparing districts and staff for implementing MI as an EBP.

There are several barriers that can impede staff's progress from adoption to implementation. First, there may be lack of planning by leadership. Without a plan e.g. How will students be determined for receiving MI services? When will services be initiated? How will MI be integrated into practice? staff lack the necessary direction to begin implementing MI. Second, too many demands on staff time can limit their ability to engage continued implementation and learning. And third, the "initial awkward stage" of adopting a new method into practice (Joyce and Showers, 2002, as cited by Fixsen et al., 2005) could discourage staff who otherwise prefer comfortable (albeit unrealistic) competence immediately following initial training. These formidable barriers strongly suggest the need for trainer consultation following initial adoption training. Through consultation, technical assistance to the leadership (district level) and ongoing support to staff (individual level) can help reduce these and other barriers so that implementation can proceed (Edmunds et al., 2013).

**Implementation**

This stage involves delivery of MI with students in the context of ongoing staff learning and skill development. Our experiences are consistent with the MI training outcome literature that shows staff can demonstrate limited MI skills following adoption training (Barwick et al., 2012; deRoten et al., 2013; Madson et al., 2009). However, initial skill gains quickly deteriorate without continued opportunities for learning and practice (Fixsen et al., 2005). Thus, the goal of training during the implementation stage is to help staff continue to integrate MI into practice while working toward proficiency.

The second author (S. K.) developed an implementation training for student services staff who had completed the above described adoption training. This training involved a monthly 3-hour workshop during the academic year (8 months, 24 hours total training time) with the following components: 1) a monthly workshop which focused on advancing staff's knowledge and skills in topics that paralleled Miller and Moyers (2006) tasks of learning MI: developing MI spirit; OARS skills; recognizing, eliciting, and responding to student change talk; effectively responding to student sustain talk (the opposite of change talk); helping students to develop a change plan and enhancing their commitment to change; and integrating MI into practice; 2) submission of three audio recorded samples practice recorded with students in the school setting using the protocol described above; 3) trainer tape reviews, coding using the MITI, and individualized feedback to each staff similar to the format of Table 3; and 4) staff development of an individualized learning plan to focus on specific skill acquisition e.g. increasing

## Chapter 8

the percentage of complex reflections of total reflections. Training methods included experiential skill building exercises, demonstration, case presentations with group discussion and practice delivering the protocol with peer and trainer feedback (MINT, 2008). In short, this implementation training was designed based on the evidence-informed learning cycle depicted in Figure 1.

To promote ongoing learning of MI during implementation, a "learning to learn" approach was taken (Arkowitz and Miller, 2008; Martino et al., 2007; Miller and Rollnick, 2002). As Arkowitz and Miller (2008) note, "the real learning is in doing, and that requires ongoing practice with feedback. As it turns out, the needed feedback is built into the process of MI..." (p. 20). Training emphasized the recognition of student change talk cues (predictive of behavior change) and sustain talk cues (predictive of no change) which enabled staff to use this immediate in-session feedback offered by students. This built-in learning mechanism of MI is based on the reciprocity of staff-student interactions: when staff hears student change talk, it encourages continued use of MI skills and adherent behaviors; conversely, when staff hears student sustain talk, it encourages a new direction (away from non-adherent behaviors) and a return to MI. Students respond accordingly and the reciprocity continues.

There are several barriers that can inhibit progression through the implementation stage. First, staff may be unwilling or unable to take the time to engage in continued learning. This is a barrier commonly identified in EBP implementation projects (Fixsen et al., 2005) and specifically in learning MI (Barwick et al., 2012; Bennett et al., 2007). In the implementation training described above, there was a fairly high rate of staff attrition (about 30%) from the start to the end of the school year. Yet implementation research consistently shows that staff who engage in more consultation activities post-adoption training evidence greater improvements in skill and fidelity than those who drop out prematurely or engage in less activities (Edmunds et al. 2013). A related barrier is that staff are often reluctant or unwilling to submit samples of their work for review. For example, Bennett and colleagues (2007) found that of total possible audio recorded practice samples that could be submitted for trainer review, only 7% were submitted during a 12-week period post-adoption training. We often hear staff express anxiety and concern about recording sessions. Yet this reluctance presents a significant barrier to implementation because there is no other valid way to ascertain fidelity of MI practice (Miller and Rose, 2009). Another barrier is that hiring an external trainer-consultant can be cost prohibitive for most school districts. School administrators may choose to not allocate already limited resources to an MI implementation project. It is a sobering thought to consider that, according to Fixsen and colleagues (2005), full implementation of an EBP (so that it becomes routine practice) takes two or more years!

There are creative ways that trainers can proactively address these implementation barriers through consultation (Edmunds et al., 2013; Fixsen et al., 2005) and the creation of "intrinsic" and "extrinsic" incentive for staff (Miller et al., 2006). The goal of consultation is to help further the process and quality of implementation.

As discussed earlier, effective outcomes of EBP will only be achieved when staff demonstrates fidelity of MI and when there is high quality implementation (see Figure 2, Condition 4). Consultation can promote quality implementation at two levels. At the district level, consultation can be used to provide guidance to the leadership for actualizing the implementation plan, such as: helping to clarify which students should receive MI and the timing of service delivery; making adaptations of practice to fit a specific student services discipline while assuring fidelity; helping to set up a data collection system to evaluate student outcomes, for example, by introducing a behavioral health screening instrument that quantifies student symptomology and having staff administer it pre-post MI intervention. Additionally, the trainer should ensure that the leadership supports any expectation that staff submit practice samples of their work. Barwick and colleagues (2012) developed a memorandum of understanding – signed by each participant in MI training – to help facilitate submission of practice samples. At the individual staff level, consultation may include: addressing staff reluctance to submit practice samples; helping staff develop an individual learning plan; identifying learning resources to supplement training; helping to set up ongoing learning support such as an MI peer learning group or MI Professional Learning Community; and addressing staff motivation for continued learning, that is, enhancing intrinsic factors to implement MI (Miller et al., 2006). Extrinsic incentives can also be put into place to maximize staff involvement in implementation such as offering continuing education units for successful completion and having meals and snacks during workshop time (Miller et al., 2006). In sum, the consultation activities described above serve to reduce implementation barriers and enhance the quality of implementation, thus contributing to the overall success of a school's MI implementation project.

**Lessons Learned**

1. Training is not an event, but one aspect of a dynamic and complex process which involves several stages e.g. exposure, adoption, implementation.

2. For effective allocation of limited training resources, it is critical that MI training be designed to "match" a district's stage of implementation. For example, exploration training need not take 1 or 2 days of valuable staff time when the purpose is to simply present basic information so that leadership and staff can decide interest in learning more (or not).

3. Planning for implementation by leadership and staff is critical to ensure that MI will become at least partially integrated into practice following adoption training.

4. To enhance fidelity and the quality of implementation, student services should be trained to use a protocol that guides the delivery of MI services.

5. Direct observation of practice via audio recorded practice samples coupled with feedback are an essential element of learning. To maximize submission of practice samples, it is important to clearly state the expectation prior to the start of training, work with the leadership to support the expectation, and during training directly address staff reluctance to audio record sessions.

116                                Chapter 8

6. An important outcome of implementation training is staff 's own behavior change. MI trainers can model MI during training in a parallel process that teaches while addressing staff's own motivation for change. Ongoing monitoring of staff's progress toward proficient practice is important and skill building exercises should be tailored to address staff specific stuck points.

7. Some staff struggle more than others to reach even basic competency in MI. These staff will require more trainer attention and access to learning resources.

8. MI trainers working with schools should be prepared for roles and tasks that go beyond just design and delivery of presentations or workshops. In particular, trainers should be versed in implementation science (Forman et al., 2013) to be able to identify and promote the factors and processes that underscore successful implementation of MI in the school setting.

## References

Arkowitz, H., & Miller, W. R. (2008). Learning, applying, and extending motivational interviewing. In H. Arkowitz, H. A. Westra, W. R. Miller, & S. Rollnick (Eds.), *Motivational interviewing in the treatment of psychological problems* (pp. 1-25). New York: The Guilford Press.

Barnett, E., Sussman, S., Smith, C., Rohrbach, L. A., & Spruijt-Metz, D. (2012). Motivational interviewing for adolescent substance use: A review of the literature. *Addictive Behaviors,* 37, 1325-1334.

Barwick, M., Bennett, L. M., Johnson, S. N., McGowan, J., & Moore, J. E. (2012). Training health and mental health professionals in motivational interviewing: A systematic review. *Children and Youth Services Review,* 34, 1786-1795.

Beidas, R. S., & Kendall, P. C. (2010). Training therapists in evidence-based practice: A critical review of studies from a systems-contextual perspective. Clinical *Psychology: Science and Practice,* 17, 1-30.

Bennett, G. A., Moore, J., Vaughan, T., Rouse, L., Gibbins, J. A., Thomsa, P., James, K., & Gower, P. (2007). Strengthening motivational interviewing skills following initial training: A randomized trial of workplace-based reflective practice. *Addictive Behaviors,* 32, 2963-2975.

Burke, P. J., DaSilva, J.D., Vaughan, B.L., & Knight, J. R. (2005). Training high school counselors on the use of motivational interviewing to screen for substance abuse. *Substance Abuse,* 26(3/4), 31-34.

Caldwell, S. (2013). Report on School Screening, Brief Intervention, and Referral to Treatment training to Department of Public Instruction. Unpublished data. deRoten, Y., Zimmermann, G., & Despland, J.-N. (2013). Meta-analysis of the effects of MI training on clinicians' behavior. *Journal of Substance Abuse Treatment,* 45, 155-162.

Edmunds, J. M., Beidas, R. S., & Kendall, P. C. (2013). Dissemination and implementation of evidence-based practices: Training and consultation as implementation strategies. *Clinical Psychology: Science and Practice,* 20, 152- 165.

Fixsen, D. L., Naoom, S. F., Blase, K. A., Friedman, R. M., & Wallace, F. (2005). *Implementation research: A synthesis of the literature.* National Implementation Research Network. Tampa: University of South Florida.

Forman, S. G., Shapiro, E. S., Codding, R. S., Gonzales, J. E., Reddy, L. A., Rosenfield, S. A., Sanetti, L. M. H., & Stoiber, K. C. (2013). Implementation science and school psychology. *School Psychology Quarterly,* 28(2), 77-100.

Frey, A. J., Cloud, R. N., Lee, J., Small, J. W., Seeley, J. R., Feil, E. G., Walker, H. M., & Golly, A. (2011). The promise of motivational interviewing in school mental health. *School Mental Health,* 3, 1-12.

Frey, A. J., Lee, J., Small, J. W., Seeley, J. R., Walker, H. M., & Feil, E. G. (2013). Transporting motivational interviewing to school settings to improve the engagement and fidelity of tier 2 interventions. *Journal of Applied School Psychology,* 29, 183-202.

Herman, K. C., Reinke, W. M., Frey, A. J., & Shepard, S. A. (2014). *Motivational interviewing in schools: Engaging parents, teachers, and students.* New York: Springer Publishing Company.

Hettema, J., Steele, J., & Miller, W. R. (2005). Motivational interviewing. *Annual Review of Clinical Psychology,* 1, 91-111.

Jensen, C. D., Cushing, C. C., Aylward, B. S., Craig, J. T., Sorell, D. M., & Steele, R. G. (2011). Effectiveness of motivational interviewing for adolescent substance use behavior change: A meta-analytic review. *Journal of Consulting and Clinical Psychology,* 79(4), 433-440.

Kaplan, S., Engle, B., Austin, A., & Wagner, E. (2011). Applications in schools. In S. Naar-King, & M. Suarez (Eds.), *Motivational interviewing with adolescents and young adults* (pp. 158-164). New York: Guilford Press.

Kelly, A. B., & Lapworth, K. (2006). The HYP program: Targeted motivational interviewing for adolescent violations of school tobacco policy. *Preventive Medicine,* 43, 466-471.

Lundahl, B. W., Kunz, C., Brownell, C., Tollefson, D., & Burke, B. (2010). A meta-analysis of motivational interviewing: Twenty-five years of empirical studies. *Research on Social Work Practice,* 20(2), 137-160.

Madson, M. B., Loignon, A. C., &Lane, C. (2009). Training in motivational interviewing: A systematic review. *Journal of Substance Abuse,* 36(1), 101-109.

Madson, M. B., Lane, C., & Noble, J. J. (2012). Delivering quality motivational interviewing training. *Motivational Interviewing: Training, Research, Implementation, Practice,* 1(1). DOI 10.5195/mitrip.2012.8

Martino, S., Carroll, K. M., & Ball, S. A. (2007). Teaching, monitoring, and evaluating motivational interviewing practice. In G. Tober, & D. Raistrick (Eds.), *Motivational dialogue: Preparing addiction professionals for motivational interviewing practice* (pp. 87-113). London: Routledge.

Masterman, P. W., & Kelly A. B. (2003). Reaching adolescents who drink harmfully: Fitting intervention to developmental reality. *Journal of Substance Abuse Treatment,* 24(4), 347-355.

McNamara, E. (Ed.). (2009). *Motivational interviewing: Theory, practice, and applications with children and young people.* Merseyside, UK: Positive Behaviour Management.

Miller, W. R., & Moyers, T. B. (2006). Eight stages in learning motivational interviewing. *Journal of Teaching in the Addictions,* 5, 3-17.

Miller, W. R., & Mount, K. A. (2001). A small study of training in motivational interviewing: Does one workshop change clinician and client behavior? *Behavioral and Cognitive Psychotherapy,* 29, 457-471.

Miller, W. R., & Rollnick, S. (2013). *Motivational interviewing: Helping people change* (3rd ed.). New York: Gilford Press.

Miller, W. R., & Rollnick, S. (2002). *Motivational interviewing: Preparing people to change* (2nd ed.). New York: Gilford Press.

Miller, W. R., & Rollnick, S. (2009). Ten things that motivational interviewing is not. *Behavioural and Cognitive Psychotherapy,* 37, 129-140.

Miller, W. R., & Rose, G. S. (2009). Toward a theory of motivational interviewing. *American Psychologist,* 64(6), 527-537.

Miller, W. R., Sorensen, J. L., Selzer, J. A., & Brigham, G. S. (2006). Disseminating evidence-based practices in substance abuse treatment: A review with suggestions. *Journal of Substance Abuse Treatment,* 31, 25-39.

Miller, W. R., Yahne, C. R., Moyers, T. B., Martinez, J., & Pirritano, M. (2004). A randomized trial of methods to help clinicians learn motivational interviewing. *Journal of Consulting and Clinical Psychology,* 72, 1050-1062.

MINT (Motivational Interviewing Network of Trainers). (2008). *Motivational interviewing training for new trainers: Resources for trainers.* Retrieved from: http://www.motivationalinterview.org/Documents/TNT_Manual_Nov_08.pdf

Moyers, T. B., Martin, T., Manuel, J. K., Miller, W. R., & Ernst, D. (2009). *Revised global scales: Motivational Interviewing Treatment Integrity 3.1* (MITI 3.1). Unpublished manual. Center on Alcoholism, Substance Abuse, and Addictions: University of New Mexico.

Moyers, T. B., & Miller, W. R. (2012). Is low therapist empathy toxic? *Psychology of Addictive Behaviors* 27(3), 878-884.

Naar-King, S., & Suarez, M. (Eds.). (2011). *Motivational interviewing with adolescents and young adults.* New York: Guilford Press.

Reinke, W. M., Herman, K. C., & Sprick, R. (2011). *Motivational interviewing for effective classroom management: The classroom check-up.* New York: Guilford Press.

Rogers, E. M. (2003). *Diffusion of innovations (5th ed.).* New York: Free Press.

Rosengren, D., & Dunn, C. W. (2012). *MI training research.* Plenary address delivered at the annual Motivational Interviewing Network of Trainers Forum, Fort Wayne, IN.

Strait, G. G., Smith, B. H., McQuillin, S., Terry, J., Swan, S., & Malone, P. S. (2012). A randomized trial of motivational interviewing to improve middle school students' academic performance. *Journal of Community Psychology,* 40(8), 1032-1039.

Wagner, E. F., Tubman, J. G., & Gil, A. G. (2004). Implementing school-based substance abuse interventions: Methodological dilemmas and recommended solutions. *Addiction,* 99(Suppl. 2), 106-119.

Winters, K. C., Fahnhorst, T., Botzet, A., Lee, S., & Lalone, B. (2012). Brief intervention for drug-abusing adolescents in a school setting: Outcomes and mediating factors. *Journal of Substance Abuse Treatment,* 42, 279-288.

Winters, K. C., Leitten, W., Wagner, E., & O'Leary Tevyaw, T. (2007). Use of brief interventions for drug-abusing teenagers within a middle and high school setting. *Journal of School Health,* 77, 196-206.

**Acknowledgement.** The authors wish to thank the following people for their support of the training projects described in this chapter: Jeannette Deloya, Steve Fernan, Brenda Jennings, Joan Lerman, Monica Wightman and Nancy Yoder.

120                    Chapter 8

# Section 2

# Motivational Interviewing: Clinical Applications

*122*

# Chapter 9

# MI and Anxiety Management

## Roger Lakin
### *East Leeds Children and Adolescent Mental Health Service (CAMHS)*

Cognitive behavioural therapy (CBT) is a well-established and effective treatment for young people with anxiety disorders (Rutter et al 2010; Cartwright-Hatton et al, 2004). However there are some young people who do not engage with the therapy fully or drop out. This chapter considers if adding a motivational interviewing (MI) approach to a CBT approach could be helpful in treating this challenging group of patients.

### Cognitive Behavioural Therapy for Young People with Anxiety Problems

Anxiety disorders are common in young people - epidemiological studies reveal that they are the most common mental disorders in this age group. They have major negative consequences at school with regard to interpersonal functioning and frequent co-morbidities (Rutter et al 2010; Cartwright-Hatton et al, 2004). Rates vary: it is thought that around 4-10% of children and adolescents have clinically significant anxiety that causes substantial distress and life interference which often persist into adult life (Goodman and Scott, 2005; Anderson et al, 1987; Carwright-Hatton et al, 2004).

CBT is perhaps the most studied intervention for anxiety in young people (Rachman and Wilson, 2008). It has been shown to have benefit over waiting list controls for anxiety in young people (Barrett, 1998; Kendall et al, 1997). Care needs to be taken when looking at the results of some studies in this area as some show efficacy for CBT but were conducted in non-clinical samples over short periods of time (Grave and Blissett, 2004). Cartwright-Hatton et al (2004) carried out a critical systematic review of ten trials using CBT for anxiety disorders in young people. There was some heterogeneity between the trials used e.g. degree of parent involvement. The authors found that overall CBT did show a significant effect suggestive of a strong positive effect for CBT when compared with a no treatment control. Less research has been conducted comparing CBT directly with other treatments.

Despite the positive results seen in the research that is available, over a third of children maintain an anxiety diagnosis at the end of treatment (Cartwright-Hatton et al, 2004). There therefore remain a significant proportion of young people who do not respond to therapy - and there are others who do not engage in the first place. There are a variety of reasons for this, including the young person's motivation. Now is a particularly relevant time to be considering how the therapy is delivered to young people as anxiety disorders are specifically highlighted in the roll out of Children's and Young People's IAPT (Improving Access to Psychological Therapies) (IAPT, 2012).

## Motivational Interviewing

Motivational interviewing evolved initially as a pragmatic solution to the problem of confrontation in counselling problem drinkers (Miller, 1983). Miller had observed that confrontation with these clients tended to elicit denial and avoidance of further discussion (Tober and Raistrick, 2007). While inspiration was drawn from Carl Rogers' (1953) work in non-directive counselling it was integrated with more active cognitive-behavioural strategies targeted at the client's stage of change (Burke et al, 2003; Prochaska et al, 1992; Ruback et al, 2005). The client centred approach described by Rogers is associated with a non-directive counselling style, but Miller applied Rogers' principles within an agenda driven, directive style while maintaining a non-confrontational approach. The challenge for clinicians has therefore been the need to reconcile these two initially seemingly contradictory components of counselling; that is, a directive style with a non-confrontational approach (Miller and Rollnick, 1991; Tober and Raistrick, 2007)

The application of MI has expanded from work with patients with alcohol dependence to a wider range of fields including drug abuse, smoking cessation, eating disorders, diet and exercise and high risk HIV behaviours (Treasure et al, 1999; Tober and Raistrick, 2007). It is also being used, predominantly with adults, in areas such as depression and anxiety.

## Combining CBT and MI

It has been suggested that the principles of CBT and MI may overlap, although there has been little research into this (Dorian, 2004). The two approaches can be compared, although CBT is a treatment while MI is a therapeutic approach.

Both are i) collaborative ii) focused and goal directive and iii) use a questioning style to let the patient articulate and consider the discrepancy between their thoughts and behaviour (Dorian, 2004; Beck, 1995; Wilson and Schlam, 2004).

Further

- MI involves hypothesising reasons for behaviour that appears contrary to the patient's stated thoughts. In particular whether the patient feels it is important to change their behaviour and how confident they feel that they can change their behaviour (Miller and Rollnick 1991; Tober and Raistrick, 2007).

- MI uses a decision matrix to motivate people to change, helping the patient think through the pros and cons of either changing behaviour or accepting the status quo.

- CBT facilitates change by using Socratic questioning, facilitating the patient to think through the advantages and disadvantages of a particular behaviour (Wilson and Schlam, 2004; Miller 2000).

## Integrating CBT and MI

Motivational interviewing was originally developed with the aim of helping problem drinkers, moving subsequently into the broader range of addictions. CBT has also been used in this area and the greatest use of their combined approach has been in the addictions field. Connors et al (2002) showed that for alcohol abuse MI was an effective pre-treatment to a treatment that had a strong CBT component. The research in healthcare shows that brief encounters (15 minutes) can also be effective but that more than one encounter with the patient increases the size of effect (Connors et al, 2002; Ruback et al, 2005).

CBT and MI have also been used to address eating disorders: however a combined approach has not been explicitly tested. Wilson and Schlam (2004) discuss the overlapping issues in this group of patients when using both approaches. When CBT and MI were compared as treatments for patients with bulimia by Treasure et al (1999) it was expected that the therapy would be best suited for those less ready for change (figure 1), whereas CBT may help those moving towards the later action stage. In fact no difference was seen. A difference may not have been seen due to the inherent overlap in styles of both approaches.

Another consideration is the validity of the stages of change model. This is widely used and can be a helpful model for therapist and client to refer to. However, its validity has been challenged by a number of authors including Willson and Schlam (2004) and Drieschner et al (2004). Criticism has included the way the stages of change are defined and measured and the idea that the proposed stages are not discrete categories (Willson and Schlam, 2004). The main research addressing the stages of change model has been carried out in areas such as smoking and drinking - which involve only a single behaviour (Willson and Schlam, 2004).

Application of the model in areas outside these such as treating anxiety disorders or eating disorders, where multiple behaviours need to be changed complicate the assessment of "stage of change". An example of this is young people with bulimia.

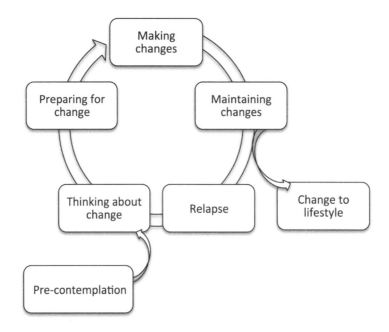

*Figure 1:* Prochaska and Diclimente's Stages of Change Model.

(Adapted from Drugtext, 2008)

They often fall into the 'preparing to change' or 'action / making changes' stage for stopping binge eating. However they are simultaneously much less motivated, perhaps being at the 'pre-contemplation' or 'contemplation' stages, for changing other behaviours such as over exercising or restricting their diet to lose weight.

**A CBT and MI Approach for Anxiety Disorders**

MI and CBT have been used in areas such as addictions and eating disorders and there is an established evidence base. The area of anxiety is an area of much more recent development for a combination of these approaches. Anxiety disorders cover a range of diagnoses including panic disorder, generalised anxiety disorder (GAD) and obsessive-compulsive disorder.

A significant amount of work addressing anxiety disorders has been carried out by Henry Westra, David Dozois and Hal Arkowitz (Westra et al 2009; Westra and Dozois 2008; Arkowitz et al 2008; Westra and Dozois 2006; Westra 2004; Westra and Phoenix 2003).

Westra and Dozois' (2006) pilot study with adults in this area randomised MI pre-treatment to twenty-five of fifty-five patients with a principal anxiety disorder (panic disorder, social phobia and generalised anxiety disorder) before group CBT. The MI pre-treatment was compared with a no pre-treatment group. MI pre-treatment consisted of three sessions given by a clinical psychologist with extensive training in MI and MI for anxiety. Treatment was based on work described in an earlier

*Chapter 9* 127

paper by Westra and Phoenix (2003) in which an evaluation of the efficacy of a manualised MI treatment was carried out. In the manual two phases of MI are discussed - phase 1 focusing on understanding and exploring ambivalence and phase 2 focusing on developing self-efficacy (Westra and Phoenix 2003; Westra and Dozios, 2006). Both groups showed significant improvements but the MI pre-treatment group had a significantly higher proportion of responders compared to no pre-treatment. Seventy-five percent of the MI treatment group were considered to have responded to therapy compared to fifty percent of the no pre-treatment group (p<0.05). Although the numbers in this study were relatively small and there was no control for the MI pre-treatment it was felt that this study did show support for the inclusion of MI as a pre-treatment to CBT, as enhancements in both engagement and response to treatment could be seen.

Another randomised trial was carried out by Westra et al (2009) and focused on generalised anxiety disorder. Their results revealed a significantly greater reduction in worry in the group who had MI pre-treatment compared to the controls (p=0.01). These gains were made during both sections of treatment i.e. MI and CBT. Therapists also rated those in the MI pre-treatment group as displaying greater homework compliance (p=0.13). Both groups showed significant gains i.e. improvement, on scores of depression, anxiety, disability and clinician rated severity. There were no significant differences between the groups. Analysis of the results showed that for those with high severity worry at baseline, a greater effect was achieved when MI was added as a pre-treatment. For individuals with a moderate severity of worry there was virtually no effect when MI was added. Limitations of the study include the MI pre-treatment group receiving four extra sessions than the control group, the CBT therapist not being 'blinded' to what pre-treatment had occurred and the lack of discriminative validity calculations.

The study by Merlo et al (2009) involved a paediatric population suffering from OCD. Sixteen young people (age 6-17 yrs) were randomised to receive CBT plus MI or CBT plus psycho-education. The CBT used was described as an intensive family based approach. The adjuncts used were given throughout therapy: both MI and psycho-education were delivered in three sessions just before the first, fourth and eighth CBT sessions and lasted twenty to thirty minutes. After four sessions the authors found that the scores on the Children's Yale-Brown Obsessive Compulsive Scale (CY-BOCS) had reduced significantly more in the CBT plus MI group than the CBT plus psycho-education group. This difference decreased over time, with post treatment scores not being significantly different: but the young people in the CBT plus MI group completed treatment on average three sessions earlier. Despite the small sample size the study does suggest that adding an MI adjunct to the CBT may accelerate treatment effect.

Thus it can be concluded that there have been some promising studies using motivational interviewing alongside or with CBT for adults and young people with anxiety disorders. The prevalence of ambivalence about change in these individuals also makes the argument for using MI compelling. Further investigation is required

128                                    *Chapter 9*

with larger numbers of participants looking at specific issues. It should also be noted that the studies discussed are of "good quality" but the majority have been carried out by one group of researchers: replication of results is therefore needed from other groups before the findings can be fully judged.

## A CBT and MI Approach for Children and Young people (CYP) with Anxiety Disorders

There is clear evidence of the benefit of cognitive behaviour therapy for young people for a range of anxiety disorders (Cartwright-Hatton et al, 2004). However a substantial number of patients refuse treatment. Often the reason given by the client or suggested by the therapist is fear or apprehension about the treatment as it may include exposure and response prevention - or the patients may state a preference to manage the disorder on their own (Maltby and Tobin, 2005). Although self-directed treatment (using books or online resources) can be helpful to certain groups of people, it does have very high attrition rates when compared with treatment with a therapist (Farvolden et al 2005). Poor insight into their condition may affect CYP uptake into therapy. The level of understanding of the condition displayed by young people can be limited, particularly younger children who may also evidence developmental difficulties that will make it less easy to think in abstract terms.

An example from the author's own experience using CBT with MI with a young person with developmental difficulties is now described.

Martin was 12 years old and had a diagnosis of OCD and Asperger syndrome. MI techniques were used throughout therapy to help maintain his full involvement in therapy. Martin's social and communication difficulties associated with his Aspergers syndrome made his understanding of his difficulties and ability to challenge thoughts very limited, despite evidencing an above average level of overall cognitive ability. His symptoms were very severe. He was unable to be in the same room as certain family members and he had stopped leaving the house. Clarity of communication was required from the therapist to avoid confusion and the use of metaphors was avoided - in the first session Martin had been troubled by the idea that somebody had told him his OCD *'had got him in a pickle'*. He described how he didn't like pickles, how it would be impossible for him to fit in one anyway. The MI technique of using a decision matrix was used to weigh up the pros and cons of change. Martin's feelings of self-efficacy were very low. This needed to be addressed. His OCD was externalised as something to fight against. It was decided to give it a name to fit in with super heroes, a particular interest of Martin. The OCD was thought of as "The Joker OCD" with Martin then taking up the role of a super hero being coached or trained by Batman. Using this approach the idea that OCD rituals can seem to help with Martin's anxiety could be approached, as Martin was able to see that at times The Joker could seem to be charming to Batman but he was always an enemy. The resistance encountered at this point was 'rolled with' to show that if The Joker OCD was suggesting to wash/

clean/avoid the young person would know that if he resisted the compulsion, then he would be working against The Joker OCD. In this situation the exposure and response prevention was put to one side until it became clear what was important to Martin and how to best describe the problem so as to increase Martin's belief about the importance of change. It could be argued that this forms part of good practice in CBT, a statement that the author would agree with, however it may be that placing more emphasis on motivation in certain cases results in better clinical outcomes. Martin did improve with regard to his OCD symptoms. He was able to get back to school, he was more comfortable leaving the house and he was able to spend time doing activities he enjoyed with his family.

Motivation in CYP attending therapy cannot be assumed to be similar to the levels of motivation common to adults attending for therapy - as CYP are often brought to treatment by parents or carers. They may not be interested in treatment or think that it 'will not work'. Dozois and Westra (2005) demonstrated that a higher expectancy on the part of the therapist of the patients' ability to change predicted more positive outcomes.

MI can be seen as a catalyst for beginning to change in populations that may be difficult to engage (Westra and Dozois, 2006). However, it needs to be considered that CBT does already address a number of issues around populations of this nature. There is a view that CBT can be a rather narrow "skills training" treatment for behaviour change. However, this view seriously misrepresents CBT, which shares a number of common principles and strategies with MI – referred to in the introduction to this chapter. Competently delivered CBT focuses on enhancing motivation in ambivalent patients. Wilson and Schlam (2004) suggest that this may explain Treasure et al (1999) findings of no difference in readiness to change between those given four session of CBT and those given four sessions of MET (Motivational Enhancement Therapy) in CYP with eating disorders.

**MI Practice Applicable for Integration of CBT with CYP**

For young people with anxiety disorders MI appears to be a promising way of tackling ambivalence about becoming involved in therapy and then engaging with the specific aspects of the therapy. MI uses a range of approaches to increase motivation to change. These include being non-judgmental, expressing empathy, avoiding confrontation, exploring ambivalence, developing discrepancy and supporting self efficacy. Some of these approaches are now considered.

*Empathy*

Empathy is a key component of both MI and CBT. Miller and Rollnick's (2002) explanation of expressing empathy in MI was to take Carl Rogers' specific form of reflective listening (or accurate empathy), and make this the foundation on which motivational interviewing is based. Through skilful reflective listening the counsellor seeks to understand the client's feelings and perspectives without judging, criticising or blaming. It is important to realise that understanding and

130                                    *Chapter 9*

accepting a client's point of view is not the same as approving or agreeing with it. It does not stop the counsellor expressing that disagreement - as long as the attitude of respectful listening is maintained with a desire to understand the client's perspective.

### *Developing discrepancy*

Developing discrepancy sits MI apart from classic client centred therapy. Specific questions and selective reflections are used to promote discrepancy between the client's problem behaviour and their broader personal values and goals. The client is encouraged to identify reasons for change – for people are often more persuaded by what they hear themselves say than by what others tell them (Miller and Rollnick, 2002). This approach is similar to the CBT strategy of examining the evidence (Westra et al, 2009). For example the author treated a young woman with panic disorder. She saw herself as outgoing and sociable. However this view of herself, and how she would like to be, differed markedly from her behaviour of not leaving the house. This difference became the main motivation for change in engaging with the treatment (exposure to her feared situations - public transport).

### *Roll with Resistance*

Resistance is described by Westra and Dozios (2008) as being one of the most important but least understood phenomena in clinical practice. In CBT resistance is often encountered. CBT recognises the negative impact resistance can have on therapy progressing and attempts to avoid or circumvent it. However this is an area where specific MI techniques help. The delicate and subtle language used can make the difference between the client becoming further resistant and 'shutting down' or engaging in change talk. Therapist questions that communicate their agenda e.g. 'wanting' the patient to talk about the pros of change, can lead to the patient and therapist getting into an argument. MI encourages therapists to get alongside (or roll with) the patients resistance. Examples of two edited sections from situations with a client from the author's casework are described below.

Alex presented with depression and social anxiety.

Alex: *"I just don't know what to do, it's depressing staying in all the time with my mother"*

Therapist: *"How do you see your depression going if you continue to stay in at home? What do you think will happen if you don't start going out?"* (amplifying resistance)

Alex: *"I don't know."*

Therapist: *"Can you tell me about a recent time you went out"*

*Chapter 9* 131

Alex: *"Actually, I went out on Sunday with my cousin"*

Therapist: *"That's great!"*

Patient: *"It wasn't, I just wanted to go home"*

In the above section the therapist initially amplifies the patient's resistance. The therapist also tries to positively reinforce the statement about having gone out, but again meets resistance. Westra and Dozois (2008) describes how in this context praise can be very useful if well timed, but praise can at times be perceived as coercive by the client: it depends on whether the client sees the agenda being served is the patient's or the therapist's. A different therapist response to a similar comment in the following session provided a different set of client responses.

Alex: *"I just stay at home all the time, people tell me to get out but it's my problem and things will just get better"*

Therapist: *"They might, that would be good. Perhaps things will just sort themselves out and be fine"*

Alex: *"My father says that he thinks things will be fine if I just pull myself together"*

Therapist: *"And what do you think of that?"*

Alex: *"I think he is wrong, I am depressed and I need help to get better. He is always getting cross and telling me there is nothing wrong."*

Therapist: *"What would things be like at home in six months time if things stayed as they are at the moment? What would the pros and cons be?"*

Alex: *"Not great, I think I would still be depressed."*

In this section of the interview it can be seen that the therapist has been able to foster Alex's freedom to express himself. The style of the therapist's first statement is in part similar to the paradoxical question used in strategic family therapy (Goldberg and Goldberg, 2007). However there are differences: Westra and Dozois (2008) observe that the use of these questions ( paradoxical questions) in MI is incompatible with MI as the therapist is attempting to control or 'trick' the patient. In this example however the therapist is trying to understand the patient's dilemma from the patients perspective, rather than coerce them into a decision.

Another method that can be employed when encountering resistance is to explicitly emphasise the choice and autonomy of the young person. This can be useful with young people who are brought to therapy by their parents or guardians as it is acknowledges that they are in charge of making decisions about what to do.

132                    *Chapter 9*

## Support Self Efficacy

Classical MI moves from resolving ambivalence to developing confidence on the part of the patient with regard to their ability to initiate and carry out a plan for change.

A client's readiness to change is related to both the importance of change for the client and the confidence the client has about making the change. This self-efficacy is an important predictor for treatment outcome. Enhancing the client's confidence in their capability to cope is therefore important to help them accomplish the desired change in behaviour. The client, not the counsellor is responsible for choosing and carrying out the change, but may be helped by the counsellor and encouraged by the success of others or their own previous success in behaviour change (Miller and Mount, 2001; Burke et al, 2003). New perspectives are invited but not imposed with a "take what you want and leave the rest" approach that is hard to fight against (Miller and Mount, 2001).

Motivational therapy is appropriate as a way of developing discrepancy between an individual's core values and the reality of their behaviour. The first stage in Prochaska and Diclemete's (1982) model (figure 1) is pre-contemplation and is characterised by denial or rationalisation of the problem. This discrepancy exists at the contemplation stage, but motivational interventions can be used to help the client move towards decisions that will match their core values. MI strategies can also be used at later stages if there are specific blocks e.g. feelings of low self efficacy. Other strategies may also be required. For example, during the action and maintenance stages the more common cognitive, behavioural and systemic approaches are useful when working with young people with anxiety problems

Figure 2 is a template for combining aspects of MI and CBT. Ideas for the template were first generated when the author was treating a young person called Emma with OCD. The formulation used was kept very simple and led on to a decision matrix being included in her therapy workbook. This aided Emma to see the OCD cycle and what she needed to do to break the cycle. The arguments put down directly on paper for resisting the OCD compulsions helped Emma recall ideas, theories and commitment talk at times of stress. The template comes from a combination of ideas from the work of Wells (1997), Miller and Mount (2001), Tober and Raistrick (2007) and the author's clinical experience.

It is intended that using the decision matrix aspect of MI may clarify a specific decision about behaviours and how they may or may not fit in with the patient's goals and beliefs about themselves. A combined MI and CBT approach could use this template (figure 2) along with specific therapist learnt skills around delivering CBT in a motivational style. Figure 3 is an example of how the template was used by the author in clinical practice with Emma.

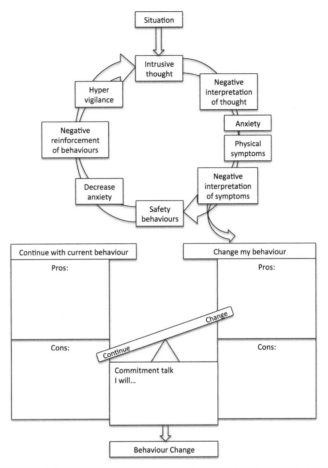

***Figure 2:*** A Template for MI to Link in with a CBT Formulation for Anxiety Disorders

## Future Research

The research described combining CBT and MI reflect the fact that the ways that MI has been employed have varied. Some studies involved the approach described by Miller and Rollnick (1991) and delivered it as a pre-treatment or throughout therapy (Westra and Dozois, 2008; Arkowitz et al, 2008). Others have used selected components of MI or added other components. It remains to be seen whether using the intervention of "pure" MI or MI-related practices added to CBT works best in research and general clinical environments.

It has been noted that CBT of 'good quality' already aims to do a number of things that are aimed for by the incorporation of MI. However, it may be that a shift of therapist approach or perspective that evokes more motivation can produce greater change in some people (Arkowitz et al, 2008). Ambivalence about change is often high in young people with anxiety disorders and a specific method of dealing with this is useful. Motivation to change could be assumed to be present if the patient

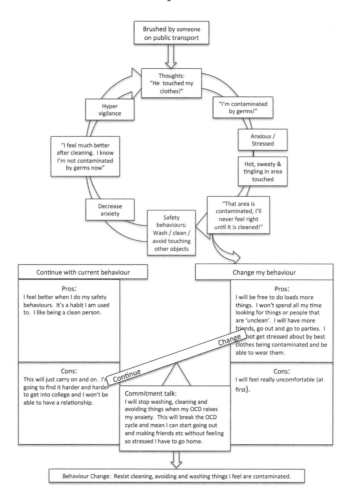

**Figure 3:** MI and CBT Template for Emma when Treating her OCD

attends sessions regularly but the high drop out rates and resistance often seen in practice suggests otherwise. This may be even less the case with regard to young people who are brought to therapy by their parents or guardian. Arkowitz et al (2008) describe how using an MI approach can help change the approach from one of 'wrestling' for change ie imposing change, to one of 'dancing' ie achieving change via a collaborative activity. This highlights the collaborative nature of MI, something that is perhaps less emphasised in CBT practice.

There are a number of possible avenues for research in this area. Studies are beginning to tease out what elements of psychotherapies such as CBT and MI are more useful/important than others eg empathy (Miller et al, 1980) and the therapeutic relationship (Arkowitz et al, 2008; Tracey and Kokotovic, 1989). This continues to be a difficult area to research and replication of results is needed. With these 'active ingredients' that may facilitate change it is important to find out more about what occurs when MI and CBT are combined: both use a number of strategies and techniques and it could be the case that some may be superfluous or at least not as useful as others.

*Chapter 9* 135

Future research will have to manage the difficulty of rating the quality of the psychotherapy. There are a variety of ways of rating the psychotherapies. MI can be rated in a number of ways with the intervention measuring both adherence to treatment and also clinical competence (Waltz et al, 1993). A number of measures for evaluating motivational interviewing have been designed e.g. the Motivational Interviewing Skills Code – MISC - (Miller, 2000), the Yale Adherence and Competence Scale (YACS) (Carroll et al, 2000), the Alcohol Treatment Trial Process Rating Scale - UKATT-PRS - (Tober et al, 2008) and The Motivational Interviewing Treatment Integrity scale – MITI - (Moyers et al, 2005a). From the above array of resources the MITI is probably the most useful way of examining some of the issues raised in this chapter - due to the shorter time it takes to complete.

Published papers on the validity and reliability of the MITI have found i) good to excellent inter-rater reliability and ii) the scale is sensitive to clinicians' behaviour change (Moyers et al, 2005b; Brueck et al, 2009).

The MITI is useful in research in this field as it is a relatively easy to use scale that can be used to assess specific and global measures in MI in sessions. Research could be carried out using the MITI (or another MI quality measurement scale) to rate sessions of CBT. This would identify current areas of overlap between CBT and MI. If the sessions were also rated using a scale typically used for CBT such as the CTRS (Blackburn et al, 2001) then it could be seen if there are correlations between practice scoring highly on CBT scales and the MI scale. A hypothesis could be that therapists scoring highly on a scale for CBT would also score highly on a scale designed to pick up MI related behaviour. This scale would help researchers see if good quality CBT, as rated on a CBT specific scale, scored more highly in certain areas than others on an MI scale. For example, it may be that CBT scores relatively well on the global scores of empathy and direction but less well on autonomy and collaboration.

Further studies could look at the introduction of MI training for CBT therapists and explore if there are therapist behaviour changes eg improvements in ratings of quality of the therapy. Longer term it would be required to demonstrate an effect on patient outcome scales to show if clinically useful change is achieved by adding MI training to CBT before wider adoption of training techniques.

One of the simplest ways of investigating a combined MI and CBT treatment for young people is to use MI as a pre-treatment to the CBT. This was method used by Westra et al (2009) for anxiety disorders and by Connors et al (2002) for alcohol misuse. For research purposes this is likely to be the best way to initially examine the question of whether this approach is clinically useful. However it is not the only way CBT and MI could be combined - as fluctuations of ambivalence and motivation are likely to occur throughout therapy. Using MI techniques when applicable throughout the CBT would appear to make most sense in a clinical setting but effectiveness would be more difficult to compare with CBT alone. Holt and Heimberg (1990) report that adult client's expectancy of treatment

136                                   *Chapter 9*

outcome was lower after the fourth session of CBT for social anxiety, than at the end of session one. This might suggest that patients' motivation may fluctuate throughout therapy. Promoting motivation at critical low motivation points may be necessary to help the client stay in therapy. Miller and Rollnick (2002) suggest that when working with adults with alcohol problems, MI is never over and that even when a patient has started to change MI strategies should be maintained throughout treatment. It seems reasonable to consider that this may also be the case with young people and anxiety disorders.

For initial evaluation research it may be that a manualised form of the therapy would be needed to keep the specificity of the intervention proposed clear. This would have benefits but could restrict the therapist when using CBT and MI techniques, both of which work best when there is flexibility of approach.

Who would benefit from an integrated CBT and MI approach is another area for research. It appears that some young people could benefit but it is unlikely that all young people would need the MI component to help treat their anxiety disorders. If clinicians were able to identify clients that might benefit most from a more MI focus, it would help with the specificity of the therapy given to patients.

**Training Implications**

If adding a motivational interviewing component does potentate CBT then how this is taught to CBT trainees needs to be considered. Miller and Mount (2001) found that using an introductory workshop to teach MI had minimal impact on the participant's subsequent practice. Yahne et al (2008) in a follow up study were able to demonstrate that following a two day MI workshop there were demonstrable changes in practice behaviour, which were large enough to make a difference in their clients' response and to reach the standard for MI competence. The question remains about how this approach could best be taught: but workshops, the most widely used current method, are probably the most effective teaching medium

**Concluding Observations**

In this chapter we have seen how both CBT and MI have been effective interventions in their specific settings. Both therapies are now being considered for use in areas outside those they have been traditionally linked with. Consideration has been given in this chapter as to whether the addition of an MI component to CBT may help in the specific area of young people with anxiety disorders. We have seen a degree of overlap with the therapies, however the idea of using MI as an added tool when using CBT for young people who are difficult to engage with appears promising. The research in this area is limited, often pilot trials and case studies. The outcomes indicate that this is an area that warrants further attention. Larger trials by different groups of researchers will continue to add to the literature and evidence base. The author has found the approach of adding MI principles and the CBT/MI decision matrix template (figure 2) to be helpful when treating young

*Chapter 9*     *137*

people with CBT for anxiety problems when they had become stuck at a particular point of therapy.

There are certainly areas of commonality and overlap between CBT and MI: however there does appear to be a distinctive style and set of techniques that MI may be able to bring to CBT to aid clinical outcomes in specific areas such as the one considered in this chapter. The research so far in this area perhaps raises more questions than it answers but further refinement will help work out the key ingredients to therapy in this hugely important area of treating anxiety disorders in young people.

## References

Anderson, J., Williams, S., McGee, R. & Silva, P. A. (1987) DSM-III disorders in preadolescent children: prevalence in a large sample from the general population. *Archives of General Psychiatry,* 44, p69-76.

Arkowitz, H., Miller, W., Westra, H & Rollnick, S. (2008) Motivational Interviewing in the treatment of psychological problems: Conclusions and future directions. In: Motivational Interviewing in the treatment of psychological problems. Eds Arkowitz, H. Westra, H., Miller, W. & Rollnick, S. New York; Guildford Press.

Barrett, P. (1998) Evaluation of cognitive-behavioral group treatments for childhood anxiety disorders. *Journal of Clinical Child Psychology,* 27(4), p459–68.

Beck, J. (1995) Cognitive Therapy: Basics and Beyond. Guilford Publications Inc.

Blackburn, I., James, I., Milne, D. & Reichelt, F. (2001) Cognitive therapy scale – revised (CTS-R), Newcastle upon Tyne, UK. Available at: http://www. getselfhelp. co.uk/docs/CTSRmanual.pdf

Brueck, R., Frick, K., Loessl, B., Kriston, L., Schondelmaier, S., Go, C., Haerter, M. & Berner, M. (2009) Psychometric properties of the German version of the Motivational Interviewing Treatment Integrity Code. *Journal of Substance Abuse Treatment.* 36(1), p44-48.

Burke, B., Arkowitz, H. & Menchola, M. (2003) The efficacy of Motivational Interviewing: A meta-analysis of controlled clinical trials. *Journal of Consulting and Clinical Psychology.* 71, p843-861.

Carroll, K., Nich, C., Sifry, R., Nuro, K., Frankforter, T., Ball, S., Fenton, L. & Rounsaville, B. (2000) A general system for evaluating therapist adherence and competence in psychotherapy research in the addictions. *Drug and Alcohol Dependence.* 57(3), p225-38.

138                              *Chapter 9*

Cartwright-Hatton, S., Roberts, C., Chitsabesan, P., Fothergill, C. & Harrington, R. (2004) Systematic review of the efficacy of cognitive behaviour therapies for childhood and adolescent anxiety disorders, *British Journal of Clinical Psychology*, 43, p421–436.

Connors, G., Walitzer, K. & Dermen, K. (2002) Preparing clients for alcoholism treatment: Effects on treatment participation and outcomes. *Consulting and Clinical Psychology*, 70. p1161-1169.

Dorian, E. H. (2004) Motivational Interviewing and cognitive behavioral therapy. *Academy of Cognitive Therapy*. Newsletter March 2004.

Dozois, D. & Westra, H. (2005) Development of the Anxiety Change Expectancy Scale (ACES) and validation in college, community and clinical samples. *Behaviour Research and Therapy*, 43, p1655-1672.

Drieschner, K., Lammers, S. & van der Stakk, P. (2004) Treatment motivation: An attempt for clarification of an ambiguous concept. *Clinical Psychology Review*, 23, p1115-1137.

Drugtext. (2008) Available at: http://www.drugtext.org/library/books/methadone/ section7.html.

Farvolden, F., Denisorff, E., Selby, P., Bagby, M. & Rudy, L. (2005) Usage and longitudinal effectiveness of a web-based self-help cognitive behavioural therapy programme for panic disorder. *Journal of Medicine Internet Research.* 7(1):e7.

Goldberg, H. & Goldberg, I. (2007) Family therapy: An Overview. 7th edition. Wadsworth Publishing Co Inc, Belmont, USA.

Goodman R. & Scott S. (2005) Child Psychiatry. Oxford; Blackwell Publishing Ltd.

Grave, J. & Blissett, J. (2004) Is cognitive behaviour therapy developmentally appropriate for young children? A critical review of the evidence. *Clinical Psychology Review*, 24(4), p399-420.

Holt, C., & Heimberg, R. (1990) The reaction to treatment questionnaire: measuring treatment credibility and outcome expectancies. *The Behavior Therapist*, 13, p214–222.
IAPT (2012) Website: http://www.iapt.nhs.uk/cyp-iapt/

Kendall, P., Flannery-Schroeder, E. Paniehelli-Mindel, S., Southern-Gerow, M., Henin, A. & Warman, M. (1997) Therapy for youths with anxiety disorders: A second randomized controlled trial. *Journal of Consulting and Clinical Psychology*, 65, p366-380

Maltby, N. & Tolin, D. (2005) A brief motivational intervention for treatment refusing OCD patients. *Cognitive Behaviour Therapy,* 34, p176-184.

Merlo, L., Storch, E., Lehmkuhl, H., Jacob, M., Murphy, T., Goodman, W. & Geffken, G. (2009) Cognitive behavioural therapy plus motivational interviewing improves outcome for pediatric obsessive-compulsive disorder: a preliminary study. *Cognitive Behaviour Therapy,* 1, p1-4.

Miller, W (1983) Motivational Interviewing with problem drinkers. *Behavioural Psychotherapy.* 11, p147-172.

Miller, W. (2000) Motivational Interviewing Skills Code (MISC). Coder's manual. University of New Mexico. Available at: http://casaa.unm.edu/download /misc1.pdf

Miller, W. & Mount, K. (2001) A small study of training in motivational interviewing: does one workshop change clinician and client behaviour? *Behavioural and Cognitive Psychotherapy,* 29, p457-471.

Miller, W. R. & Rollnick, S. (1991) Motivational interviewing, preparing people to change addictive behaviour. New York; The Guilford Press.

Miller, W. R., & Rollnick, S. (2002) Motivational interviewing: Preparing people for change. New York; The Guilford Press.

Miller, W., Taylor, C. & West, J. (1980) Focused versus broad spectrum behaviour therapy for problem drinkers. *Journal of consulting and clinical psychology,* 48, p590-601.

Moyers, T., Martin T., Manuel, J., Hendrickson, S. & Miller, W. (2005a) Assessing competence in the use of motivational interviewing. *Journal of Substance Abuse Treatment.* 28; p19-26.

Moyers, T., Martin, T., Manuel, J. & Miller, W. (2005b) The Motivational Interviewing Treatment Integrity Code: Version 2.0 (MITI 2.0). University of New Mexico, Centre on Alcoholism, Substance Abuse and Addictions (CASSA). Available at: http://casaa.unm.edu/download/miti.pdf.

Prochaska, J. O., DiClemente, C. & Norcross, J. (1992) In search of how people change: Applications to addictive behaviours. *American Psychologist.* 47, p1102-1114.

Rachman, S. & Wilson G. (2008) Expansion in the provision of psychological treatment in the United Kingdom. *Behaviour Research and Therapy,* 46 p293–295.

140    *Chapter 9*

Rogers, C. R. (1953) Client-centred therapy. Its current practice, implications and theory. Boston; Houghton Mifflin.

Ruback, S., Sandbaek, A., Lauritzen, T. & Christensen, B. (2005) Motivational interviewing: a systematic review and meta-analysis. *British Journal of General Practice,* 55(513), p305-312.

Rutter, M. , Bishop, D.. Pine, S., Scott, S., Stevenson, S., Taylor, E. & Thapar, A. (2010) Rutter's Child and Adolescent Psychiatry 5th Edition. Blackwell Publishing Ltd.

Tober, G., Clyne W., Finnegan O., Farrin A. & Russell I. (2008) Validation of a Scale for Rating the Delivery of Psycho-Social Treatments for Alcohol Dependence and Misuse: The UKATT Process Rating Scale (PRS). *Alcohol and Alcoholism,* 43(6), p675-682.

Tober, G & Raistrick, D. (2007) Motivational Dialogue. Routledge, an imprint of Taylor & Francis Books Ltd.

Tracey T., & Kokotovic A. (1989) Factor structure of the Working Alliance Inventory. Psychological Assessment. *A Journal of Consulting and Clinical Psychology,* 1:207–210.

Treasure, J. L., Katzman, M., Schmidt, U., Troop, N., Todd, G., & de Silva, P. (1999) Engagement and outcome in the treatment of bulimia nervosa: First phase of a sequential design comparing motivation enhancement therapy and cognitive behavioural therapy. *Behaviour Research and Therapy,* 37, p405–418.

Waltz, J., Addis, M., Koerner, K. & Jacobson, N. (1993) Testing the integrity of a psychotherapy protocol: Assessment of adherence and competence. *Journal of Consulting and Clinical Psychology,* 61(4) p620–630.

Wells, A. (1997) Cognitive Therapy of Anxiety Disorders, A Practice Manual and Conceptual Guide. Chichester; John Wiley & Sons Ltd.

Westra, H. (2004) Managing resistance in cognitive behavioural therapy: the application of motivational interviewing in mixed anxiety and depression. *Cognitive Behaviour Therapy,* 33(4), p161-175.

Westra, H., Arkowitz, H. & Dozois, D. (2009) Adding a motivational interviewing pretreatment to cognitive behaviour therapy for generalized anxiety disorder: A preliminary trial. *Journal of Anxiety Disorders,* 23 (8), p1106-1117

Westra, H. & Dozois, D. (2006) Preparing clients for cognitive behavioural therapy: a randomised plot study of motivational interviewing for anxiety. *Cognitive Therapy Research,* 30, p481-498.

Westra, H. & Dozois, D. (2008) Integrating motivational interviewing into the treatment of anxiety; In: *Motivational Interviewing in the Treatment of Psychological Problems.* Eds Arkowitz, H. Westra, H., Miller, W. & Rollnick, S. New York; Guildford Press.

Westra, H. & Phoenix, E. (2003) Motivational enhancement therapy in two cases of anxiety disorder: new responses to treatment refractoriness. *Clincial Case Studies,* 2, p306-322.

Wilson, G. & Schlam, T. (2004) The transtheoretical model and motivational interviewing in the treatment of eating and weight disorders. Clinical *Psychology Review,* 24 p361–378.

Yanhne, C., Miller, W., Moyers, T. & Pirritano, M. 2008. Teaching motivational interviewing to clinicians: a randomised trial of training methods. Poster presentation available at:

http://casaa.unm.edu/posters/teaching%20motivational%interviewing%20 to%clinicians.pdf.

*142*                                    *Chapter 9*

# Chapter 10

# Motivational Interviewing and Diabetes Mellitus

## John Roberts
### *Independent Practitioner in Cognitive and Behavioural Therapy and MI Trainer*

### Introduction

Motivational Interviewing (MI) was developed initially as a method of assisting people decrease alcohol and drug misuse. It has been empirically supported and is a promising intervention for encouraging changes in health behaviour in a variety of settings - either as a stand-alone intervention or alongside more traditional interventions (Rollnick et al, 2002).

People with chronic conditions make day to day decisions about how to self-manage their conditions. The reality of living with a chronic condition and taking self-management decisions has important implications - as a range of condition specific issues are invoked. These decisions can range from disease complications in the future to healthcare cost burdens for provider systems and from deferment of longer term benefits in exchange for more immediate gratification. In the management of a chronic condition the relationship between healthcare provider and patient also becomes significant. Modern healthcare-patient relationships have increasingly moved away from traditional consultative-directive advice given by a healthcare provider to a patient towards more collaborative models of care provision – as the consultative approach has been found to be disengaging and disempowering to healthcare consumers.

Arising from these new models of care (Bodenheimer et al 2002) patient-healthcare provider relationships have moved towards collaborative and self-management/ educative forms. Within these paradigms the facilitation of problem solving skills for particular conditions becomes important. Enhanced patient problem solving skills are linked to increased self-efficacy in condition management. Self-efficacy,

144                                    *Chapter 10*

the confidence to reach expressed goals by undertaking a specific behaviour, is linked to reduced healthcare burdens, prevention of disease specific complications and psycho-social benefits.

In the field of diabetes research it has been shown that effective glycaemic control i.e. controlling the levels of blood sugar, can prevent long term complications (UKPDS, 1998). The management of diabetes mellitus is complicated by multiple factors. These factors are of importance with respect to achieving as near as possible optimal glycaemic control. They include creating a healthy lifestyle and using that lifestyle to avoid long term complications of diabetes. They also feature managing excessive blood sugar levels or hypo-glycaemic events. Achieving optimal or at least patient-preferred glycaemic control can be problematic as the majority of diabetic management is undertaken by the individual in the absence of 'expert' healthcare professional guidance.

Primarily, diabetes is a chronic disease of self management. Professional recommendations to adhere to lifestyle changes e.g. diet, exercise, alcohol consumption, smoking and recreational drug use, are dependent on patients (and in the case of young people, their carers) being willing to collaborate with healthcare professionals and self manage their condition. In other words, client compliance with professional recommendations to adhere to medication regimes, insulin dosing, foot care and a range of other diabetes specific self care regimens, are dependent on the willingness of the individual to adhere to the recommendations between infrequent consultations.

## Young People and Diabetes

Young people with diabetes face developmental hurdles and are subject to multiple psycho-social influences. These can range from peer or media pressure to taking part in 'unhealthy' activities e.g. smoking, alcohol consumption or psychoactive drug taking, to finding an identity or individuation from their family of origin e.g. belonging to a youth culture, spending time away from a family. Psychosocial influences also exist in an increasingly complex milieu and demand a young person's attention. Advertising for the consumption of 'unhealthy foods' or sugary drinks and the role of alcohol in socialising or peer activity both play a significant role. These can be important to a young person as they are frequently founded on notions of peer acceptability. In this context helping young people make choices about their self-care health behaviours can become problematic.

In this chapter I outline the types of diabetes and provide a brief and selective overview of some research issues undertaken into MI with diabetic children, young people and their families. I then examine some of the developmental issues facing the MI clinician when working with diabetic youngsters and finally review some of the practice tools and techniques that I have found to be useful when using MI with diabetic children, young people and their families.

## Type 1 Diabetes

Type 1 Diabetes (T1DM) can occur at any age. However, it is most often diagnosed in children, adolescents and young adults. Insulin is a hormone produced by beta cells in the pancreas. Insulin is needed to move blood sugar (glucose) into body cells, where it is stored and later used for energy. In T1DM the beta cells produce little or no insulin.

Management of T1DM must include insulin management. Insulin allows sugar to leave the bloodstream and enter cells to be stored for energy. Insulin is injected under the skin and in some cases is delivered by a pump. People with T1DM are encouraged to manage their blood sugars by frequent testing and then titrate insulin injections accordingly. Supplemental care of T1DM involves managing diet and exercise, foot care and a range of measures to prevent further complications. There is no way to prevent T1DM. T1DM is the most common paediatric metabolic disorder. The incidence is approximately 1.7 per 1000 of young people under the age of 20.

## Type 2 Diabetes and Maturity Onset Diabetes of the Young (MODY)

Type 2 Diabetes Mellitus (T2DM) accounts for 90-95% of people with diabetes. T2DM occurs when the body develops insulin resistance, a condition where the cells of the body fail to use insulin sufficiently. Incidence of T2 DM is increasing, particularly in developed nations.

The first-line treatment of T2DM is diet, weight control and physical activity in order to prevent long term complications e.g. heart disease, strokes, and circulatory problems. If this fails to adequately control blood glucose levels medication (and sometimes insulin) is used.

MODY (Maturity Onset Diabetes of the Young) is a form of diabetes more likely to be inherited than the other forms of diabetes as there is a stronger genetic risk factor. It affects 1-2% of those who have diabetes and has been compared to T2DM as it shares a number of similar symptoms. The treatments for the 6 types of MODY are similar to those of T2 DM.

### Diabetes and Quality of Life

Beside the health and economic burdens associated with diabetes, T1DM and T2DM impose a range of physical and emotional burdens on children, young people and their families. It has a profound effect on quality of life (Edgar and Skinner, 2003). Even though good glycaemic control can help prevent long term complications, psycho-social influences become difficult to separate from a young person's regimen of self care. Young people are growing, adapting and developing; factors influencing these processes and the formation of habits of self care implemented at this time will be of profound importance in later adult self-care regimens.

## 146        *Chapter 10*

**Self Regulation and Impulse Control**

Young people are in the process of developing self-regulation skills and learning to manage their impulses. Self regulation and impulse control are important in the management of diabetes as appetitive regulation is a feature of management regimens. Self-regulation is defined as the conscious, purposeful and effortful control of behaviour, thoughts, emotions, impulses and attention. Social factors such as care giving support, peer or sibling relationships and social norms have a role to play in the development of self control (Kalvana, 2010). For example, poor family functioning e.g. the presence of parent mental health problems, violence, and substance or alcohol misuse in childhood may predispose an individual to poor self-control in adulthood. In contrast, factors such as social support, parental monitoring of behaviour or appropriate discipline foster a structured environment that promotes self control amongst children and adolescents. When children and young people develop, innate factors in combination with socialising influences result in manifestations of self-regulation skills such as goal setting, impulse control and the delay of gratification. The MI professional needs to understand and integrate understandings of this developmental context to self-regulation and impulse control when developing successful MI interventions for this client group.

**Treatment Compliance**

Young people often experience great difficulty completing prescribed treatment regimens as they are often complex and burdensome (Rapoff, 1999). High rates of non-adherence to treatment, estimated at 50% or more (Drotar, 2006), indicate that this condition is under treated in comparison to available medical standards. Such non-adherence/under treatment may account for raised morbidity, the development of complications, increased healthcare utilisation and limitations in quality of life.

Many service users report being asked to take on complex self-management tasks for long term benefits rather than for immediate and obvious gain (Ridge et al, 2012). For young people immediate gratification often appears more attractive as long term adherence can be quite problematic and complex. Long term complications are often not considered by young people as these complications are not experienced in the 'here and now'. The young person often believes them to be too 'far away' to be meaningful. Simply put, they sometimes express a wish to deal with them "when I get there" or, at worse, "why does this matter? I am going to die anyway."

Clinicians sometimes perceive that young people and their carers are often dissatisfied with the help they receive – reflected sometimes in non attendance at clinics (Channon et al, 2003). Thus, recognition of the importance of promoting engagement to better, choice led diabetic care among children and adolescents has led to an interest in the development and evaluation of MI for this disease.

*Chapter 10*                                                                                       *147*

## Motivational Interviewing

Research into diabetes and MI applications is still in its infancy: but some has been carried out e.g. Naar-King and Ellis (2010), Naar-King et al (2006), Channon (2007). The outcomes of these studies are promising. e.g. showing that integrating MI into the intervention results in better glycaemic control and improved psychological well-being (Channon et al, 2005, Channon et al, 2007). Channon and colleagues (2005), working with teenagers with T1DM, showed MI to be an effective intervention - contributing to improvements (lasting over 2 years) in glycaemic control. Participants also reported greater and sustained improvements to their quality of life and to psychological well-being. Though this study had a relatively small sample size (n=66) and a relatively short follow up period (approx 2 years), it shows MI to be i) an effective method of facilitating behavioural change for promoting regimen adherence ii) a means for delivering improvements in glycaemic control at 12 months and 24 months and iii) a means of promoting significant psychological benefits.

## Eating Disorders and Co-present Mental Health Problems

Eating disorders and sub-threshold eating disorders are common psychological problems in T1 and T2DM (Ismail, 2008). Eating problems are associated with poor diabetic control, complications and raised mortality rates. Motivational approaches need to take account of risk factors for the presence of an eating disorder, especially if poor diabetic control is present – as sometimes young people with T1DM and an eating disorder skip use of insulin as a means of purging for weight loss (Jones et al, 2000). There have been insufficient studies to develop a robust evidence base for MI approaches to managing co-present psychological problems with young people with diabetes, for example, eating problems, needle phobia, depression, hypoglycaemia phobias, or social phobias characterised by hiding an illness from peers, refusing to monitor blood glucose in front of others for fear of shaming and so forth.

The challenge then is to develop MI interventions for young people in (brief) healthcare consultations which are developmentally flexible, teachable to professionals; that can account for co-present mental health problems and which are specific enough to enable research evaluation. Additional research into intervention processes, delivery, intra-individual and psychological processes is needed. Research into the relation of these processes toward outcomes is called for (Michie and Abraham, 2004).

## Developmental Issues when Working with Children and Young People.

Providing children and young people with developmentally appropriate explanations of their chronic conditions and treatment recommendations is a component of any MI intervention. This is challenging as there has been limited research into how children and young people understand and conceptualise

148                              *Chapter 10*

health, illness and treatment (Erikson, 2005). As the period of growth from childhood through to adolescence and then into early adulthood is a period of fairly rapid, always uneven development and change, it is unlikely that any MI tool or technique is going to be effective for all youngsters across this time span. Developing MI interventions for diabetic youngsters necessarily involves an understanding of young people's changing causal reasoning, their language competencies and self-understanding over this time span. In addition a thorough appreciation of their environmental context, family, school, peer relationships and so forth, is relevant. Finally, the MI professional may find an overview of some of the biological changes that occur in adolescence useful.

Developmental psychology and psychopathology has provided a lexicon for clinical observations e.g. developmental trajectory, risk, protective processes and so forth, (Kendall and Holmbeck, 2002). MI approaches have often been developed for adult populations and not always from research with young people. MI has thus sometimes been extended downwards to 'fit' younger age groups. It is suggested here that in order to be effective, that 'fit' between the client and MI is likely to be enhanced if the MI clinician adopts an approach that is matched to a young person's unique trajectory of development. In short, the MI clinician needs to have at least some knowledge of the young client's overall functioning.

Adopting a developmental perspective in MI for children and adolescents gives rise to opportunity for a number of unique questions about implementing MI with young people. For example, why are some groups of young people harder to work with than others? How does one engage with an 8 year old? What does a good scaling tool look like for a 9 year old? What types of MI questioning techniques are likely to best work with adolescents? A developmental perspective assists the MI professional to differentiate between behaviours that are seemingly maladaptive - even though they may be fairly typical for the developmental period e.g. with teenagers, experimentation with alcohol or smoking. Such differentiation clarifies the differences between typical and atypical – and provides a framework for the MI professional to engage with young people.

## Glycaemic Control and Adolescence

As children enter adolescence involvement with healthcare professionals in their self care tapers away before increasing again in early adulthood (Wysocki et al, 1996). Adolescence is of interest to the MI professional as it is a period that presents with profound problems of engagement. It is also a period of opportunity – the opportunity to create and establish adaptive lifetime healthcare habits.

Patients with insulin dependent diabetes often have poor metabolic control during puberty as pubertal growth hormones can disrupt glycaemic control (Amiel et al, 1986, Borus 2010). Pubertal development is accompanied by rapid growth and an almost doubling of lean body mass. This poses challenges to the provision of nutrition and the subsequent insulinisation of young people with Type 1 DM. It is also normal at this time for a young person to wish to increase their personal autonomy. They often do this by decreasing healthcare behaviours, even though they could be required to step up blood sugar testing and manage more complex insulin dosing regimens.

These additional requirements may threaten to overwhelm a young person's motivation for entering into positive self-healthcare regimens. At the same time as such additional demands to manage a regimen there is often the additional challenge of minimising undesirable health behaviours. For the adolescent this can mean more regular monitoring of blood glucose, more complex administration of insulin and medication along with closer attention to diet and lifestyle. Poor adherence in this period can result in lower glycaemic control and the risk of further complications. All this can be off-putting to the person who just wishes to be 'normal' and enjoy the things non-diabetic youngsters enjoy. It therefore seems quite normal for a large proportion of diabetic youngsters to become ambivalent or resistant to attempts by healthcare professionals to introduce healthier treatment regimens.

The challenge here is to meet this ambivalence or resistance creatively as often the young person has become dispirited. They may feel that they will "never ever get it right". In the MI paradigm, expressing empathy for the young person's situation and skilful reflective listening is helpful. Recognition that this sort of ambivalence is entirely normal will also be part of the clinicians approach. When faced with the dispirited youngster struggling with glycaemic control the MI professional should avoid active disputation and facilitate a process of self-presentation of rationales for change or perseverance. In summary, it is important for the MI professional to help the young person place a positive spin on these difficulties – as the amount of testing and monitoring required falls back in late adolescence. Thus reflection on past achievements, efficacy and praise for hard work is often the mode of delivery in MI through this sometimes difficult period.

**Features of effective MI with Diabetic Children, Adolescents and their Families.**

Motivational Interviewing differs from traditional health coaching approaches in that it is not based on information giving, does not rely on 'scare tactics' and is not confrontational.

Motivational Interviewing, suggested as a "way of being with people" (Miller and Rollnick, 2002) enhances intrinsic motivation to change by exploring ambivalence and perspective. Rather than coercion, MI with young people with diabetes visits the status quo and sets about facilitating change through open exploration of values, interests and concerns. The emphasis is on collaboration, past achievements, the promotion of self-efficacy and an elicitation of the young person's own ideas about change

## Chapter 10

Thus a primary consideration is ensuring that the young person plays a full and active role in the shaping of the treatment decisions. When working with children and their families distinguishing between competing goals and agendas vis a vis those involved in a young person's healthcare is paramount. For example, are parental goals in conflict with the young person's? Do the treatment team wish to implement a new model of diabetes management or change the type of insulin compound? Is the treatment team prematurely focussing on change? Does the young person have a view that this is "just another boring healthcare visit" or are they genuinely wishing to enter a period of change?

*Goal specification* becomes particularly important in this context. It assists a reduction of ambivalence about change and increases a young person's intrinsic motivation, especially if the goals are relevant and meaningful to them. Goal specification does not mean that the MI clinician will necessarily counter the previously held beliefs of the young person. Indeed, an MI clinician working with youth will typically make no direct attempt to confront, deny, or dismantle irrational or maladaptive beliefs – the cognitive-behavioural approach - and above all they will not cajole or persuade. Confrontation of young person's beliefs can damage rapport and build defensiveness on the part of the young person rather than produce confidence and engagement. The MI clinician helps the young person think about and verbally express their goals. They help the young person find the reasons for and against change. They assist the young person in discovering how their current behaviour or health status affects their ability to achieve their life goals. In essence when adapting MI for diabetic young people the clinician elicits intrinsic motivation to make changes and encourage the young person to find their own solutions.

The clinician wishing to adopt MI with young people with diabetes acknowledges that the client and clinician work in partnership – for genuine rapport or alliance is crucial in exploring attitudes and practical difficulties associated with lifestyle change. The young person is provided with a non-judgemental, genuine, warm and open environment in which to articulate their concerns. In turn the practitioner demonstrates empathy and clearly values the young person's perspective. This is achieved by the use of open questions, reflections of responses and summaries. Above all the practitioner dispenses with the idea of being superior or 'the expert'. They imaginatively enter the young person's experience of living with diabetes and attempt to understand their difficulties, viewpoints and the dilemmas of having such a condition. Appropriate consultations should bias the balance of 'talk time' in favour of the patient and involve plenty of clear positive affirmations and demonstrations of empathy and acceptance from the clinician.

In practical terms MI can involve the use of compliments/praise and statements of understanding or empathy. The MI clinician supplements these skills with techniques such as "Importance Scaling" and "Affirmatory Feedback". The clinician pulls together and reinforces discussed material thereby eliciting change talk. These practical techniques are underpinned by the principles of open unconditional acceptance of the young person. The MI clinician is concerned with collaboration, reflecting and reviewing options with their client. The clinician supports the young person's autonomy to select and then enact change. Examples of basic MI techniques specific to diabetic youngsters are provided below:

## MI Techniques Applied to Diabetic Youngsters

### Open ended questions:

*How does drinking lots of coke fit with diabetes?*
*How does missing insulin shots fit with diabetes?*

### Closed questions:

*How many bags of crisps have you eaten today?*
*Did you test your blood before every meal?*

### Reflective listening:

*You're fed up with having diabetes and being different*
*It's hard work having diabetes and not being able to eat the same as other kids*
*You've had to do this for 12 years and it's not fair that you have to stick to this diet for longer*

### Affirmations:

*Coming in all the time for reviews sucks, but you're doing really well sticking to it*
*I'm impressed by how you are handling this new testing system*
*Fantastic! You seem to be getting the results you want. Look at the benefits...you're now going out with friends more and feeling better.*

### Summaries:

*I can see it's important for you to fit in with your friends. Sometimes testing blood in public makes this difficult.*
*Yes, you can see that when you skip insulin you don't feel well and find it harder to keep up in class. Do you want to add anything more to that?*

### Change Talk: to be Promoted

*I will test my blood sugars more*
*I will change my diet*
*I wish I could manage hypos better*
*I wish I could lose weight and go for a run.*

152                                Chapter 10

**Importance Scaling:**

*On a scale of 1-10, where 1 is the most important and 10 is the least important to you where is "Going on a Dose Adjusted for Normal Eating (DAFNE) course"?*

*You told me that going on a Dose Adjusted for Normal Eating course is a "5"... what would be necessary for you to get from a 5 to a 3?*

**Agenda Setting Tools.**

Healthcare professionals using MI when working with young people have an immediate window of opportunity to collaborate and establish rapport or alliance. Simply put, 'getting things right' from the moment their young client enters their consultation rooms. It is a process of focussing on the young person 'beyond their diabetes' (Doherty and Roberts, 2002) and it moves consultations beyond technical, medical or administrative considerations toward patient-focussed and highly individualised personal aspirations.

However, diabetes is a complicated condition demanding knowledge of multiple self-care behaviours. This is often reflected in the packed nature of healthcare consultations. Meetings therefore come with the risk of multiple conflicts and competing aims. Practitioners will be tempted to 'run' meetings as they have their jobs to do and wish the young person to benefit from their service. Young people, parents and others involved with a young person's treatment will have their own agendas. These may not necessarily be congruent with those of the healthcare providers.

These possible competing aims and components – screening, reviewing self-management, developing rapport or alliance, information giving, identifying and resolving problems, addressing patient priorities and striking a balance between them - are of importance with regard to reducing the chances that the young person disengages with a service and 'opts out'. Meetings are also limited by practicalities e.g. i) time allotted (the busy clinic or client lateness) ii) , the setting - the cramped consultation room iii) the family attending with a fractious sibling iv) administrative tasks and v) time since last review.

Meetings should be as naturalistic in style as possible. The introduction of a collaboratively agreed agenda and structure to the meeting i) aids cohesion and ii) minimises the effects of competing aims. Collaborative agendas elevate client priorities and promote a productive and beneficial service to the service user meeting.

**Visual Tools**

Young people often enjoy the use of visual tools and the inclusion of plenty of choice into their consultations. This is particularly true at the beginning of meetings. The 'menu of strategies' (Channon et al, 2007) or diabetes 'notice board' appears to be a useful approach to take. A flipchart, a felt notice board or a white board can be used. Felt notice boards and blank counters or tokens are placed on a table. The young patient's aspirations for the meeting are then elicited by the use of open questions. Their responses are then written on the counters and collaboratively arranged or ranked in order of importance. They are then placed on the notice board for the duration of that consultation. An element of 'forced choice' can be introduced here with some 'standing items' being conveniently present – it sometimes helps to suggest to the young person that some of the standing items have proved helpful to other young people. The author uses the picture below (Figure 1) as a trigger stimulus for agenda items. Ranking in terms of importance to the young person then occurs. The agenda items are then 'managed' according to time allotted to the consultation. If items 'fall off' the agenda they can be put back on again at the next consultation. The speech bubbles are typically left blank. Extra pieces of blank card or paper are also left adjacent to the picture so that the young person can write anything that crops up for them. Other pieces of paper or card containing diabetes specific subject areas are left near the picture:

*Figure 1:* Agenda setting: Choice and Topics.

154                           *Chapter 10*

When engaged in setting the agenda the MI clinician introduces plenty of choice-led questions. This stimulates the young person toward setting their priorities and begins the longer term process of identifying goals for behavioural change. Some exemplar agenda setting questions are listed below:

**Agenda Setting Questions:**
Choices and multiple diabetes self care behaviours.

### (i) Type 1DM

1. *I am concerned by these hp1AC results...how do you feel about a structured programme to manage this?*

2. *How do you think eating chocolate is affecting your diabetes?*

3. *You say you don't like having hypos...should we talk about how to manage them better?*

4. *I am worried that you skip insulin whilst at school. Tell me more about that. Should we think about that today?*

5. *What would you like to talk about today? You told me you have lots of hypos after going clubbing. Is that important to you?*

### (ii) Type 2DM

6. *What would you like to talk about today? We could talk about decreasing sugar intake, watching less TV, doing more and eating more healthily. What do you think? Is there something more important you would like to discuss?*

7. *Would you like to talk about how you can improve your health today? Or is there something else I can help you out with?*

8. *Which diet or type of exercise are you ready to talk about today?*

9. *Some people think that taking more exercise helps them reduce weight. What do you think?*

### Questions for Dealing with Single Self Care Behaviours

1. *Some people think that teenagers with diabetes who drink lots increase the risk of future complications. What do you think?*

2. *I am concerned that you do not test your blood glucose when out with your friends. What do you think about that?*

3. *I am worried that you miss insulin sometimes. What effects do you think that has? Why is that concerning?*

When setting agendas with young people clinicians sometimes encounter 'road blocks' or impasses in the development of sessions. For example, the non-communicative young person, the young person who wishes to talk about anything but diabetes, or the young person who appears to have multiple crises in their lives that impede discussion of diabetes relevant subject matters. It is important for clinicians to 'roll' with this sort of resistance. Reframing provides the opportunity to develop collaboration and reinforce alliance.

### Responses to Client Resistance to Agenda Setting:

- *I can see that talking about your exams is important to you. How does this get in the way of discussing diabetes?*

- *On a scale of 1 being important and 10 being unimportant how important is it to you that we deal with managing hypos today?*

- *I can see you are upset by your friend. Would you like to talk about them first or later?*

Common road-blocks in agenda construction also include clinician behaviours. 'Shoe-horning' agenda items in or packing a session with too many items are common errors. 'Shoe horning' conveys a power differential to young people and will interfere with developing a shared understanding of problems, issues or goals. It is important to be flexible as possible in the construction of the agenda. Letting the young person go first and acting as a stimuli by using open questions will elicit productive material. If a young person appears non-committal or unconcerned, the clinician can use further questions to find out why.

Sometimes though, young people can seem outwardly 'non-co-operative' or inaccessible. If this seems to be the case the author has found the technique of taking the 'temperature' or mood in the room helpful when beginning the session. An exemplar mood temperature gauge is illustrated in Figure 2. The clinician tests the mood in the room on a Likert scale; the young person places an object or shape on the corresponding number. The clinician can then 'test out' the temperature in the room. Some exemplar mood testing questions are illustrated below:

156                           *Chapter 10*

*Figure 1.2:* Mood Temperature Gauge Tool.

**Mood Temperature Questions for Opening Sessions.**

- *On a scale of 0-10, where 0 is very unhappy and 10 is very happy, where are you right now?*

- *On a scale of 0-10, where 0 is very calm and 10 is very angry, where are you right now?*

- *On a scale of 0-10, where 0 is very chilled and 10 is very anxious, where are you right now?*

The clinician can then probe further for more data and client explanations by the use of reflections, summaries, empathetic statements and requests for further information.

*Chapter 10*                                                                157

## Behavioural Change: Importance, Confidence and Willingness to make Change.

MI, first described by Miller (1983) and then elaborated on by Miller and Rollnick (1991), highlights a process of the provision of empathy in the form of direct feedback on a service user's comments. Through this dialogue a development of awareness of discrepancies between existing healthcare behaviours and possible goals is then developed. Discussions are supplemented by further open ended exploration of apparent discrepancies between beliefs and behaviour (Channon et al, 2007). Sessions include combinations of awareness building, eliciting alternatives, problem solving segments, decision making and goal setting sections.

Sessions also include elements of awareness building that aim to assist the young person express conflicting views about behavioural change. The MI clinician assists the young person to make decisions about behavioural change by facilitating calculation of the advantages and disadvantages of that healthcare behaviour change. The clinician typically investigates all domains of a young person's life – as perceived costs may be social, emotional, financial or health-related. It is normal for the young person to sometimes express ambivalence about making these changes. The clinician's role is to facilitate this. It then becomes easier to explore and elicit discrepancies and then assist the patient to become aware of them. The clinician can do this in the following ways:

- *Alternative Exploration - once the young person has developed awareness of apparent discrepancies; the costs and benefits of their healthcare behaviours and the alternatives can be considered.*

- *Elicit Problem solving – the costs and benefits, the pros and cons to the alternatives are explored, ranked and weighed up.*

- *Choice/priorities for action – the selection of the choice/priority solution is then owned by the patient*

- *Goal setting –once the choice has been made the patient and clinician together can then develop Specific, Measurable, Achievable, Realistic and to a Timescale (SMART) goals*

- *Use of Appropriate Monitoring tools when implementing preferred solution.*

When engaged in the above activities I like to use a set of small weighing scales with weights to help the young person balance up their decision/pros and con things. I also like to use a 'traffic light system' – counters coloured red, green and yellow are placed against a priority list and acted accordingly. Further I have found the use of Paul Stallard's "Think Good Feel Good" resource (Stallard, 2002) productive.

The MI clinician will need to ascertain whether or not their young service user is ready for change. Importance scaling tools, as illustrated below, can be adapted for use by young people. Often teenagers will wish to see their language and expressions utilised in their scales. The clinician will need to admit the young person's language and utterances into their contacts as more formal language can seem disempowering or at worst, irrelevant to the young client. Using the client's own language, references and terms helps cement a good working MI Alliance and makes importance, confidence and willingness to change scaling tools more meaningful to the young person. An example of an Importance scaling tool for an adolescent, using language from a session is illustrated below:

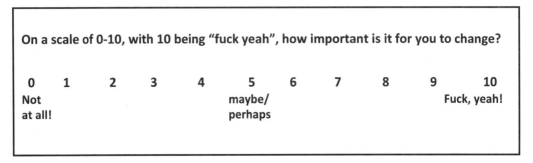

**Figure 3:** Importance of Change

Often MI clinicians will assume that young people are ready for change. Attendance at clinic is not necessarily an indication that a young person is invested in change. Often young people attend as they have been told to by a parent or carer or are "going along with things just to keep everyone at home happy". Awareness of the difficulties involved in change can help validate the young person's experience. It will be an important step toward considering the advantages and disadvantages of change. Thus evaluation of whether youngsters are invested in action oriented change will be useful. In particular clinicians need to check out, scale and evaluate the advantages and disadvantages of change – and whether the idea was theirs or someone else's. In short, checking out for readiness, confidence and willingness to change at all stages of consultation will be important.

*Developing Discrepancies.*

In this component the clinician should adopt a curious role, exploring issues that concern the young person and assisting them in articulating simultaneously held but occasionally conflicting beliefs about health behaviour change. Here, the MI clinician is paving the way towards the young person making decisions to discontinue, continue or change a healthcare behaviour. The young person is weighing up the benefits of change or maintenance against perceived personal costs across personal, social, health and emotional domains. Any ambivalence elicited will thus reflect a balance of costs and benefits – the role of the MI professional is simply to enable awareness of the advantages and disadvantages of change.

The practitioner should avoid giving information or advice until the client has presented their own understandings or their own ideas for overcoming obstacles to change. The provision of information is done in a neutral but curious way. The young person is asked to do the interpretation of information. In this fashion the clinician avoids falling into the trap of providing "pre-digested" health messages. This permits a young person to process information and avoids clinician-client persuasion-disputation traps. The MI professional should build up a repertoire of useful statements and questions. Some exemplar statements and questions are illustrated below:

### Exemplar Statements Designed to Elicit Discrepancy.

(Type 1) "Whilst it seems important to you to achieve good diabetic control, you say that eating sugary foods makes this difficult. What do you make of that?"

(Type 2) "You say it is important for you to achieve weight loss by taking exercise. But so much good stuff on TV makes this tricky. What do you think about that?"

After raising awareness it then becomes possible to consider the costs and benefits of the particular healthcare behaviour under consideration. Once the young person has become aware of the costs and benefits of their healthcare behaviours, alternates to the behaviour can be considered. Brain storming or list writing is a helpful technique. MI clinicians should include ideas from the young person, even if they seem outlandish or unreal. Alternatives can be considered item by item.

### Exemplar Pros and Cons of Moderating Drinking with an Adolescent (Type 1).

Whilst evaluating with a young person the costs and the benefits of change via

| Pros | Cons |
| --- | --- |
| **No change:** Getting pissed is fun | Getting drunk is harming my health |
| I like getting pissed with friends | Getting pissed costs a lot of money |
| All my friends get drunk | Dad bollocks me when I am drunk |
| **Change:** My health will get better | I'll miss out on stuff |
| Save money | This will be difficult to stop |
| I'll get fewer hyper-glycaemias | My friends will think I am boring |
| Dad will get off my case | |

the alternatives use of scaling tools, rankings or decisional balance worksheets can be useful:

## 160 Chapter 10

**Decisional Balance Work Sheet:**

| | |
|---|---|
| *What am I going to change?* | *Testing blood sugar more frequently.* |
| Good things about testing: | Good things about changing |
| *I know whether I am going to hypo* | *It will help me balance my blood sugars better* |
| *Helps me avoid long term problems* | *It will be part of my plan to get healthy* |
| Not so good things about testing | Not so good things about changing |
| *I have to remember* | *I use a lot of strips* |
| *This will take effort* | *It takes time* |

The MI clinician should be careful not to impose their solutions or 'obvious' choices on the young person. At all times they must guard against entering into confrontation as this will increase resistance and argumentation. The MI clinician will be open and curious in order to elicit concerns, goals and choices. Once decisions about change have been evaluated and the young person has committed to change, monitoring tools can be used to evaluate and assess progress to goals.

## Parent Concerns

To have a child newly diagnosed with diabetes can be overwhelming to parents. In cases of very young children, parents must acquire new sets of skills to manage this irreversible condition. Parents of the very young with T1DM are required to administer insulin, test blood glucose levels and respond to fluctuations. Often parents can find this very hard as they may have the belief that they are 'hurting' their child or perhaps damaging their relationship with them. Practically, injecting a screaming, wriggling 3 year old in a busy household also has its own complications! Thus the MI professional needs to be skilled in helping the parents manage both the behavioural responses of the child as well as the emotional responses of the parent. When given the diagnosis many parents report feeling abandoned, alone or isolated. They also sometimes report feeling incompetent, lacking in confidence, and under stress in providing chronic disease care. A diagnosis of diabetes may put parents at risk of mental health problems such as depression or anxiety (Landholdt et al, 2002). The MI professional meeting the parents of young people with diabetes should retain a flexible outlook and be vigilant to the occurrence of problems such as these. Referral to appropriate adult mental health services can be an extremely useful adjunct to the provision of MI in a family context.

*Chapter 10*   161

Parents/carers need to integrate complex, disease related new skills into effective daily routine management. This increases stress and has the effect of decreasing motivation over the longer term (Streisand et al, 2008). Thus if family plans for change lack collaboration and mutual goal setting they are likely to elicit defensiveness in parents. In the same way that plans relying on direct persuasion or guidance issuing by the professional often fail with young people so also they may fail with parents. Traditional educational information provision about diabetes is therefore unlikely to have an impact on parents (Weinstein et al 2004). This may be especially the case if a diabetes regimen is complex and demanding and if the child/young person is too young to 'lead' the regimen adequately without consistent support and assistance from their carer/parent. As pre-school and junior school children depend much more on their families than adolescents, the MI professional needs to factor in knowledge of parental disciplinary styles into their undertakings – as this may be a more specific indicator of diabetes outcome than other indices of family functioning (La Greca et al, 1990). In the same way that young people may often express doubt and ambivalence about the benefits of healthcare behaviour change, so too at times will parents and carers. Moreover, some parents and carers will be anxious to get things 'absolutely right' and strive to be over-compliant. This sometimes will be at the expense of their relationship with their child. The MI clinician needs to be attuned to these nuances. Empathy, affirmation and rolling with resistance delivers better healthcare outcomes for this group of patients.

**Summary and Conclusions.**

This has been a brief review of some of the issues that face an MI clinician working with a chronic healthcare condition such as diabetes. A range of issues affecting healthcare behaviour change in this context has been highlighted. These include considering the family context, the developmental level or attainment of a young person, their temperament and personality and their ability to participate collaboratively in treatment. In the context of the growth of the emotional well-being agenda and psychological approaches to chronic condition management further research into MI applications with this population group is called for.

**References**

Amiel, S.A., Shewin, R.S., Simonson, D.C., Lauritano, A.A., and Tamborlane, W.V. (1986). Impaired Insulin Activity in Puberty. *New England Journal of Medicine,* 315, 215-219.

Bodenheimer, T., Lorig, K., Holman, H., and Grumbach, K. (2002). Patient self management of Chronic Disease in Primary care. *Journal of the American Medical Association,* 288, 19, 2469-2475.

Borus, J.S. (2010). Adherence Challenges in the management of type 1 diabetes in adolescents: prevention and intervention. *Current Opinion in Paediatrics* 22, 4, 405-411.

Doherty, Y., and Roberts, S. (2002). Motivational Interviewing in Diabetes Practice. *Diabetes Medicine* 19, 1-18.

Drotar, D. (2006). *Promoting adherence to medical treatment in childhood chronic illness: Concepts, methods and interventions.* Mahwah: NJ: Lawrence Erlbaum Associates.

Erikson, S.J. (2005). Brief Interventions and Motivational Interviewing with Children, Adolescents and their Parents in Paediatric Health Care settings. *Archives of Paediatric and Adolescent Medicine,* 159, 1173-1180.

International Diabetes Federation, (2003). *Cost Effective approaches to Diabetes Care and Prevention.* Brussles: International Diabetes Federation.

Ismail, K. (2008). Eating Disorders and Diabetes, *Psychiatry,* 7, 4, 179-182.

Jones, J.M., Lawson, L.L., Daneman, D., Olmstead, M.P., and Rodin, G. (2000). Eating disorders in adolescent females with and without type 1 diabetes: cross sectional study. *British Medical Journal* 320, 1563-1566.

Kalvana, T.V., Maes, S., and De Gucht, V. (2010). Interpersonal and self regulation determinants of healthy and unhealthy eating behaviour in Adolescents. *Journal of Health Psychology,* 15: 44-52.

Kendall, P., and Holmbeck, G.N. (2002). Introduction to the special section on Clinical Adolescent Psychology: Developmental Psychology and Treatment. *Journal of Consulting and Clinical Psychology,* Vol 70, 1-5.

La Greca, A.M., Follansbee, D., and Skyler, J.S. (1990). Developmental and behavioural aspects of diabetes management in youngsters. *Children's Health Care,* 19, 132-139.

Landholdt, M.A., Ribi, K., Laimbacher, K., Vollrath, M., Gnehem, H.E., and Sennhauser, F.H. (2002). Post-traumatic stress disorder in parents of children with newly diagnosed Type 1 Diabetes. *Journal of Paediatric Psychology,* 27: 647-652.

Michie, S., and Abraham, C. (2004). Interventions to change health behaviours: evidence-based or evidence-inspired? *Psychological Health,* 19, 1, 29-50.

Miller, W.R. (1983). Motivational Interviewing with Problem Drinkers. *Behavioural Psychotherapy,* 11, 147-172.

Miller, W.R., and Rollnick, S. (1991). *Motivational Interviewing: Preparing people to change addictive behaviours.* New York, Guildford Press.

Miller, W.R., and Rollnick, S. (2002). Motivational Interviewing: Preparing people for Change. New York. Guilford Press. 2nd Edition.

Naar-King, S., and Ellis, D.A. (2010). Self care for Chronic Medical Conditions. In: *Motivational Interviewing with Adolescents and Young Adults.* Sylvie Naar-King and Mariann Suarez. Pp145-150.

Rapoff, M.A. (1999). *Adherence to Paediatric Medical Regimens.* New York: Kluwer Academic/Plenum Publishers.

Ridge, K., Treasure, J., Forbes, A., Thomas, S., and Ismail, K. (2012). Themes elicited during motivational interviewing to improve glycaemic control in adults with Type 1 diabetes mellitus. *Diabetic Medicine, 29,* 1, 148-152.

Rollnick, S., Mason, P., and Butler, C. (2002). *Health behaviour change: a Guide for Practitioners.* London. Churchill-Livingstone.

Streisand, R., Swift, E., Wickman, T., Chen, R., Holmes, C. (2008). Paediatric parenting stress among parents of children with Type 1 Diabetes: the role of self-efficacy, responsibility and fear. *Journal of Paediatric Psychology, 30,* 513-521.

UKPDS (1998). UK Prospective Diabetes Study (UKPDS) Group. Intensive blood-glucose control with sulphonylureas or insulin compared with conventional treatment and the risk of complications in patients with Typ2 2 Diabetes. *Lancet.* 352: 837-853.

Weinstein, P., Harrison, R., and Benton, T. (2004). Motivating Parents to prevent caries in their young children. One Year Findings. *Journal of the American Dietetics Association,* 135: 731-738.

Wysocki, T., Taylor, A., Hough, B.S., Linscheid, T.R., Yeates, K.O., and Naglieri, J.A. (1996). Deviation from developmentally appropriate self-care autonomy; association with diabetes outcome. *Diabetes Care,* 19, 119-125.

164 Chapter 10

# Section 3

# Motivational Interviewing in the Community

*166*

# Chapter 11

# Application of Motivational Interviewing with and about Looked After Children (LAC)

## Eleanor Thomas
### *Chartered Clinical Psychologist: the Together Trust (Children's Charity)*

Motivational interviewing (MI) techniques have been described as a helpful means of bringing about behavioural change in adults in a non-confrontational way e.g. Rubak (2005. There is considerable research on working with adults with alcohol e.g. Brown and Miller (1994) and other substance misuse problems e.g. Miller and Yahne, (2003); Stotts, Schmitz, Rhoades and Grabaowski (2001). There is also an emerging body of literature on the use of MI principles with children and adolescents in health education e.g. diabetes management (Channon et al., 2007), substance misuse (McCambridge and Strang, 2004) and within educations settings e.g. Atkinson and Woods (2003); see Erickasson, Gerstle and Feldstein (2005) for a review.

This chapter focuses on the application of MI techniques to the Looked After Children (LAC) population and those caring for them. Concerns are often raised vicariously about a LAC's needs and difficulties by their carers/other involved professionals. Typically the LAC may not see a problem or if they do, may struggle to define it and seek appropriate help. To set the scene for this, the needs and risks of the LAC population will first be considered, then the application of MI with carers of LAC, then directly with LAC. Case studies will highlight key issues.

### Overview of MI and the Transtheoretical Model of Change

MI originated from work by Miller and Rollnick (1991) in their work with people who struggled to overcome addictions to alcohol and drugs and is based upon the premise that clients attending therapy are often not ready to change behaviour.

168                                    *Chapter 11*

Without a readiness to change, or if this is actively opposed, traditional therapeutic approaches can flounder as they are dismissed.

Traditionally MI has been allied to the transtheoretical model (TTM) of change first proposed by Prochaska and DiClemente (1982) which classifies readiness to change across six explicit stages. However this model has come under criticism for issues including lack of predictive utility, poor stage definition and arbitrary and unhelpful categories to which clients may be wrongly assigned e.g. Wilson and Schlam (2004). Criticism has been levelled by practitioners and researchers, including the founders of the MI approach (Miller and Rollnick, 2009), at those that assume the use of MI necessarily involves the use of the TTM e.g. West (2005).

However, there have also been consistent reports that this model can be used effectively across populations, including with disaffected young people e.g. Kittles and Atkinson (2009) and use of the TTM can be consistent with the principles of MI which include: expressing empathy, developing discrepancy between current and ideal situation, rolling with resistance and supporting self efficacy.

For these reasons, and because it can be helpful in developing awareness in those around the client of how/why they do what they do, the TTM model has been used throughout the work described in this chapter.

**Looked After Children**

LAC are defined as those children in public care who are placed with foster carers, in residential homes or with parents or other relatives. They may be subject to a full or interim care order or an emergency protection order or be accommodated under Section 20 of The Children's Act (1989) whereby their parents retain parental responsibility and consent to the placement. This population does not technically include those who are adopted, although many children within the care system have experienced the breakdown of an adoptive placement.

Children within foster placements significantly outnumber those in residential placements. Outcomes are generally more positive for children placed within a family setting compared with a residential setting, and thus these are sought initially (Care Matters, 2006). The LAC population has been increasing over the past 30 years (Department of Education, 2011), although there are geographical variations. This population is reported to have significantly increased risks of mental health problems e.g. Meltzer et al. (2003), Young Minds Foundation (2012) and are at risk of being socially excluded, e.g. Stein, 2006. This group presents with increased learning needs/difficulties in processing information, alcohol and substance misuse e.g. Ward (1998), teenage pregnancy e.g. Haydon (2003), deliberate self harm (NSPCC, 2009), truanting and school refusal, anti-social and criminal behaviour (Department for Children, Schools and Families, 2009), have a statement of special educational needs (Ford, Vostanis, Meltzer and Goodman, 2007), conduct or oppositional defiant disorder (ibid) and (CSE) - child sexual

## Chapter 11

exploitation – (CEOP, 2011) and gang involvement. Some CSE gangs seem to focus their recruitment upon the LAC population, possibly because their risk profile makes them more amenable and less resistant.

In summary, risk is significantly greater for these young people and the nature and causes of these risks are multifarious and subsequently complex and challenging to manage. In the long term, those who have been in care are over-represented among teenage parents, drug users and prisoners (Care Matters, 2006). Outcomes are poor even when compared to other children with roughly comparable backgrounds and problems (ibid). Moreover the LAC population is associated with far fewer resilience and protective factors making risk reduction, proactive support and therapeutic work far more challenging. Furthermore those LAC who present with the most alarming risks are often those with the greatest unwillingness or insight to acknowledge or discuss these risks. Typically they are resistant to attempts by others to change what they see as acceptable, often culturally validated, behaviour.

### Carers

Those employed to provide care for LAC are foster carers and residential social care workers (RSCW). They are responsible for day to day provision of 'corporate parenting' responsibilities. This includes helping young people to keep safe and enjoy positive physical and mental health. As such active efforts are made to promote healthy lifestyles, reduce the likelihood of illicit drug and alcohol use and promote positive self-esteem and coping strategies in the face of adversity. In the UK progress against these and other goals are generally guided by the Five Outcomes proposed within the Every Child Matters guidance (2004). These are: be healthy, stay safe, enjoy and achieve, make a positive contribution and achieve economic wellbeing.

### Placements

LAC placed within residential care homes generally present with more complex needs and higher risk. They may have experienced multiple placement breakdowns. Like LAC in foster placements they are significantly more likely than their non-cared for peers to present with dysfunctional attachment and interpersonal styles. While 'adaptive' in neglectful, unsuitable and/or abusive environments, these styles can create significant difficulties for them, their peers and carers in a new care environment. They may lack sufficient communication skills and adaptive coping strategies to make sense of their experiences and form positive, pro-social relationships.

Within a residential setting RSCWs will generally try and work as proactively as possible to reduce risks and promote positive, adaptive behaviours. However, crises frequently occur and reactive, crisis-response measures are often used. Guidance and regulations on how LAC can be supported in Children's Homes, as

## 170 Chapter 11

well as in foster placements, is carefully structured (Children's homes regulations, HM Gov, 2011; National Minimum Standards for care homes, 2011; Fostering regulations, 2011, both Department of Education). These guidelines generally advise against restrictive measures. So, for example, it is generally forbidden to lock the doors in children's homes to prevent escape/absconsion. The balance between keeping to these regulations whilst adhering to other guidance which stress the importance of keeping vulnerable LAC safe from harm and exploitation can be a difficult one for all involved in supporting LAC.

Clearly the role for carers in both residential and fostering contexts is very challenging when engaging with this high risk and low resilience population.

### The Role of the Clinical Psychologist with LAC

Theoretically all LAC have access to mental health support within the NHS, whether it is via a generic CAMHS (Child and Adolescent Mental Health Service) or a specialist LAC provision. Additionally, carers typically have access to consultation and training by clinical psychologists and other mental health professionals to help them understand and support the needs of LAC.

There are a wide range of reasons that a LAC may be referred for psychological care including diagnosable mental health conditions such as depression or an anxiety disorder such as post traumatic stress disorder. More ambiguous referrals relating to interpersonal difficulties, which are typically underpinned by poor quality early attachment relationships, are common. Ultimately it appears that concerns about 'problem' or 'challenging behaviour', including deliberate self harm, are likely to drive the majority of referrals. This may be with the intent that the young person is seen for therapeutic intervention to explore the issues which underpin these behaviours. Alternatively/in addition, carers may be seen for consultation to provide advice and support in managing the behaviour and coping with its impact.

Unsurprisingly, it is commonplace for LAC to be referred for a psychological intervention and not have a strong desire to attend for assessment and treatment. This may be because:

- They do not believe that what they do is problematic most or all of the time

- They do believe that what they do is problematic but for a variety of reasons they do not wish to change

- There is acknowledgement of a problem/disadvantages as to how they are coping but this is coupled with a belief that there is no-one capable of understanding or helping with the problems

- There is a desire to change but a refusal to engage with services, perhaps because of negative experiences in the past such as lack of trust. For example, the idea that 'psychologists are bad... one wrote the report that took me from my family'.

*Chapter 11*                                                                    *171*

Underpinning the high risk profile of this population are important features relevant to the use of an MI approach. They include:

- An emerging sense of identity, especially around adolescence, and emerging language skills to make sense of and describe this - common to all young people.

- Repeated and ongoing exposure to unhelpful/maladaptive messages and role models.

This population are more likely than their peers to have:

- Disrupted processing and reasoning abilities. This is relevant when they are making decisions, weighing up pros and cons. This is because of the now well documented impact of abuse, neglect and trauma upon brain development e.g. Perry and Pollard (1998).

- A history of feeling disenfranchised and disempowered both within the family and the care system.

- Considerable experience of being told what they do is wrong/bad and that they must stop/change, without such informational feedback having any influence on their behaviour.

**Service Context**

In this author's experience, because of the paucity of resources, LAC with complex needs may be denied treatment from a CAMHS. This may be because they do not meet the eligibility criteria due to their complex and multi-faceted difficulties. However due to inconsistent geographical provision of highly specialised mental health services – referred to as "Tier 3 Services" - they may also struggle to access this provision.

Many residential and foster carers talk of 'battles with the system' to get a LAC referred and be seen by a mental health professional. Related to this is that the preferred and relevant intervention may well be one that requires long-term professional involvement. Therapeutic interventions such as Dialetical Behaviour Therapy (Linehan, 1993), Theraplay (Jernberg and Booth, 2001) and Dyadic Developmental Psychotherapy (Hughes, 2007) which are often used with LAC can have extensive treatment times, especially the latter (Golding and Hughes, 2012). Service structures and funding are not always supportive of such long-term interventions.

The barriers to successful engagement in a therapeutic process are therefore significant. As such the role of a clinical psychologist with LAC is often to support and 'skill up' the carer(s) supporting the child because this can ensure greater consistency and therefore effectiveness in a support package.

# Chapter 11

172

## Application of MI with Carers

*"Sometimes it's just so hard to know what's going on in their head and if you're doing the right thing. I often think I might be failing her"*

Quotation from a foster carer in a consultation

Given that much of a Professionals work with LAC takes place indirectly via their carers, it is often focused around exploration and development of the carer's understanding of the reasons for the young person's presentation. Specifically:

- Developing the carers curiosity and understanding of why the young person operate as they do

- Understanding and accepting the impact of early life experiences upon current functioning

- Enhancing the carers empathy for the young person's struggle

- Enhancing the carer's sense of self-efficacy as a carer; that they can play a valuable role in supporting the young person through their difficulties

- Developing a plan for how they might implement this increased awareness and maintain it in the face of likely challenges.

## Case Study of a Foster Carer

Suzanne had been the foster carer of Hannah, 15 years of age, for 9 months at the time of referral and was finding it hard to cope with Hannah's refusal to engage in school work. Hannah was the subject of a full Care Order - meaning the Local Authority had parental responsibility.

As ex-teachers Suzanne and her husband knew of the importance of having good qualifications and were alarmed at Hannah's disinterest and regular refusal to do any homework. They tried to talk it through with her but this could escalate into arguments and did not result in change. They tried to explore underlying emotional difficulties. This also led to them feeling 'stuck'. Suzanne seemed to be in the contemplation stage of the TTM (Transtheoretical model). A consultation with the clinical psychologist was arranged. During this Suzanne's attitudes towards the value of Hannah gaining qualifications were explored. What follows are excerpts from the consultation. An important caveat is that, as within any therapeutic approach, tone of voice is a crucial element of communication. This cannot be inferred from transcripts alone. Throughout this (and subsequent transcripts) it is important to note that vocal tones and body language attempted to convey acceptance and empathy to the client.

# Chapter 11

173

|  |  |
|---|---|
| **Hannah's story** | **Suzanne's story** |
| As soon as I get up I know they're going to nag me. On and on. Whatever. | Why won't she realise how important it is to have qualifications? It's vital, especially these days |
| Listening to them takes my mind off the horrible stuff but when I try and explain what's going on the words get muddled in my head and don't come out how I want. | She just doesn't seem to care. |
| | I know she's not good at thinking about the future and consequences because of how she's developed. |
| I can't explain myself. | That means she can't see the effect that no qualifications will have for her. That really worries me. |
| I don't care about school. What's the point? I can't do it and I never will. Doing it just makes me feel more stupid. | We have parental responsibility. That means we need to do what it takes to help her get qualifications. |
| Why do people say they care when no-one really does? | |

Suzanne

*Kids really need a good education these days. There is so much competition out there but Hannah doesn't care. She is so stuck in her world that she can't think about the future but we know what this can mean for her.*

Psychologist

*So you're both worried about her future and what it will be like if she doesn't apply herself to school work now. You see yourselves as responsible for ensuring this happens.* (Summarising and reflecting)

Suzanne

*Yes we do. It's our job as foster carers. We especially worry about education.*

Psychologist

*So you believe that you would not be doing your job properly, that you would be letting her down, if you did not push the homework. (Summarising and reflecting)*

Suzanne

*Yes absolutely. I wonder if really we may not be the best carers for her. Maybe we just can't give her what she needs.*

Psychologist

*You really aren't sure how to help her best are you? And that's caused you to doubt your caring skills. (Summarising)*

174                                   *Chapter 11*

*We've talked about the really difficult early life that Hannah had and you mentioned that you feel overwhelmed thinking about the abuse she suffered. I wonder what impact that carrying that round all the time has on her ability to get on with day to day tasks now.*

Suzanne            *I think it must be massive. What happened was so terrible; it went on for so long. I think it must be in her head a lot of the time.*

Psychologist       *The psychologist then shared with Suzanne a formulation incorporating abuse experiences, attachment relationships and Hannah's role within the family.*

*It's hard for us to imagine what it must be like to carry round those memories, those experiences isn't it? They may invade her mind and disrupt her concentration at any time. Some of the behaviours you describe suggest that she is often reminded of the abuse by a random trigger and gets overwhelmed by it. When that happens our brain goes into 'fight, flight or freeze' mode and our options are limited.*
(Reflection and formulation)

The psychologist then discussed at length the neurobiological impact of abuse and anxiety and the impact on cognitive functioning.

Suzanne            *I suppose when that happens she can't focus on.....well anything really. Poor Hannah, she must think about it all the time.*

Psychologist       *It sounds as though she might be so pre-occupied with those thoughts and feelings that it is almost impossible for her to concentrate on some activities in the present. That includes when you talk with her sometimes, it includes school work.*

Suzanne            *Yes, thinking about your homework when you have all that in your head must be impossible. I didn't think of it like that. But all that won't help her in the future when she has no qualifications. That could make a bad start worse. She's already so disadvantaged.*

Psychologist       *She's had a very difficult start in life and you are both trying to compensate for that. You are doing the best you can for her. When we think about what Hannah has been through and how that has affected her relationship skills, communication skills and general understanding of the world we can begin to imagine what might be going on for her.*

*The* psychologist made reference to Maslow's hierarchy of needs (Maslow, 1943) with which Suzanne was familiar.
*I wonder which needs Hannah is most focused on meeting.*
(rolling with resistance, continuing to develop discrepancy)

Suzanne

*Hmmm, I think she is stuck at trying to meet her safety needs. She doesn't feel safe does she? I mean, she knows she's safe here, she must know that by now, but if she was abused for that long at home, I mean…she must have been so scared. And helpless.*

Psychologist

*I think you could be right there. I think she may often feel very unsafe. This environment, its still relatively new to her isn't it? She spent the vast majority of her life in an unsafe environment and she may have a constant drive to seek safety. I'm imagining feeling that unsafe and what I would be able to think about on top of that. Would I be able to choose matching outfits, eat proper meals, think about homework? I'm not sure I would.*
(Supports self-efficacy and continues to develop discrepancy)

Suzanne

*Yes. She can't think about school. Maybe we've been going about this the wrong way. I didn't really think about it like that. You know, talking to you, I think we need to stop bothering with forcing the school issue; give up some of that fight. Its not helping is it?*

Psychologist

*It sounds like she can't manage it with everything else she has going on. You've been trying your best to do what's right and I think you've both done so well for her, you've done your best. We can think together about how you could both tweak what you're doing a little to work at the level we imagine she's stuck.*
(Supports self-efficacy, introduces change talk and develops collaborative plans)

**Intervention and Outcome**

Following this meeting the psychologist, foster carer and her supervising social worker developed a plan to change Suzanne and her husband's approach in subtle ways. To get to this point the psychologist used the core principals of motivational interviewing to move the carer from a contemplative state to one of determinism for action, so that this plan could be developed. A range of collaborative, therapeutic skills consistent with the MI were used in this process.

This meeting was followed up with:

- Another consultation to foster carers

- Consultation and supervision to their supervising social worker

*176* *Chapter 11*

- Telephone liaison with CAMHS

- A consultation summary letter with handouts appended as further information.

- A post-consultation evaluation form completed by foster carer and social worker

The foster carer evaluated the intervention as 'very helpful' and rated her ability to make changes as 'significantly increased'. This suggests her sense of self-efficacy as a foster carer was improved via this relatively brief and short-term intervention. The ratings of her social worker were consistent with this.

In many ways this was an 'easy' intervention because the foster carer was in the contemplative phase and was relatively open to consideration of alternatives. This may have been because she had experienced repeated failures; certainly she had been desperate for the meeting and had become frustrated with the lack of involvement from other services.

There are many other situations in which this approach will require a greater level of input when the foster carer is at a pre-contemplative state and, for various reasons, is resistant to a change of perspective and approach with their foster child.

## Other Ways of Using the Principles of MI with the Carers of LAC

*Consultation to a staff team*

The following describes consultation with a team of residential care workers and their assistant manager and manager.

MI skills can be invaluable in exploring the experiences of a staff team as well as individual professionals and carers. The application of these skills at different stages of staff team change as assessed within the TTM is illustrated in figure 1 (page 178) with respect to the case study of Sophie.

It is important to facilitate/support the team to explore key issues in a non-judgemental manner so that the skills of MI are role-modelled with the team. This means that all present can experience firsthand the impact of active listening skills and a curious and empathic approach to their predicament.

This can of course be very challenging for a clinical psychologist, or any professional, as the desire to dispel unhelpful assumptions and attitudes can feel overwhelming at times. In addition risk and safeguarding issues must be dealt with appropriately and in accordance with policy and legislation. A key part of this process is the validation of each team member's experience of interacting with the young person, their complex needs, how they meet these needs and what behaviour is hardest to understand/empathise with.

The value of this validation is that it encourages open exploration of the attitudes and beliefs that underpin care approaches; failure to explore these can increase the chance that unhelpful ones persist unnoticed and continue to inform unhelpful interactions/care approaches. Staff members can present with a range of value judgements about a behaviour or a young person; this is especially the case if the young person has assaulted a staff member (seriously or recently) or if they are engaged in a pattern of behaviour that (some of) the team find difficult or abhorrent e.g. restricted eating, cutting, sexually harmful behaviour towards other young people, bullying.

The use of MI skills can help raise awareness of these judgements and their influence on how the staff member interacts with the young person. It can help the staff member to approach the young person in a more helpful way as they attempt to provide support and manage risks.

Typically residential staff and foster carers report finding it helpful when they are supported to reflect on:

- What has happened when they've tried to change a behaviour (themselves and with a young person)

- What had constituted helpful vs. unhelpful support from others (in both scenarios)

- Their ideal outcome for the young person: if this differs from realistic outcomes a formulation of need may help determine realistic expectations

- How they think they are most likely to achieve that outcome

The author has found it constructive to link staff/carers own experiences of being cared for (linking to their attachment histories) with their beliefs about how young people should best be cared for. It is imperative that this is done in a safe way and thus typically with a single carer or very small group.

The author has also found that staff and carers often confuse MI skills such as active listening with lack of boundaries and exculpation of behaviour they see as inappropriate; they seem to find it reassuring that this is not the case. It is important to emphasise to the staff team that there are different times for different skills. Active listening skills are appropriate in one situation, but in the event of a significant risk then crisis management skills are required.

## Case Study in Holding a Residential Staff Team Consultation

Sophie, 13, was admitted on an emergency basis into a residential children's home. It soon emerged that she was a regular user of cannabis and sometimes self harmed by cutting her arms. This vignette focuses upon the cannabis use. The team were concerned by the risks they thought she was exposed to when seeking dealers to purchase from and smoke, cannabis with.

In accordance with the service protocol, the following happened:

**Sophie's story**

They have no idea. They think smoking weed is bad. It isn't, pretty much everyone I know does it and they are not bad!

I'm not going mental with it and I don't really care if it gets in the way of education.

They say they care about me and that's why they go on. They don't care! They don't know me!

It helps me cope with feeling crap and it stops me cutting myself so it's got to be a good thing.

**The staff team's story**

We know she smokes cannabis. She doesn't even really try and hide it.

It's bad for you. It's linked to serious mental health problems, like psychosis. She reckons it's safe but it definitely isn't.

Her social worker's been on at us again, they might end the placement if we don't get on top of the cannabis issue.

We've got to stop her doing it. That's our job. We care about her.

**Figure 1:** Pattern of Support

*Use of questionnaires*

The clinical psychologist created a simple form (completed for Sophie) and carers were requested to record their concerns about a child, their level of confidence in managing the child's needs, their desire for help and their perception of to what extent change in their caring capacity/understanding was possible. Additional information was sought at the discretion of the clinical psychologist depending on the nature of the referral. This commonly includes the 'Carer Questionnaire' compiled by members of the network of Clinical Psychologists working with Looked After and Adopted Children (CP-LAAC).

*Intervention with the Team* - The consultation

A session took place with the majority of the staff team to explore their concerns. The following are excerpts of the conversation to highlight key issues:

*"She's not safe, anything could be happening to her out there. We have to keep her safe".*

*"She seems to smoke a lot of cannabis. It's always in the news that it can cause psychosis. We are not stopping that".*

*"If we keep reporting her missing from home then it's going to cause issues with the police and her social worker....more strategy meetings"*

*"She's out till late, what if she gets into trouble with these dealers?....they could do anything to her"*

*"When she self harms it's superficial. She always shows us where the cuts are.... but what if she cut too deep by accident?"*

**Summarising and Reflecting the Concerns**

The clinical psychologist reflected back the dilemma that the team faced: they felt compelled to keep her safe, as agreed with the local authority, but could not compel Sophie to do what they believed would keep her safe; she would not comply. This created feelings of panic among some of the team and there appeared to be a split within the team in terms of how people dealt with her, with some challenging her less and being perceived to condone her risky behaviours and others being inflexible/hard lined in their approach, driven by the belief that 'we must have rigid, consistent boundaries'.

**The Path to Contemplation**

A team meeting, arranged for one week later was used to extend the exploration of the different approaches to the management of Sophie's behaviour.

A collaborative formulation was completed on a flip chart, with staff helping the clinical psychologist to complete it. It focused upon functioning in the here-and-now but linked back to key life events. This is crucial because it allows for an

180                                          *Chapter 11*

educational element to come in which is vital in helping to reformulate some of the negative errors of attribution that can be in evidence. For example, the team found it helpful to consider life through Sophie's eyes as a toddler and young child in her early environments. This helped them make links between her early care and the strategies she used in the present to meet her needs and cope with demands.

The formulation was complicated by the fact that, as so often with LAC, there were no definitive accounts of some key parts of Sophie's childhood and so the team had to tolerate uncertainty when formulating how her current presentation linked to early, adverse experiences and attachment relationships. This ability to tolerate uncertainty, risk and the fact that we cannot always "fix things" is crucial in helping a team develop a balanced understanding of their roles and responsibilities. However it must always be counterbalanced by reasons to be hopeful for change/improvement.

This process also helped the team members to reflect on the pros and cons of Sophie's alarming coping strategies and also of their responses to her strategies, both in terms of behavioural theories e.g. operant conditioning and reinforcement schedules, and in terms of attachment theories.

## Preparing for Change and Developing Action Plans

The team struggled to explore the pros and cons of Sophie's behaviour with her and so Sophie often appeared alienated and was unable to talk with some of the team members about what thought processes underpinned her self harm and cannabis use.

The staff were also more aware of team dynamics which created inconsistent approaches to care. However, members were feeling increasingly competent as a team to make some changes to their approach, changes which they believed were consistent with expectations of other agencies e.g. Local Authority social worker, Provision Commissioner, Police, Youth Offending Team.

The plan was to:

- Run training on active listening skills with an emphasis on role play

- Revisit the formulation in subsequent team meetings to ensure it continued to guide the staff team's approach

- Ensure Sophie had regular slots to explore her coping strategies with a staff member using MI principles (non-judgemental, curious and empathic approach).Examples of specific skills included summarising and reflecting, wondering 'Columbo-style' (McNamara, 2009, p 29) with Sophie about the benefits and costs of the behaviour, rolling with resistance and avoiding arguments and power battles

- Make available the option for Sophie to meet with the clinical psychologist if appropriate/helpful

- Share the formulation with Sophie, and the wider multi-agency team so that there was greater consistency in approach

- Increase the level of proactive planning so that key risk times were populated with forced choice options of activities inconsistent with the risky behaviour

- Monitor and review effect of action plan implementation

## Reviews and Outcomes

The team worked enthusiastically and the frequency of occurrence of high risk behaviours dropped significantly. The majority of the team and Sophie reported that interactions were calmer and more positive. The team reported an increased confidence in their behavioural management and care skills.

Relapse occurred with regard to both cannabis use and self harm during an episode when Sophie absconded and was missing all night. She also disclosed that she had unprotected sex with a stranger. When this relapse occurred team members responded in a variety of ways. Some felt let down and frustrated and some felt that it indicated that the change in approach was not sufficient or effective. Others were able to reflect that it fitted with Sophie's default coping styles and attributed the relapse to a major stressor - a distressing family contact.

The ongoing use of MI skills in a further team meeting helped the team express and explore these issues. All reported that they continued to believe that the formulation was still the most appropriate working hypothesis to explain Sophie's behaviour. This shared agreement highlights the importance of exploring realistic expectations, which can polarise between desperation for a panacea i.e. the 'magic wand' and hopeless/dismissive attitudes i.e. 'what's the point, nothing can change'. Helping a team to consider the impact of their expectations has proved to be a pivotal element of intervention; it certainly seems to improve a team's experience and judgement of an intervention as measured by post-intervention questionnaire. Sophie also reported more positive interactions with the team.

## Other Indirect Uses of MI Skills

MI skills can also be used in group supervision meetings. The author has used MI techniques with management groups, at school staff meetings and when meeting with fostering social work teams. Positive feedback was generally received. MI techniques also work well when supervising an individual staff team member, foster carer or professional, e.g. teacher, with regard to their approach/engagement with a young person when it is not possible or desirable for the clinical psychologist to work directly with that young person.

Consistent feedback is received from such professionals that using MI principles to inform their interactions with young people results in significant improvements in the quality and subsequent quantity of interactions. The interactions no longer feel like battles or fights. This feedback is consistent with findings in the MI literature.

Figure 2 is a diagrammatic representation of how Motivational Interviewing (MI) and the Trans-Theoretical Model (TTM) model of change can be used with a staff team who care for look after children. It demonstrates how different techniques may be helpful at different stages.

**Figure 2:** Diagrammatic Representation of How Motivational Interviewing Skills and the Transtheoretical Model of Change Can Be Used with a Staff Team Who Care for LAC

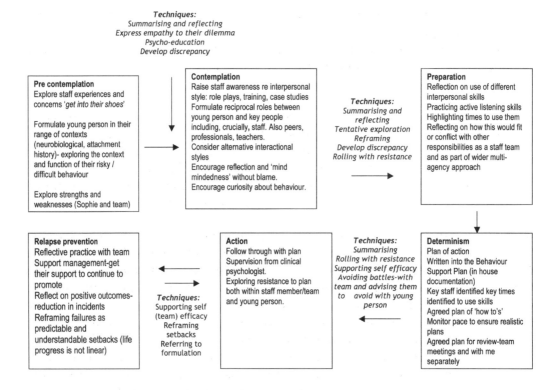

### Case study: a Resistant Residential Team

Soon after commencing post the author was invited to meet with a residential staff team who were working closely with a non-directive play therapist. This therapist left soon after by coincidence but it is possible that some staff may have thought that the newly appointed clinical psychologist was supplanting the role of play therapist. Some of team were strongly in favour of non-directive play therapy and perhaps sceptical of a psychological approach. The way in which the two professionals worked differed significantly, although there was overlap in how they viewed the needs of looked after children.

*Chapter 11*                                                                                    *183*

*Building Relationships with the Team*

The clinical psychologist attended several team meetings, initially informally and later to provide consultation around particular issues, typically the behaviour of a young person.

The clinical psychologist began to notice signs of resistance to their recommendations and involvement: these included:

- Some staff presenting as disengaged in team consultations, e.g. texting on their phone at the time

- A failure to follow through with some recommendations

- Jokey comments within meetings, framed as 'playful' but which hinted at concern, a lack of understanding or negative opinions about the role and presence of the clinical psychologist

- Evidence that although several staff members responded positively to formulations or recommendations there was no subsequent shift in attitude (towards a behaviour or issue), as such things did not change in that instance

- Staff not turning up for/not engaging in training provided specially for the service

*The Way Forward*

Initially the subtlety of the resistance made it difficult to respond to. It seemed as though it was being tacitly supported by the manager of the service who seemed to role model it to the team in a manner which was both almost imperceptible but powerful.

Several attempts were made to explore the perceived mistrust from the manager towards the clinical psychologist. These included using curiosity, a standard part of a reflective approach particularly with a pre-contemplative staff member e.g. *"I wonder if it might feel quite different working with a clinical psychologist"*. This was met with denial. It seemed that continuing with this approach could lead to the entrenchment of mistrust. Therefore a motivational interviewing approach was used with the staff team – initially on an individual basis and then with the group. Concurrently it was important to demonstrate the potential value of the Clinical Psychologist's role for both for the team and young people they cared for.

*The use of MI Techniques with the Team*

Although a minority of team members were clearly very positive about the role of the clinical psychologist and what it could bring to the team, a stance was taken to assume the team in general was functioning at the pre-contemplative state described in the TTM.

184 *Chapter 11*

*Activities with the pre-contemplative team*

- Setting up an informal and accessible referral system for consultations at team meeting; quick response time to requests

- Team formulation sessions of a young person with the aim of linking their history and internal working model (IWM; their attachment style) to their current coping strategies and behaviour

- Exploration and validation of staff experience of behaviour; consideration of the reciprocal roles that staff and young people operate within.

- Access to training on the impact of abuse and neglect on the developing brain, attachment styles and IWM, the mixed cognitive profiles of LAC, mental health labels, self harm

- Support and advice around positive behaviour support practices

- Opportunities to provide verbal and written feedback on the service they received

- Individual meetings with key workers exploring their views and concerns re their key child

- Specific activities of value such as an assessment of neuropsychological functioning and attachment style for a young person, attendance at multi agency review meetings, telephone calls and letters with/to other professionals

- Debriefing the team following significant incidents

*Addressing Resistance*

Here follows a conversation between the clinical psychologist and a resistant member of staff, *Tom* about a child *David* about whom they had previously met.

David had become increasingly withdrawn and had reported feeling depressed. They talked about how Tom could follow this up. Previously Tom had presented with covert resistance in team meetings and in casual interactions with the clinical psychologist. David had been snapping at and bullying two younger children which had been separately addressed.

Tom  *I tried to have the chat you suggested, but it didn't work. He just walked out and said he wanted to play on the Playstation. I tried again later and he just talked over me.*

Psychologist  *So it didn't go according to plan (summarising), I sense that you expected more from that.*

*Chapter 11*  185

Tom

*Yeah! I was all ready after our chat and the plan we talked about. I waited for a time when there was just him in, no other kids, and I thought he'd be pleased but he seemed like he wasn't bothered. I'm not saying you don't know your job, I'm sure you're good but I can't see the point in it now really.*

Psychologist

*And you feel disappointed, perhaps like we got it wrong? I suppose part of you might think it's a waste of time talking with me now? That would make sense (Reflecting, wondering, rolling with resistance) I know I don't work here like you do, several days a week. It makes sense that you would know far more about these young people than I do. In that way Tom, you are the expert. (Validation, supporting self efficacy)*

Tom

*Don't get me wrong I've got nothing against you. But maybe...I mean if he doesn't want to talk about it I think I should just leave it; I don't want to stress him out and I might get it wrong.*

Psychologist

*Well first of all please don't think I will take offence if you tell me you don't agree with what I'm saying, or don't understand me. I won't. I much prefer you to let me know like this, then at least I know how you're feeling. That helps a lot. (Clarification, reframing conflict/disagreement)*

*Now about David, it sounds like you've been thinking that his response was a clear sign that talking about it was uncomfortable, that he wanted you to back off. And if he wants you to back off, if it really bothers him, then the last thing you want to do is bring it up. You're worried that you might mess it up and make it worse? (summarising, reflecting, wondering)*

Tom

*Yes. Yes, that's it. These kids have been through so much. What if I say something that brings stuff back for him. But then.....*

Psychologist

*So it sounds as though you are treading very carefully around David. Not wanting to make things harder..and yet? You are unsure about this? (Reflecting, wondering)*

Tom

*Yes. Well I don't want to make things harder for him but at the end of the day when he's in the real world people will say whatever to him and he'll have to deal with it won't he? So maybe we're not doing him any favours.*

Psychologist

*Aaah, this seems important. I think what you're saying is that you're concerned that this home is a bubble for him, which is*

186                             *Chapter 11*

                                      *unlike how people operate 'out there' in shops, College and on the street. You worry that David might explode in response to someone saying the sort of things that some staff here avoid saying. That he's being protected here and that won't help him out in the future.*
*(Reflecting, wondering)*

Tom

*Yeah. That's right. People out there don't talk like we do; they won't let these kids get away with what they do in here. Like when he bullies Connor. He wouldn't get away with that at school and he doesn't do it there. The parents would go mad at him.*

Psychologist

*So maybe a sense here is that David is getting away with things he shouldn't do? But you're not sure how best to work with him? (summarising, reflecting a dilemma, avoiding confrontation/ telling what to do)*

Tom

*Yes. I think. I don't know. Then I read his file and I feel really bad for him. His family treated him like crap. They just don't want to know. Maybe I'm getting it wrong.*

Psychologist

*This sounds tough for you Tom, and the team. These kids present us with really tricky dilemmas don't they? And David is no exception.*
*(Reflecting, being with discomfort, empathy for Tom's situation)*

*He had this really difficult start in life. Parents drinking heavily, taking drugs and fighting. He was stuck, a helpless baby in the middle of it, never sure if someone would come when he cried, never sure if they would be sober, high or straight. Nothing was predictable for him, he probably felt unsafe most of the time.*

*He had to learn to be very watchful of carers and do what he could to get his needs met, even if it was at the expense of his brothers. He may have ceased noticing some of his needs if they were repeatedly not met and so it might be hard for him, even now, to work out what's going on inside and what he needs to sort that out.*
*(Formulation)*

*Now he's out of that environment but those strategies can persist, even though he's been here two years. So he can make us all feel as though we are the unavailable and abandoning carers, even when we try not so hard not to be. That's even when we are doing our best to help, like I think you are now Tom. I think you are doing the best job you can for him with all the resources*

*Chapter 11*  187

> *you have, just like David is doing the best he can. But it's such a challenging job and that's why we can all feel a little hopeless and overwhelmed at times.*
> *(Validation, normalisation, supporting self efficacy)*

Tom
> *You're telling me! But hearing that I feel proper sad for David. That is so unfair, what he's been through.*

Psychologist
> *You care for him and his past upsets you because you care.*
> *(Reflecting)*
>
> *Being able to care, having empathy is a vital part of what you do. I don't think anyone can do this job well without that and I think you do so many things well with David*
> *(supporting self efficacy)*
>
> *I think there are more things we can do to help him make sense of his past, and how he copes now. He is likely to find those things difficult, especially if they are a change from his normal conversations. But that may not mean that he doesn't want someone to notice his struggles and talk with him, it may mean we need to think about how you do that from a different angle. I think you would have lots of ideas about that. What do you think?*
> *(supporting self efficacy, developing discrepancy)*

Tom
> *Yeah. Maybe not approach him directly. He loves his rap music I could start a conversation like that. Especially in the car. He loves going out for a drive with staff and putting one of those CDs on, he talks more in the car.*

Psychologist
> *You know it sounds like you already have some great ideas, and kids do tend to talk more in the car. Maybe it's the lack of eye contact, who knows.*
> *How about we talk about more informal options for you approaching these things with him and you let me know how realistic you think these plans are?*
> *(supporting self efficacy, introducing change talk)*

Although this conversation progressed positively, versions of it were repeated in the months that followed although Tom seemed less resistant to working with the clinical psychologist after this point. A crucial factor seemed to be the use of a formulation of David's needs that enabled Tom to relate David's past to specific current presentation. The formulation presented here is significantly truncated but the full version made more explicit links and seemed to chime very much with Tom and his colleagues as it reflected specific comments and actions by David. This had the effect of increasing Tom and the team's trust in the value of the clinical psychologist as someone who 'might just get it'.

188                           *Chapter 11*

*Follow up*

Not long after, a change in the assistant manager seemed to intensify in some respects the covert resistance within one faction of the team who, perhaps coincidentally, were all male. This included Tom. Not long after, the manager left the service and although she had begun to speak in increasingly positive terms about the role and value of the clinical psychologist, it seemed that some covert resistance remained.

The clinical psychologist decided to run, with a social work colleague, a two day training course on attachment specifically for residential management teams, and invited the assistant manager. This was an amended version of the two day attachment training that all staff are invited to attend, although management teams typically do not - due to work demands. The training was deliberately focused on imagining the early lives of LAC, via case studies and the young people the attendees work with, and acknowledging the difficult emotions this raised for those in attendance.

During and following this training the assistant manager reported a significant shift in his understanding of how attachment needs manifest in the behaviour of the young people at the home. He rated the training as excellent and valuable and wished all his team could attend soon. In some respects he became a champion for promoting the link between negative past experiences and current difficulties to help his team make sense of complex presentations. He also presented as increasingly interested in working with the clinical psychologist. Over time this seemed to permeate the attitudes of his team.

In this final example, the training course seemed to work at the pre-contemplative level, after which different MI techniques were employed to build upon the shift in attitudes towards both the value of clinical psychology and the most helpful ways to support the young people. This work is ongoing and whilst teams and individual staff members will move around the TTM, different MI techniques can be correspondingly employed to support them in their work.

**Summary and Concluding Observations**

Working with a high risk group of children and young people can be emotionally draining and burn out among residential care staff, foster carers and professionals can be high. This may in part be a function of the expectations people have for LAC and for their role in changing behaviour and making a difference. While such positive expectations are laudable and vital in this area, there is clearly a place for balanced expectations which do not engender hopelessness or regular frustration and feelings of being let down.

One of the many challenges for a clinical psychologist working with residential staff teams and foster carers is the need to identify and then change discreet attributional errors and unhelpful attitudes. Training can be successful but cannot

*Chapter 11*

fully address individual sources of resistance/misunderstanding and does not typically allow for lengthy consideration of a specific child.

This chapter describes i) how MI skills can be used in a variety of settings with those that care for LAC and ii) how their use can result in significant positive shifts in the care practices of those that support young people who are sometimes hard to empathise with and whose behaviour can be hard to support and understand.

In an era of emphasis on evidence-based practice incorporating outcome measurement and sometimes payment by results it is important for clinicians to gather data to demonstrate efficacy and impact. This can be difficult in cases where there are multiple, complex factors influencing behaviour. However, it is possible. The evidence can be 'hard' empirical outcome data such as incidents of aggressive behaviour, number of absconsions, psychometric data and so on. The evidence can also consist of 'softer' outcomes measures such as quantified judgements regarding progress towards a goal, e.g. how well a young person or a team member/carer feel they are coping with an issue, scaled from 1-10 (goal-based outcomes, Law, 2013).

When working indirectly via primary carers the progress a young person can make can be measured not only by behavioural indicators but also by shifts in staff or carer's beliefs about the following:

- the extent to which they believe they understand the behaviour
- the extent to which they believe they can manage the behaviour
- their beliefs about the possibility of change
- their ability to reflect upon progress to date
- their commitment to action plans to change behaviour

These can be evaluated via simply constructed questionnaires and rating scales. Although subjective, they are helpful in attempting to assess change in attitudes and expectations.

## References

Atkinson, C. & Woods, K. (2003). Motivational Interviewing Strategies for Disaffected Secondary School Students: a case example. *Educational Psychology in Practice,* 19(1), 49-64.

Brown, J. M. &. Miller, W.R. (1994). Impact of Motivational Interviewing of participation and outcome in residential alcoholism treatment. *Psychology of Addictive Behaviours,* 7, 211-218.

CEOP. (2011). *Out of Mind, Out of Sight: Breaking down the barriers to looked after children risk sexual exploitation.*

## Chapter 11

Channon, S.J., Huws-Thomas, M.V., Rollnick, S., Cannings-John, R.L., Rogers, C., & Gregory, J.W. (2007). A multicenter randomized controlled trial of motivational interviewing in teenagers with diabetes. *Diabetes Care,* 1390-1395.

Department for Children, Schools and Families. (2009). Children looked after in England (including adoption and care leavers) year ending 31 March 2009.

Department of Education. (2011). Children's Homes: National Minimum Standards. HM Government.

Department of Education. (2011). Fostering Services: National Minimum Standards. HM Government.

Department of Education. (2011). *Children looked after by local authorities in England:* year ending 31 March 2011.

Department for Education and Skills. (2004). Every Child Matters: Change for Children. HM Government.

Department for Education and Skills. (2006). *Care Matters:Transforming the Lives of Children and Young People in Care.* HM Government.

Erickson, S.J., Gerstle, M. & Feldstein, S.W. (2005). Brief Interventions and Motivational Interviewing With Children, Adolescents and Their Parents in Pediatric Health Care Settings: A Review. *Archive of Pediatric Adolescent Medicine.* 159(12), 1173-1180.

Ford, T., Vostanis, P., Meltzer, H., & Goodman, R. (2007). Psychiatric disorder among British looked after children by local authorities: comparison with children living in private households. *British Journal of Psychiatry,* 190, 319-325.

Golding, K., & Hughes, D. (2012). *Creating Loving Attachments. Parenting with PACE to Nurture Confidence and Security in the Troubled Child.* Jessica Kingsley Publishers.

Haydon, D. (2003). *Teenage Pregnancy and Looked After Children / Care Leavers.* London: Resource for Teenage Pregnancy Co-ordinators. Barnardos.

HM Government. The Children Act. (1989). London: HMSO.

HM Government. Tyhe Children's Homes (Amendment) Regulations. (2011). London HMSO.

Hughes, D. (2007). *Attachment-focused Family Therapy.* Norton and Company.

*Chapter 11* 191

Jernberg, A.M., Booth, P.B. (2001). *Theraplay: Helping Parents and Children Build Better Relationships Through Attachment-Based Play.* San Fransisco, USA,: Jossey Bass publishers.

Kittles, M., & Atkinson, C. (2009). The usefulness of motivational interviewing as a consultation and assessment tool for working with young people. *Pastoral Care in Education* 27(3), 241-254.

Law, D. (2013). *Goals and Goal Based Outcomes (GBOs). Some useful information.* London: CAMHS Press.

Linehan, M. (1993). *Skills Training Manual For Treatment of Borderline Personality Disorder.* New York Guilford Press.

Maslow, A. H. (1943). A theory of human motivation. *Psychological Review,* 50(4), 370-396.

McCambridge, J., & Strang, J. (2004). The efficacy of single-session motivational interviewing in reducing drug consumption and perceptions of drug-related risk and harm among young people: results from a multi-site cluster randomized trial. *Addiction,* 99((1)), 39-52.

McNamara, E. (2009) Motivational Interviewing with Children and Young People: Theory, Practice and Applications with Children and Young People positivebehaviormanagement.co.uk

Meltzer, M.,Gatward,R., Corbin,T., et al. (2003). The Mental Health of Young People Looked After by Local Authorities in England.TSO (The Stationery Office).

Miller, W. R., & Rollnick, S. (1991). Motivational interviewing: Preparing people to change addictive behavior. New York: Guilford Press.

Miller, W.R., & Rollnick, S. (2009) Ten things that Motivational Interviewing is Not Behavioural and Cognitive Psychotherapy, 2009, 37, 129-140.

Miller, W. R., & Yahne, C. E. (2003). Motivational interviewing in drug abuse services: A randomized trial. *Journal of Consulting and Clinical Psychology,* 71(4).

NSPCC. (2009). Young people who self-harm: implications for public health practitioners. Retrieved from www.nspcc.org.uk/Inform/research/briefings/ youngpeoplewhoselfharmpdf_wdf63294.pdf

Perry, B. D., & Pollard, R. (1998). Homeostasis, stress, trauma, and adaptation: A neurodevelopmental view of childhood trauma. *Child and Adolescent Psychiatric Clinics of North America,* 7(1), 33-51.

Prochaska, J.O., & DiClemente, C.C. (1982). Transtheoretical therapy: towards a more integrative model of change. Psychotherapy: *Theory Research and Practice,* 276-288.

Rubak, S. S. (2005). Motivational interviewing: a systematic review and meta-analysis. *The British journal of general practice: the journal of the Royal College of General Practitioners.,* 55, 305–312.

Stein, M. (2006). Research review: Young people leaving care. *Child and Family Social Work,* 11, 273-279.

Stotts, A. L., Schmitz, J. M., Rhoades, H. M.,& Grabowski, J. (2001). Motivational interviewing with cocaine-dependent patients: A pilot study. *Journal of Consulting and Clinical Psychology,* 69(5), 858-862.

Young Minds Foundation. (2012). Improving the mental health of 'Looked After Young People: an exploration of mental health stigma.

Ward, J. (1998). Substance Use Among Young People 'Looked After' by Social Services. *Drugs: Education, Prevention and Policy,* 257-267.

West, R. (2005). Time for a change: putting the transtheoretical (stage of change) model to rest. *Addiction,* 100 (8), 1036-1039

Wilson G. T.,& Schlam, T. R. (2004). The transtheoretical model and motivational interviewing in the treatment of eating and weight disorders.
[Review]. Clin. Psychol. Rev. 24, 361–378

# Section 4

# Integrating Motivational Interviewing and Therapeutic Interventions

194

# Chapter 12

# Motivational Interviewing and Cognitive Behavioural Therapy

## Garry Squires

### *University of Manchester*

Working with children, young people and adults in schools is a rewarding experience. Often a problem is presented and work is undertaken to help the other person change their thinking, emotional responses or behaviour. Therapeutic approaches such as cognitive behavioural therapy (CBT) have been found to be beneficial in this respect (Rait, Monsen, and Squires, 2010; Squires, 2001b, 2002; Squires and Caddick, 2012). This goes well when the other person wants to engage and is clear about the changes that they want to make. But what happens if they do not want to change? Or, if they are resistant to change? Or ambivalent about change? Or perhaps there is initial commitment to change only for the client to drop out of the intervention at a later point and return to their original behaviours and habitual unhelpful thinking. These scenarios have been cited as one of the reasons that a practitioner might turn to Motivational Interviewing (Miller and Rollnick, 1991, 2002) in order to improve client engagement (Atkinson, 2009; McNamara, 2009; Rollnick, Heather and Bell, 1992).

While both approaches are cognitive approaches and concerned with thinking, motivational interviewing and cognitive behavioural therapy are not the same and they have slightly different purposes. In this chapter, I want to explore how the two approaches are similar and how they might complement each other. I will draw upon the Transtheoretical Model of change (Prochaska and DiClemente, 1982). This model is still widely used in thinking about how to deal with ambivalence, however, there are critiques levelled at this model and distancing of some MI authors from the model e.g. Wilson and Schlam, (2004).

## Basic Counselling Skills Link MI and CBT

It is worth starting with an obvious similarity; MI and CBT both require one person (the therapist) to work with another or group of others (the clients). Both are seen as therapeutic approaches that involve talking in order to evoke change. Both approaches draw upon open ended questioning techniques to elicit reflective thinking in the client (such as Socratic questioning). However, MI differs from other therapeutic approaches in that there is no assumption that the other person wants to change. In CBT, the adult clients usually refer themselves and this effort suggests that they are already committed to making changes. This assumption cannot be held when using CBT with children who have been referred by teachers or parents.

An understanding of client centred counselling (Rogers, 1951) helps when developing cognitive based interventions and building a therapeutic relationship with the client in which there is mutual trust, mutual respect, good rapport, empathy shown towards the client and unconditional positive regard (see Figure 1). These are important features of the therapist client relationship that are common to many therapeutic approaches, including MI and CBT.

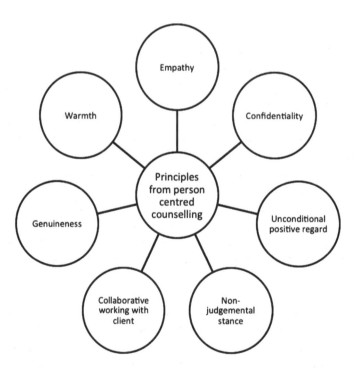

*Figure 1:* General Principles of Counselling (Adapted from Squires, 2002)

However, both MI and CBT might be considered to be less client-centred than Roger's approach in that they have a behavioural dimension and are target focussed with a high degree of therapist direction. Unlike person centred approaches, MI and CBT are not totally open ended or non-directive. There is business to be done,

*Chapter 12* 197

a pace to be set and a clear process to be followed. The therapist acts in a more active and directive role in which there is a clear structure to each session and the therapist sets the pace of the session.

The possibility of different viewpoints around the same set of issues is taken from a constructivist perspective. This acceptance of differing realities makes a non-judgemental approach easier with the client's viewpoint being as valid as that of the therapist. This leads to both MI and CBT taking an approach that is collaborative and in the spirit of Kelly's notion of working with the client as a 'co-scientist' to explore the client's construction of their experience and their lived reality (Dalton and Dunnett, 1992; Greig, 2007; Kelly, 1955; Overholser, 1993; Squires, 2002, 2006; Stallard, 2005).

Clearly, schools like all organisations have rules that may be congruous with the rules of the individual or not. Difficulties arise when individuals choose to disregard rules. But difficulties also arise when children misinterpret the rule or the situation, or do not have the personal resources that are required in order to comply. For example, the rule might be that fighting and acts of aggression are discouraged in the classroom. A child is teased by others, becomes angry and the only response that they know is to kick those who tease. Is the child doing the wrong thing, or is it that they just have limited options? If the view is that the child has limited options, then skills can be identified for the child to learn to increase the range of responses available to them.

By taking a different perspective, it might be considered that it is the organisation that might need to change in order to be more accommodating to the child - for example, by providing a differentiated response or exploring new ways of organising activities e.g. increasing supervision on the playground to reduce the opportunities for teasing, improving anti-bullying work across the curriculum. These can be achieved through consultation that takes into account adult perspectives and desire to change organisational structures and it could be argued that there is a role for either MI based consultation (Blom-Hoffman and Rose, 2007; Kittles & Atkinson, 2009) or CBT based consultation (Squires, 2010) in increasing the capacity of the organisation to accommodate the child.

In another situation, a child acts aggressively towards others when their feelings of frustration increase and they have difficulty managing their emotions and their behaviour. It could be perceived that in this situation, the child is kicking out because they lack self-control. Both MI and CBT may have the common goal of trying to help the child take more self-control (McNamara, 1992; Squires, 2001a, 2001b; Squires and Caddick, 2012), and this may be achieved through individual work or by making use of social support networks (Atkinson and Woods, 2003; Squires, 2008, 2010; Squires and Caddick, 2012).

The language used in describing MI and CBT techniques differs, often hiding similarities, though care must be taken in understanding the purpose of the

198                                    *Chapter 12*

technique in each approach. The tendency to overgeneralise is referred to as 'all or nothing' thinking in CBT and often is dealt with by exaggerating situations further. In MI two techniques do the same thing, these are 'overshooting', to make the client refine their estimate of occurrences, or 'undershooting', underplaying the comments made by the client to make them reflect on their true feelings with more intensity. More examples of MI techniques can be found in McNamara (1998, 2002). For example, when Alice told me that her teachers were, "on her back 24/7" (all or nothing thinking) this allowed me to play with this idea with her:

- "So, they telephone you in the middle of a Saturday night to have a go at you".

- "No! Not at weekends"

- "Okay", grinning, "so they call round at your house in the evening"

- "No… I mean just in school"

- "Oh, I see…. At lunchtime?"

- "No"

- "At break time?"

- "No"

- "Oh, so not 24/7? When then?"

- Pause and grin (realising that her thinking needs to be more specific). "Well, actually it is mainly my maths teacher and just in his lessons"

The realisation helped Alice appreciate that change was not needed in all parts of her life and that problems only existed in maths. This matched with school concerns about her acting aggressively towards the maths teacher and often being asked to leave the lesson. I will return to Alice later.

**MI Complements CBT**

There is a fundamental difference between the two approaches. CBT has a focus on the relationship between thoughts, feelings, bodily sensations and behaviours and clients underlying assumptions and core beliefs. There is an interaction between all of these with an inner voice mediating responses in feelings and behaviours. Faulty thinking is considered to underpin dysfunctional behaviour. The role of the therapist is to help the client restructure their cognitions and learn new skills to moderate emotional and behavioural responses so that these are more appropriate and functional (Beck and Emery, 1979; Beck, Emery and Greenberg, 1985; Beck, Freeman, and Associates, 1990; Beck, Rush, Shaw and Emery, 1979). CBT assumes that the client is ready for change and fully engaged in the process.

One of the difficulties of using CBT in schools is that the clients are usually pupils who are referred because of a problem identified by someone else, usually a teacher. The teacher believes that the child needs to change because they are challenging the school system. The child may not share this view and may not see the need to change. Equally, if the therapist or psychologist tries to work with the teacher to consider how the organisation may change in order to accommodate the child then they may be faced with a teacher who does not see the need to change. A degree of ambivalence exists in both scenarios. MI would focus on helping the client overcome their resistance or ambivalence to change. The transtheoretical model is useful to assess whether a client is ready for change to help those who are ambivalent increase their motivation for change. The goal of motivational interviewing has been described as allowing clients to explore the conflict between continuing as they are and changing their behaviour. It helps clients in expressing their reasons for their concerns and their arguments for change (Rollnick, et al., 1992).

The transtheoretical model of change (Prochaska and DiClemente, 1982) is presented here:

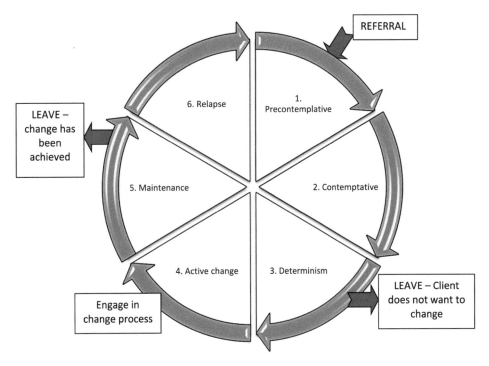

*Figure 2:* Prochaska and DiClemente's transtheoretical model

If the transtheoretical model is simply used as triage tool to screen who wants to change and who does not, then three outcomes are possible:

- Not ready for change – the agenda for change belongs to someone else: the teacher in the case of the child described above, the psychologist in the case of the teacher. The child might not see a problem with their behaviour (precontemplative stage) or may be determined to continue with their behaviour despite it being a problem for the teacher (determinism stage). In either case, change is not desired nor seen as being useful or appropriate. The psychologist might make the decision not to use CBT but to take a different approach or to deploy resources elsewhere to those who are ready to change.

- The client is ready for change and the agenda is owned by the client who sees the need for change. They are ready to engage in CBT and are determined to do so (determinism stage). The psychologist makes the decision to continue with CBT with the client to help them become active in making the change (stage 4) and setting up protocols to help maintain change (stage 5) and reduce the chances of relapse (prevent stage 6).

- The client is ambivalent. They see some reasons for change and may be weighing up the pros and cons and contemplating whether there is a need to change. There is no clear engagement with the change process at this stage. The psychologist might decide to monitor the situation and wait until the client is ready for change or until there is a clear picture that the client will not engage with further work.

An innovation on the model described above is the consideration of readiness to change existing on a continuum along which the client can move backwards as well as forwards (Rollnick, et al., 1992). The role of MI now becomes one of helping the client become ready for the therapeutic intervention that follows, while at the same time, reducing forces that would take the client further away from readiness.

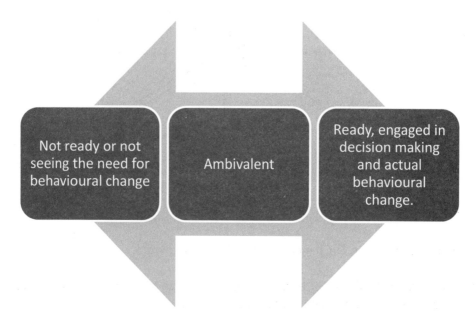

*Figure 3:* Readiness to change based on Rollnick et al, (1992)

*Chapter 12*

When used in this way, the transtheoretical model ceases to be a triage model and now allows those who are ambivalent to work with the psychologist to improve their readiness for change and prepare to undertake CBT. The 'wait and see' period is removed with a more active engagement in preparing and engaging the client.

An example from casework illustrates this further. An adolescent aged 14 was referred to me by his teachers because they were concerned about his aggressive responses to what seemed to them to be minor provocations by other pupils. For example, another child had simply looked in his direction and Jonathon swore at him and threatened to hit him; he was bumped into accidentally in the corridor and had to be restrained by a teacher when he pinned the other child against the wall. At this stage, Jonathon was being referred to me because someone else perceived his behaviour to be a problem. His behavioural response was dysfunctional for the school in which he was studying. There seemed to be a strong emotional response leading to the behaviour. CBT looked like it might have something to offer.

When I first met with Jonathon, he was not concerned at all. On the estate where he lived, any sign of weakness would lead to severe consequences for Jonathon – in that setting his behaviour was perfectly well adapted and functional. He was considered to be a tough individual by many of his peers. From his point of view there was no problem with his behaviour in school, it exactly matched what made him successful on the estate. If other pupils did not respect him then that made him angry and he would have to make sure that they did in the future; and, if the teachers could not understand his behaviour then it was their problem. Jonathon was at the pre-contemplative stage and not ready for change. We could have stopped at that point.

Instead, we met again with the aim of exploring alternative perspectives and seeing whether we could draw up lists of pros and cons for his behaviour and alternative ways of responding. A curious and non-judgemental approach was taken to explore ways that Jonathon could be relating to peers. Socratic questioning was used to consider a typical day and the good and bad things that happened (MI technique). We also used a recent event analysis (CBT technique) of an incident reported by teachers to discuss this by taking the role of different people (Jonathon, peers, teachers). This allowed information to be provided about the school's system of sanctions and the increasing likelihood of permanent exclusion (educative function). We considered his hopes for the future which included to succeed in education and to get a good job. This was used to encourage reflection by considering the pros and cons of continuing in the same school, having a managed move to another school, changing the way that he behaved in school, and maintaining the way that he behaved outside of school. A re-evaluation of whether or not Jonathon shared teacher concerns about his behaviour and then a decision about whether or not he wanted to work with me to explore how he might change and what he might change. Typical questions that helped at this point were, "OK, having thought about all of that, where does this leave you now?" and, "Do you want to meet again so that we can explore what you are going to do now?"

202                                    *Chapter 12*

It is tempting at this point to think that Jonathon has moved to the determinist stage, however, the work has only led him from pre-contemplative to contemplative. Two further sessions were held with him. These included homework tasks - in CBT a homework task acts as an extended therapy and can be used to help people become more aware of thoughts, feelings or behaviour or to practice skills. Jonathon's homework tasks were focused on helping him continue to weigh up the pros and cons of his current behaviour and to think about whether he wanted to change, and what he wanted to change. Diaries were prepared to get him to be reflective about the behaviours that got him into trouble with teachers - what was happening, what he thought, what he did, what he wished he had done. These were then used in further discussion with a teaching element that explained the link between thoughts, feelings and behaviours (CBT techniques).

**Improved Outcomes from Combined Approaches**

Several authors have discussed how MI can be combined with other therapeutic approaches and some have more strongly argued that MI works best when it is combined with other therapeutic approaches (Hettema, Steele and Miller, 2005). This leads to different considerations of how MI and CBT can be used together:

- Approaches such as Solution Focussed Approaches, Personal Construct Psychology and CBT can be mapped onto the transtheoretical model and the techniques used in those approaches can be linked to principle stages of the transtheoretical model, e.g. using solution focussed approaches to ask a client to scale a problem during the contemplation phase; identifying strategies to prevent relapse (Atkinson and Amesu, 2007; Atkinson and Woods, 2003). In this approach the transtheoretical model is central to the intervention and the other therapeutic strategies and techniques are systematically used to support MI.

- Another integrated approach uses both MI and CBT together, drawing on each model when necessary. The structure and principles of MI are consistent with those in CBT, with similar techniques which can be used together to deal with ambivalence and resistance when these occur. In particular the emphasis on spoken language and Socratic questioning can cue the therapist's attention towards looking for this during the CBT sessions, even after commitment has been made by the client - acknowledging that the client can move away from a desire to change as easily as they can move towards it.

- MI can lead other approaches or be used to deal with issues that arise in the chosen therapeutic approach. This could see MI being used prior to CBT to strengthen the CBT processes:

  o When there is ambivalence about two courses of action e.g. 'continuing to behave in a challenging way to teachers to earn peer respect' and 'moderating emotional responses to peers so that

*Chapter 12*                                                            *203*

behaviour is less challenging to teachers', then MI can help resolve the ambivalence and prepare the client for CBT (Britton, Patrick, Wenzel, and Williams, 2011; Burke, 2011; Bux and Irwin, 2006)

o   Promoting self-efficacy and agency in shaping behaviour enabling the client to take responsibility for change (Britton, et al., 2011; Bux and Irwin, 2006)

o   Reducing high rates of attrition and drop out (Burke, 2011; Geller and Dunn, 2011)

o   Improved skill building and client compliance to homework tasks is reported in some studies (Geller & Dunn, 2011; Heapy, Stroud, Higgins and Sellinger, 2006; Kertes, Westra, Angus and Marcus, 2011) but not in others (Westra, 2011)

o   Improving client perceptions of collaboration between the therapist and the client (Kertes, et al., 2011)

o   Improved treatment outcomes when combined approaches are used compared to CBT alone for obsessive-compulsive behaviours (Meyer et al., 2010) and anxiety disorders (Westra, 2011)

However, caution should be exercised when combining the two approaches since the underlying theories may lead to different decisions which may not always agree (Burke, 2011). Supposing that the client reaches the decision at the end of the contemplative stage not to engage any further, then an MI therapist would go with that decision. A CBT therapist would want to explore whether the thinking that led to the decision was based on rational thoughts or was evidence of dysfunctional thinking. When working with Alice (above), she had decided that her maths teacher was problematic to her and she was at the point of deciding that there was no need to change her behaviour. This seemed rational because her challenging response was adaptive in that she was excluded from the lessons and did not need to tolerate him picking on her. If MI practise had been followed then that would have been the end of the intervention, a conversation could have followed with school managers about adjusting her timetable so that she did not have this particular teacher. However, using CBT model to guide decision making led to the next step of checking out whether her thinking was in anyway distorted. Alice engaged with an experiment which she designed with a little help. She kept a tally of the number of times that her maths teacher picked on her and how many times he picked on other pupils. When she returned to the next session with me, she proudly presented her tally chart as evidence and cheerfully said, "Well he does pick on me.... But not as much as he picks on the other kids!" This instant cognitive restructuring, driven by evidence that Alice had collected, allowed her to see the teacher as acting in an equally harsh way towards all the pupils in the class. She no longer saw herself being treated unfairly and her reactance to his behaviour reduced. There was no need to change teachers and her engagement with the lesson improved.

## Conclusions

MI and CBT are complimentary cognitive approaches that both rely on a good therapeutic relationship and collaborative but fast paced, therapist led sessions. They are not the same and have different purposes but they do share common techniques e.g. Socratic questioning. The two approaches can be integrated to different levels: MI may lead CBT and help increase client readiness for change; CBT can be structured around the transtheoretical model so that different therapeutic sessions match the stages of change; CBT can be the main theoretical model with MI drawn upon to increase engagement, compliance with tasks and skill development and reduce attrition. A number of researchers and practitioners are reporting that when the two approaches are combined there is an improved outcome for clients than when either approach is used alone. Some tensions are inevitable in combining different models and this is true of any eclectic practice. The practitioner needs to ensure that they understand the principles and theoretical models associated with the intervention.

## References

Atkinson, C. (2009). MI in educational settings: Using MI with children and young people. In E. McNamara (Ed.), *Motivational Interviewing: Theory, Practice and Applications with Children and Young People* (pp. 59-72). Ainsdale: positivebehaviourmanagement.co .uk

Atkinson, C., & Amesu, M. (2007). Using Solution Focused Approaches in Motivational Interviewing with Young People. *Pastoral Care, June,* 31-37.

Atkinson, C., & Woods, K. (2003). Motivational Interviewing Strategies for Disaffected Secondary School Students: a case example. *Educational Psychology in Practice,* 19(1), 49-64.

Beck, A. T., & Emery, G. (1979). *Cognitive therapy of anxiety and phobic disorders.* Philadelphia: Center for Cognitive Therapy.

Beck, A. T., Emery, G., & Greenberg, R. (1985). *Anxiety Disorders and Phobias: A cognitive perspective.* New York: Basic Books Inc.

Beck, A. T., Freeman, E., & Associates. (1990). *Cognitive Therapy of Personality Disorders.* London: The Guilford Press.

Beck, A. T., Rush, A., Shaw, B., & Emery, G. (1979). *Cognitive Therapy of Depression.* New York: The Guilford Press.

Blom-Hoffman, J., & Rose, G. S. (2007). Applying Motivational Interviewing to School-Based Consultation: A Commentary on "Has Consultation Achieved its Primary Prevention Potential?", an article by Joseph E. Zins. *Journal of Educational & Psychological Consultation,* 17(2), 151-156.

Britton, P. C., Patrick, H., Wenzel, A., & Williams, G. C. (2011). Integrating motivational interviewing and self-determination theory with cognitive behavioral therapy to prevent suicide. *Cognitive and Behavioral Practice,* 18(1), 16-27.

Burke, B. L. (2011). What can motivational interviewing do for you? *Cognitive and Behavioral Practice,* 18(1), 74-81.

Bux, D. A., Jr., & Irwin, T. W. (2006). Combining Motivational Interviewing and Cognitive-Behavioral Skills Training for the Treatment of Crystal Methamphetamine Abuse/Dependence. *Journal of Gay & Lesbian Psychotherapy,* 10(3-4), 143-152.

Dalton, P., & Dunnett, G. (1992). *A Psychology for Living: Personal Construct Psychology for Professionals and Clients.* Chichester: John Wiley and Sons Ltd.

Geller, J., & Dunn, E. C. (2011). Integrating motivational interviewing and cognitive behavioral therapy in the treatment of eating disorders: Tailoring interventions to patient readiness for change. *Cognitive and Behavioral Practice,* 18(1), 5-15.

Greig, A. (2007). A framework for the delivery of cognitive behavioural therapy in the educational psychology context. *Educational and Child Psychology,* 24(1), 19-35.

Heapy, A. A., Stroud, M. W., Higgins, D. M., & Sellinger, J. J. (2006). Tailoring Cognitive-Behavioral Therapy for Chronic Pain: A Case Example. *Journal of Clinical Psychology,* 62(11), 1345-1354.

Hettema, J., Steele, J., & Miller, W. R. (2005). Motivational interviewing. *Annual Review of Clinical Psychology,* 1, 91-111.

Kelly, G. A. (1955). *The Psychology of Personal Constructs.* New York: Norton.

Kertes, A., Westra, H. A., Angus, L., & Marcus, M. (2011). The impact of motivational interviewing on client experiences of cognitive behavioral therapy for generalized anxiety disorder. *Cognitive and Behavioral Practice,* 18(1), 55-69.

Kittles, M., & Atkinson, C. (2009). The usefulness of motivational interviewing as a consultation and assessment tool for working with young people. *Pastoral Care in Education,* 27(3), 241-254.

McNamara, E. (1992). Motivational Interviewing: The gateway to pupil self-management. *Pastoral Care in Education,* 10(3), 22-78.

McNamara, E. (1998). *The Theory and Practice of Eliciting Pupil Motivation: Motivational Interviewing — a form teacher's manual and guide for students, parents, psychologists, health visitors and counsellors.* Ainsdale, Merseyside: positivebehaviourmanagement.co.uk

McNamara, E. (2009). The theory and practice of MI. In E. McNamara (Ed.), *Motivational Interviewing: Theory, Practice and Applications with Children and Young People* (pp. 3-42). Ainsdale: positivebehaviourmanagement.co.uk

Meyer, E., Shavitt, R. G., Leukefeld, C., Heldt, E., Souza, F. P., Knapp, P., et al. (2010). Adding motivational interviewing and thought mapping to cognitive-behavioral group therapy: Results from a randomized clinical trial. *Revista Brasileira de Psiquiatria,* 32(1), 20-29.

Miller, W. R., & Rollnick, S. (1991). *Motivational interviewing: Preparing people for change.* New York: Guilford Press.

Miller, W. R., & Rollnick, S. (2002). *Motivational interviewing: Preparing people for change* (2 ed.). New York: Guilford Press.

Overholser, J. C. (1993). Elements of the Socratic Method: 1. Systematic Questioning. *Psychotherapy: Theory, Research, Practice, Training,* 30(1), 67-74.

Prochaska, J. O., & DiClemente, C. C. (1982). *The Transtheoretical Approach: Crossing traditional boundaries of therapy.* Homewood: Dowe Jones/irwin.

Rait, S., Monsen, J. J., & Squires, G. (2010). Cognitive Behaviour Therapies and their Implications for Applied Educational Psychology Practice. *Educational Psychology in Practice,* 26, 105-122.

Rogers, C. (1951). *Client Centred Therapy: Its Current Practice, Implications and Theory.* Boston: Houghton Mifflin.

Rollnick, S., Heather, N., & Bell, A. (1992). Negotiating behaviour change in medical settings: the development of brief motivational interviewing. *Journal of Mental Health,* 1, 22-37.

Squires, G. (2001a). Thoughts, Feelings, Behaviour: Helping children understand themselves and take more control of their behaviour. *Special Children,* 134, 15-18.

Squires, G. (2001b). Using cognitive behavioural psychology with groups of pupils to improve self-control of behaviour. *Educational Psychology in Practice,* 17(4), 317-335.

Squires, G. (2002). *Changing Thinking and Feeling to Change Behaviour: Cognitive Interventions Ainsdale:* Positive Behaviour Management.

Squires, G. (2006). *Using CBT in Educational Settings.* Paper presented at the International School Psychology Association 28th Annual Colloquium. Retrieved from http://www.ispaweb.org/Colloquia/China/Squires.pdf

Squires, G. (2008). *Cognitive Behavioural Therapy: A model for understanding the link between thoughts, feelings and behaviour.* Paper presented at the Professional Development Opportunity Conference, "Therapeutic Interventions: Why? How? When? and by Whom?", Kingston Centre, Staffordshire.

Squires, G. (2010). Countering the argument that educational psychologists need specific training to use cognitive behavioural therapy. *Emotional and Behavioural Difficulties,* 4, 279-294.

Squires, G., & Caddick, K. (2012). Using group cognitive behavioural therapy interventions in school settings with pupils who have externalising behavioural difficulties: an unexpected result. *Emotional and Behavioural Difficulties,* 17(1), 22-45.

Stallard, P. (2005). *A Clinician's Guide to Think Good - Feel Good. Using CBT with children and young people.* Chichester: John Wiley and Sons Ltd.

Westra, H. A. (2011). Comparing the predictive capacity of observed in-session resistance to self-reported motivation in cognitive behavioral therapy. *Behaviour Research and Therapy,* 49(2), 106-113.

Wilson, G., & Schlam, T. R. (2004). The transtheoretical model and motivational interviewing in the treatment of eating and weight disorders. *Clinical Psychology Review,* 24(3), 361-378.

208                    Chapter 12

# Chapter 13

# Motivational interviewing, Choice Theory and the Freedom to Choose New Behaviours

## Geraldine Rowe

### *The Jubilee Academy Harrow*

Although Motivational Interviewing (MI) has become a recognised and useful approach for helping individuals who are resistant to change, it has been recognised that there is variability in outcomes both across and within studies (Miller and Rose, 2009). This variability suggests that there is a need for more analysis about the relationship between MI delivery and the resulting changes in the client's thinking and behaviour.

In this chapter, I introduce readers to William Glasser's Choice Theory (CT) and compare approaches based on CT with the use of MI. Both are useful and highly compatible approaches for understanding and tackling the concept of resistance to change. I intend to show how CT explains the underlying processes of MI on both relational and technical levels. Miller observes "after three decades of research...a testable theory of its mechanisms is emerging." However, he acknowledges that there may be "active ingredients" yet to be identified, that play an important role in the effective application of MI (Miller and Rose op. cit.).

It is my belief that CT provides a rationale to explain some of the underlying mechanisms by which MI assists individuals to make decisions about behaviour change. It also offers a holistic approach for helping clients to make decisions about behaviour change in a way that does not always require a focus on the "problem behaviour".

## The Importance of Identifying and Addressing Basic Needs.

In my experience as an Educational Psychologist specialising in behaviour and motivation, it is my observation that many individual behaviour plans (IBPs) are written without first clarifying what is causing the behaviour. In my opinion, much time is wasted on interventions that fail to identify the individual needs of the child. This results in a number of problems:

- The causes of the difficulty are not identified and so are not addressed;

- Teachers feel that they are failures and are more likely to direct the blame at the child and his or her family;

- The greater the number of interventions that fail, the more 'bad' or 'complex' the child is seen to be; and

- The child, teachers and parents get fed up with trying one plan after another and end up feeling helpless.

Marzano (2003 in Petty, 2006) highlights the need for educational professionals to have a good understanding of where behaviour is coming from if they are to respond effectively to the behaviour from students. This suggests that it is important to understand and reflect on the factors underlying the behaviour. Others refer to the importance of identifying and understanding the underlying causes of behaviour if plans are to be effective (House of Commons Education Select Committee, 2011; Institute of Education, 2011). This is summarised well by the following quote from the Department of Education:

> 'Research into the causes of disruptive behaviour tends to focus on 'characteristics' of individuals who display behaviour problems, such as SEN (Special Educational Needs), being in care, entering school after the usual entry time and low socio-economic status, but fail to look for the underlying mechanisms that operate in these individuals which would go some way to explaining their conduct difficulties.'
> (DfE, 2012)

## The Concept of Formulation.

The term 'formulation' is a term commonly used in Clinical Psychology (Johnstone and Dallos, 2006). A formulation is an attempt to identify the causes or contributing factors underlying an individual's behaviour. This is sometimes referred to as a 'case conceptualisation' in the medical professions. I value this concept of 'formulation' and it has been recognised as an important process in the design of effective interventions.

Needs-based theories of behaviour such as Choice Theory (Glasser, 1998) and Self-Determination Theory (SDT) (Deci and Ryan, 1987) explain human behaviour as a response to the the need for our basic psychological needs to be in balance, and contribute substantially to the identification of causes of the behaviour in question.

There is a grounding in the literature that a needs-based framework such as William Glasser's Choice Theory and the counselling approach that uses this framework, previously referred to as Reality Therapy, are appropriate and valid approaches for use by professionals whose role is to assist individuals in behaviour change (Litwick, 2007; Schwitzer and Rubin, 2012). The importance of teaching the ability to construct a formulation to psychiatrists and psychologists continues to be promoted in the professional journals of these professions (for example, HCPC, 2012; Mace and Binyon, 2005). In essence, people behave in a certain way for a variety of reasons and the formulation is the helper's attempt to find out the unique set of reasons behind this particular person's behaviour. It is no less important for teachers to identify underlying factors and the student needs behind behaviour in order for interventions to be successful (Institute of Education, 2011; McPhee and Craig, 2009; Sheridan and Elliott, 1991).

**Motivational Interviewing - why it cannot stand alone.**

Like all quality practitioners and researchers, Miller and Rollnick continue to develop and rethink the nature and practice of MI. Having felt uneasy about MI being described as a 'technique' they more recently described MI as 'a form of guiding to elicit and strengthen motivation for change' (Miller and Rollnick, 2009).

There are many things I value in MI, as a practising Educational Psychologist, and find that use of MI results in positive outcomes for the students I work with. However, the identified limitations of MI include the lack of conceptual refinement to explain why MI works, and a failure to analyse different types of motivation (Vansteenkiste and Sheldon, 2006). I believe that the integration of Choice Theory and MI can lead to a highly practical and theoretically sound approach.

**Choice Theory**

It has been said that "there is nothing more practical than a good theory" (Lewin, 1952). When it comes to a theory for helping people to feel empowered to choose new behaviours then Choice Theory is an excellent place to start, for reasons of simplicity and for its relatively jargon-free language.

I first came across William Glasser's Choice Theory from an Australian teacher working in one of the UK schools where I was working as an Educational Psychologist. During a conversation we were having about the psychology of school detention, she told me that in her previous school they had stopped using all forms of punishments and sanctions. By training all staff in Choice Theory they had managed to substantially reduce the frequency of disruption in their school to the extent that there was no longer a systemic discipline problem - although

## Chapter 13

there were still incidents of disruption. This school had previously experienced high levels of verbal and physical aggression and was in a neighbourhood where drive-by shootings were not unknown.

I next came across MI a couple of years later at a conference for Educational Psychologists and was struck by the many ways in which the two approaches resembled and complimented each other: both were born out of the analysis of what had been implicit models of practice for authors Miller (MI) and Glasser (CT).

Since that time, I have met William Glasser, qualified as a Basic Week Instructor in Choice Theory (CT) and Reality Therapy (RT - the counselling/coaching application of Choice Theory) and have used these approaches in my casework, team management, and in my work on school and staff development. I have met many inspiring professionals at international conferences who are developing successful applications of CT/RT in the fields of Health, Education, Addiction and Social Care and have visited a school in Slovenia where all staff are trained in Choice Theory.

CT places an emphasis on our genetically determined impulse to meet five basic needs: the first tenet of CT is that all behaviour is generated as a result of a process that continually compares our perception about how well these five needs are being met with a mental picture of our ideal world i.e. our wants which are stored in what Glasser refers to as our "Quality World" (QW). Glasser contends that an individual's behaviour is generated by a homeostasis system not unlike the system for regulating the individual's physical needs such as the need for sleep and hydration.

**The Five Needs of CT are:**

> **Love and Belonging -** the need to connect, care for, love and be loved
>
> **Power -** the need to feel significant, effective, valuable and competent
>
> **Freedom -** the need to have autonomy of thought and movement, freedom from pain and slavery and freedom to make choices about one's own life
>
> **Fun -** the need to enjoy, explore and learn
>
> **Survival -** the physical need for nutrition, warmth, sleep, dreaming, rest and health.

These five basic needs not only drive all behaviour but also influence the way in which an individual perceives the world.

*Chapter 13*     *213*

Practitioners applying Choice Theory in a student counselling, therapeutic or coaching situation first identify with the student which needs they are attempting to meet by their current behaviour. If these needs are ignored, and the focus becomes limited to the eradication of the 'unwanted behaviours' then there is a danger that new, equally unwelcome behaviours will be created in their place. This idea is similar to the concept of "symptom substitution" in psycho-analytical psychology.

One focus of MI is to 'enhance intrinsic motivation to change' (Miller and Rollnick, 2002). I have found that this is greatly assisted by first helping the student to identify which basic need(s) they are currently trying to meet through their current behaviour. For example, if a student is trying to meet their need for fun and enjoyment through their classroom antics and through MI you help them to find ambivalence between their wish to get good grades and their current clowning around, but fail to identify their unmet need, there is a danger that this need will re-emerge in another form.

**Total Behaviour**

Choice Theory describes our behaving as 'Total Behaviour' consisting of four elements:

- **Acting:** speech, movement, facial expression.

- **Thinking:** assumptions, thought habits, self-talk.

- **Feeling:** emotions and moods.

- **Physiology:** our biology/body chemistry and body's responses/reflexes.

At any one time, all these elements are active and are inter-dependent; when one of these changes the Total Behaviour (consisting of all four of the above) can also change.

It is not difficult to imagine that the Acting and Thinking aspects of our Total Behaviour are more under our direct control than the other two, with Acting being easier for most of us to control than Thinking.

When we change our actions, this often brings about change in our thoughts, feeling and physiology. In MI, the counsellor focuses on evoking and strengthening the client's own verbalised reasons for making a change in their behaviour. This "stating of reasons" is an Acting element of Total Behaviour, a change which, according to CT, automatically induce changes on the individual's Total Behaviour. That is, when the student chooses to act in a different way this brings about a change in their thoughts, emotions and physiology.

*214*                                         *Chapter 13*

*Example of using the Total Behaviour concept*

> GR: *I've heard that you have managed to get George to stay in class all this week, how did you manage that?*
>
> Teacher: *I just used some humour and asked George if he could try to act like he was happy and pretend that I was the best teacher in the world! We kept up the game for the rest of the day and he then kept it up himself. He then said that he felt better when he was putting more into it. I asked him what he was now saying to himself when he felt like leaving the room, and he said that he was thinking about what he could do to be more actively involved in the lesson.*

**Resistance to Change.**

In my experience, no-one is resistant to change but some people just don't like being told what to do. CT teaches us that when people perceive that they are being controlled by others, there is a natural inclination to "control back". This is especially true of those individuals who have a strong need for power and self-worth.

William Glasser, in his book Choice Theory (Glasser, 1998), builds on the observation that we are only in control of our own behaviour and that we cannot force others to change – which is also a central tenet of MI. All change has to come from within the individual. The influence that another person can have on us is increased if that person is in our QW.

Choice Theory explains how all our behaviour is caused when our brains perceive a discrepancy between what we want (QW pictures) and what we perceive we are getting.

Even when we understand clearly that we cannot control other people, we may continue to try to control them. When we do, we threaten the relationship. Glasser identifies seven behaviours that we commonly practice in an attempt to control others: He calls these the "Seven Deadly Habits that destroy relationships".

- Criticising
- Complaining
- Nagging
- Blaming
- Threatening
- Punishing
- Rewarding to control

When we start to employ these Deadly Habits, we begin a disconnecting process that may result in us being "thrown out" of the QW of the person we are trying to help.

*Chapter 13* 215

Practitioners of MI will be familiar with a similar list: Thomas Gordon's 12 Roadblocks to Change

1.  Ordering, commanding, directing.
2.  Warning, threatening.
3.  Moralizing, preaching, giving "shoulds" and "oughts".
4.  Advising, offering solutions or suggestions.
5.  Teaching, lecturing, giving logical arguments
6.  Judging, criticizing, disagreeing, blaming.
7.  Name-calling, stereotyping, labelling.
8.  Interpreting, analyzing, diagnosing.
9.  Praising, agreeing, giving positive evaluations.
10. Reassuring, sympathizing, consoling, supporting.
11. Questioning, probing, interrogating, cross-examining.
12. Withdrawing, distracting, being sarcastic, humouring, diverting

(Miller, W. and Rollnick, 2002:68):

It is not too difficult to see how, once an individual perceives that there is an intention to control, coerce or manipulate, any of the above could increase resistance.

In contrast to employing the Deadly Habits, when we employ the Seven Connecting Habits, we make it more likely that we will be perceived as a needs-satisfying person and secure our place in the other's QW. The Connecting Habits are:

- Encouraging
- Supporting
- Listening
- Caring
- Negotiating
- Trusting
- Befriending

The similarity between these Connecting Habits and of the "spirit of MI" is recognisable.

**Relationships**

Both MI and CT practitioners realise that relationships may either contribute to resistance to change if they are negative or reduce resistance to change if they are positive. When we say "The relationship is good" what does that mean psychologically?

216                              *Chapter 13*

In CT terms, we place a person in our QW if we feel good in their company or we either feel we have something in common or admire that person in some way. Once we have placed a person in our QW we will go to some trouble to please them and keep the relationship good or to emulate their lifestyle or habits. We are far less prepared to put a similar effort into doing things for people who are not in our QW.

If a person is in our QW, then we are likely to put effort into doing things for that person, as we have already recognised that person as someone who is need-satisfying. The person who is in the role of teacher, manager, counsellor or supervisor will have greater influence if they are in the individual's QW.

## The Quality World

The concept of 'the Quality World' is central to CT. From the time of birth we are continually creating an internal mental store of pictures of those people, experiences, things, beliefs and places that we perceive satisfy our basic needs. Research over the past couple of decades indicates that even experiences in the womb can have a recognisable impact on our future perceptions (Hepper, 1991). Glasser refers to this stored picture album as the Quality World; a kind of personal Shangri-la of the people, places, objects, values and activities that we would repeatedly experience if we had the chance.

Every Quality World (QW) picture represents one or more basic needs. Finding out what is in an individual's QW is the first step to understanding what is motivating their current behaviour and is an excellent guide to selecting the motivating features of any new plan for change.

The processes by which we come to place people, activities, places and so on in our QW or how we make the decision to take them out are unclear. What is certain is that the better we understand a person's QW, the better chance we have of helping them to meet their needs in a more satisfying and responsible way.

What I have discovered through using Choice Theory with previously-labelled 'reluctant students' is that they all have Quality World pictures, even if some lack detail and specificity. They can often say what they don't want, but need help to say what they do want. Once they have a clearer picture of what they want for and from themselves and others and start to understand their own basic needs, the path to change becomes more evident to them. Rather than having to accept the changes the teacher/psychologist/parent wants them to make, they see what they want for themselves and feel more in control of any process to make that change.

*Chapter 13* 217

*A conversation to explore a Student's QW*

> GR: *So tell me, Jake, where do you go when you are not in school?*
>
> J: *I usually go off on my bike as soon as I get home from school and stay out until it is time to eat*
>
> This indicates that Jake may be satisfying his needs for freedom and survival
>
> GR attempting to explore which needs he perceives are met by this activity: *Do you go on your own?*
>
> J: *I sometimes just cycle round to explore new places.* (meeting his needs for Freedom and Fun) *but sometimes I meet up with some mates over the Harlequin Centre and just hang out.* Meeting needs for Love and Belonging (meeting Friends) and Freedom ("hanging out" and not be directed by others).
>
> GR Exploring the need for Power/self-worth: *Is it important what kind of bike you have?*
>
> J: *Not really, I sometimes just borrow my brother's if mine isn't around.*
>
> Another boy might have said that his bike is really important to him as it is the latest design - indicating that the bike also meets his need for Power and Self-worth.

As this conversation developed I learned that Jake had a strong need for Freedom and Love/Belonging and a relatively low need for Power and Self-Worth. This was reflected in the difficulties he was having in school: poor attendance, low level of engagement in the curriculum and failure to follow teacher instruction.

Jake's relatively low level of need for Power and Self-Worth explained in part why previous attempts to encourage his engagement using arguments based around improved competency had not been successful.

I explained Choice Theory to Jake. He was interested in this interpretation of his behaviour and contributed other examples of his high need for freedom such as wanting to choose his own place to sit in class Then we made a plan.

The planning was led by Jake and focused on improving the relationship between Jake and key members of staff through "getting to know each other" sessions. Increasing the choices available to Jake met his need for Freedom whilst remaining in school. Jake and his teachers also discussed ways of helping him to feel more valued in school. For example, he was encouraged to contribute to a school newsletter article about safe cycle routes around the town.

Once Jake started to see school as a place where he felt he belonged, felt free and had more of a say about what he did, his attendance and engagement in lessons and wider school life improved.

*218*                              *Chapter 13*

## MI and the Quality World

As our Quality World contains all our perceived 'wants' it is important for MI practitioners to explore the Quality World of the client for a number of reasons. Firstly, to know what it is necessary to do in order to put oneself into the QW of the student, so that they perceive that when they are with you, they feel good about themselves – for without this, the counsellor, psychologist or teacher will have little influence with that student; secondly, to find out what the student is visualising as their preferred reality; thirdly, to question the student about their quality world, and identify which basic needs are represented by the 'pictures' in their QW. This sets the scene and provides the material for discussions to create the dissonance necessary to promote 'change talk' needed in MI.

## Using Knowledge about an Individual's QW to Inform a Plan

Desmond was 15 with many fixed term exclusions to his name and although he had little time left in school, his teachers wanted to make a final attempt to teach him to read - despite many failed attempts. Through exploring his QW it was concluded that Desmond had not only thrown reading and writing out of his quality world, but also teachers and teaching assistants as well. I felt that he would only learn to read if this was facilitated by a new person who did not remind him of previously rejected teachers.

We discussed the possibility of using a male volunteer from a local Rotary group or someone similar.

The following week I received a call from the school. They had recently advertised two Teaching Assistant posts and one of the successful applicants was Jeff, a retired police inspector. They had no hesitation in identifying him as the person to make a relationship with Desmond. For the first week, Jeff and Desmond spent time together getting to know each other. Jeff's brief was to let Desmond see that they had some things in common (they discovered that they had a joint interest in power tools), have some fun together and help Desmond to feel that when he was with Jeff he was free to make his own choices and free from threats and coercion.

Quite soon Jeff was able to engage Desmond in reading and writing, because Desmond wanted to do things with Jeff now that he had placed Jeff in his QW. As with MI, Jeff had to take care to avoid engaging in any of the Disconnecting Behaviours that had previously been experienced by Desmond from other staff, who were trying to encourage Desmond to do things he didn't want to do i.e. reading and writing.

The 12 Roadblocks to change (Gordon, 1970) that may unintentionally increase resistance, such as criticising, praise, advising, giving solutions, etc. and which are avoided in MI are also avoided in CT/RT approaches. CT explains why these

*Chapter 13* 219

'roadblocks' strengthen resistance: in an individual who is seriously failing to meet their need for Power and Self-worth, the slightest perception that another person is trying to manipulate or control them will lead to that person being pushed out of the student's Quality World, and along with it, any influence they might otherwise have had with that student. For CT practitioners, the MI notion of 'rolling with resistance' is a very useful one, and describes that stage where the 'helper' is maintaining their place in the student's QW whilst helping them to reflect on the discrepancy between the pictures in their QW (what they want) and their Total Behaviour (what they are doing, thinking, feeling and experiencing physiologically).

There are techniques in Reality Therapy (counselling with CT) that can be used to help an individual to be more aware of their QW and their perceptions, and to encourage them to question and evaluate their current perceptions about a situation. In this way, they are freed up to put new pictures into their QW and experience their environment in a new way.

These techniques overlap with MI strategies of eliciting concern (often by generating information) which in turn contribute to cognitive dissonance.

*An example of how a parent used CT to help her son perceive French lessons in a new way.*

> James had been saying how much he hates French lessons and how he is no good at French. I asked whether anyone in the class enjoyed French and how he knew this. What did these students do in lessons? He said that they asked lots of questions, got down to writing quickly and put their hands up when the teacher asked questions or volunteered to have a go at new things. I suggested that James try out some of these things to see what it felt like. A couple of weeks later he was talking about a French lesson in quite an animated way and had started to do and feel much better. He is even starting to talk about having a French pen friend.

The information generated, as in MI, included observations of the actions of other students. As a result of her son changing what he did (Acting), his Thinking and Feelings about French lessons also changed. It may also be that his physiology was also changed in that the release of endorphins and other feel-good chemicals were a likely contribution to higher levels of successful engagement.

By asking the question about the other students in the class, the helper is inviting the student to create some dissonance of his own, in MI terms, by describing the behaviour of the other students. In CT terms, the helper is suggesting that some other students have French in their QWs and by inviting the student to explore these other students' behaviours, he might perceive French differently.

## The Technical Aspects of Behaviour Change in CT and MI

Both MI and CT recognises that it is the personal choice of students to change their behaviour. Although there is a 'paucity of work examining underlying causal

## Chapter 13

mechanisms' of MI (Moyers, Miller and Hendrickson, 2005), both the therapeutic relationship and the eliciting and reinforcement of client change language are hypothesised causal mechanisms for the effectiveness of MI (Moyers op cit).

William Glasser devised Choice Theory as a way to explain the changes in behaviour made by his clients in psychiatric and educational settings. He found inspiration in William Powers' Perceptual Control Theory, which explained that humans behave not to change the world, but to change their perception of the world. The mechanisms of CT consist of changes in perception that come about either when new behaviours are tried out, or when existing perceptions are exposed and explored. Behaviour change comes about as a result of helping the student to identify their unmet needs and to find new and satisfying ways of meeting these needs.

### W.D.E.P. Questions.

A colleague of Glasser's (Wubbolding, 1991, 1992) has formulated the WDEP system, with each letter representing a cluster of skills and techniques for helping clients to take better control of their own lives and thereby fulfil their needs in ways satisfying to them and to society.

> **W**ant - Ask clients what they want - Explore their QW
>
> **D**oing - Ask clients what they are doing and their overall direction - Explore Total Behaviour and increase their perceptions of what they are doing
>
> **E**valuation - Ask clients to conduct a self-evaluation - Is what you are doing helping or harming you? Getting you closer to what you want or farther away?
>
> **P**lan - Ask clients to make Plans to more effectively fulfill their needs.

*Example of a WDEP conversation.*

Cherrie is close to exclusion for her defiant behaviour and disruption of lessons.

---

GR: *So how has this week been? (Opening up possibilities for Cherrie to reflect on what she has been* **Doing (D)**

C: *I walked out of Geography and got another detention* **(D)**

GR: *I can't imagine you wanted yet another detention, so what did you hope you would get by walking out?* (Clarify her **Wants (W)** )

C: *I didn't like the way Miss J was talking to me, showing me no respect*

GR: *So you want her to treat you with respect?*

---

> C: *Yes, she thinks I'm a piece of rubbish.*
>
> GR: *So you'd like her to think more highly of you?* (Clarifying **Wants**)
>
> C: *Yes, I'm just as brainy as the rest of them but she doesn't give me a chance.*
>
> GR: *So what kind of student do you want teachers to see you as?*
>
> C: *Well they just need to give me a chance to show them that my ideas are as good as the others' and let me get on with the work instead of giving me c\*\*p all the time. They don't respect me and they don't respect my family.*
>
> GR: *So what kind of student would they think you are if you continue to walk out of your classes?* (Offer Cherrie the opportunity to **Evaluate (E)** whether what she is doing is getting her what she wants.
>
> C: *Well, they probably won't get the chance to see what I am able to do if I'm not in class.* **(E)**
>
> GR: *What might you do instead of walking out?* (Invitation to make a **Plan (P)** )
>
> C: *I could just look out of the window for a while and try to calm down* **(P)**.

By the end of this conversation, Cherrie had described many positive aspects of the QW picture of herself as a successful student who was respected by teachers. By enabling her to strengthen this image and bring the QW picture into clearer focus, I was then able to invite her to reflect on whether her Total Behaviour (walking out, her assumptions - telling herself that teachers had it in for her - and the concomitant emotions and physiology) was helping or harming her. What I found was the clearer the picture she made of herself as a successful and respected student, the more effort she wanted to put into achieving it.

Approaches using MI would have many similarities, such as reflections of conflict 'You'd like her to think more highly of you', but subtle differences such as replacing the expression of concern used in MI with questions to elicit self-evaluation from the student 'Well, they probably won't get the chance to see what I am able to do if I'm not in class'. What both MI and CT have in common, although using slightly different questioning and selective reflections, is that a state of dissonance is an important mechanism for change. What CT adds to this situation is that although there is dissonance between what the student wants (QW picture) and what they are doing (Total Behaviour) there is agreement that the behaviour has as its roots an unmet need, which is identified and worked with explicitly during the process, whereas in MI, no cause for the current behaviour is explored.

## Conclusions

Viewing Motivational Interviewing through a Choice Theory lens, we can see that the empathetic stance taken by MI practitioners works because that person becomes part of the student's Quality World.

Rather than seeing the student in MI terms as 'lacking motivation for change' CT sees the student as being motivated by one or more basic needs, which need to be identified and explored.

I believe that the added attention to a student's basic needs would enrich an MI approach, both in how these needs relate to the current and preferred behaviours and their usefulness in the therapeutic relationship.

In conclusion, I believe that Choice Theory and Motivational Interviewing are highly complimentary approaches that help the student to feel free to make changes in their behaviour. The addition of the explicit exploration of basic needs provides MI with a deeper level of discussion, and the framework of CT explains the mechanisms by which MI elicits change. In turn, MI enhances the skills and extends the vocabulary of change for the CT practitioner.

## References

Deci, E. L., & Ryan, R. M. (1987). The support of autonomy and the control of behavior. *Journal of personality and social psychology,* 53(6), 1024–37.

DfE. (2012). Pupil behaviour in schools in England. *Research Report DFE-RR218.*

Glasser, W. (1998). *Choice Theory: A New Psychology of Personal Freedom.* New York: HarperCollins Publishers.

Gordon, T. (1970). *Parental Effectiveness Training.* New York: Wyden.

HCPC. (2012). *Standards of Proficiency - Practitioner Psychologists.* London: Health and Care Professions Council.

Hepper, P. G. P. G. (1991). An examination of fetal learning before and after birth. *The Irish Journal of Psychology,* 12(2), 95–107.

House of Commons Education Select Committee. (2011). *Behaviour and discipline in schools.* London: The Stationery Office.

Institute of Education. (2011). Behaviour and Discipline in Schools: Memorandum submitted by the Institute of Education, University of London. Retrieved April 24, 2013, from http://www.publications.parliament.uk/pa/cm201011/cmselect/cmeduc/writev/behaviour/we28.htm

Johnstone, L., & Dallos, R. (Eds.). (2006). *Formulation in Psychology and Psychotherapy: Making Sense of People's Problems.* Hove: Routledge.

Lewin, K. (1952). *Field Theory in Social Science: selected theoretical papers by Kurt Lewin.* London: Tavistock.

Litwick, L. (2007). Basic Needs - A retrospective. *International Journal of Reality Therapy,* XXVI(2), 28–30.

Mace, C., & Binyon, S. (2005). Teaching Psychodynamic Formulation to Psychiatric Trainees: Part 1: Basics of formulation. *Advances in Psychiatric Treatment,* 11(6), 416–423.

Marzano, R. et al. (2003). *Classroom Management that Works.* Alexandria: ASCD.

McPhee, A., & Craig, F. (2009). *Disruptive behaviour within the classroom: an ecosystemic view of pupil behaviour.* University of Glasgow. Retrieved April 30, 2013, from https://dspace.gla.ac.uk/handle/1905/805

Miller, W. R., & Rollnick, S. (2002). *Motivational Interviewing: Preparing People for Change* (2nd ed.). The Guilford Press.

Miller, W. R., & Rollnick, S. (2009). Ten Things That Motivational Interviewing Is Not. *Behavioural and Cognitive Psychotherapy,* 37(2), 129–140.

Miller, W. R., & Rose, G. S. (2009). Toward a theory of motivational interviewing. *American Psychologist,* 64(6), 527–537.

Moyers, T. ., Miller, W. R., & Hendrickson, S. M. L. (2005). How Does Motivational Interviewing Work? Therapist Interpersonal Skill Predicts Clinet Involvement Within Motivational Interview Sessions. *Journal of Consulting and Clinical Psychology,* 73(4), 590–598.

Petty, G. (2006a). *Evidence Based Teaching.* Nelson Thornes.

Petty, G. (2006b). Evidence Based Teaching. *Geoff Petty.* Retrieved June 24, 2013, from http://geoffpetty.com/geoffs-books/evidence-based-teaching-ebt/

Schwitzer, A. M., & Rubin, L. C. (2012). *Diagnosis and Treatment Planning Skills for Mental Health Professionals A Popular Culture Casebook Approach.* London: SAGE Publications Ltd.

Sheridan, S. M., & Elliott, S. N. (1991). Behavioral Consultation as a Process for Linking the Assessment and Treatment of Social Skills Treatment of Social Skills. *Journal of Educational and Psychological Consultation,* 2(2), 151–173.

Vansteenkiste, M., & Sheldon, K. M. (2006). There's nothing more practical than a good theory: integrating motivational interviewing and self-determination theory. *The British journal of clinical psychology / the British Psychological Society,* 45(Pt 1), 63–82.

Wubbolding, R. (1991). *Understanding reality therapy.* New York: Harper Collins.

# Chapter 14

# Motivational Interviewing and Solution Focused Approaches

## Mawuli Amesu
### *Solution Focused Practitioner/Training Consultant*

Parents are often worried and concerned about their children's risk taking behaviours but often the child does not deem their action to be of concern - thus neither sharing their parents anxieties nor seeing the need to change. Some parents often feel responsible for not always being able to influence their children to make better choices.

MI is based on the premise that people are not always at a stage of readiness to change behaviours which are perceived by others to be problematic eg smoking, drinking, drug use.

Miller and Rollnick (1991) linked MI to the Transtheoretical Model of Change proposed by Prochaska and DiClemente (1982). The latter looked at over 200 psychotherapeutic interventions and identified a series of stages that people pass through when changing their behaviour. McNamara (1992) later adapted this model for evaluating pupil readiness to change within academic settings.

In the case of self referral to therapeutic counselling or working with families to resolve difficulties in their relationships, often an individual or the family will seek help and sometimes give their consent to the intervention. In these type of situations engagement can be straight forward as there is a willingness and readiness to address issues.

From my experience, a lot of other cases are not as straight forward. The fact that someone has a concern about a family member's behaviour or situation does not necessarily mean the person in question acknowledges or sees the situation in the same way.

226                                  *Chapter 14*

This is a point where a skilful mediator is needed to employ the joint approach of MI and SF (Solution Focused) as a valuable tool to use with the family - meeting them where they are and going on to nudge them through the process of change.

Lewis and Osborn (2004) have identified similarities between both the theory and practice of MI and Solution Focused Counselling (SFC) and called for them to be used together in therapeutic practice. SFC examines the individual's ability to make positive changes to his or her life by accessing and using their inner resources, strengths and skills. Solution Focused Brief Therapy (SFBT) was pioneered by de Shazer (1985) and has become a popular approach in therapeutic and educational settings.

Amesu (2004) reported that solution focused language and questioning is a useful tool which he has used to help children young people and their families to explore and problem solve behavioural/family relationship issues.

The approach has also been used to help to facilitate movement through the stages of change.

In the case study that follows I describe more fully issues that has been presented by a family at each of the stages of change and how I used different solution focused language at each of these stages – language which also had the collateral benefit of nudging family members from pre-contemplative to contemplative (by eliciting information and concern) and then from contemplative to a decision to change (by promoting feelings of self efficacy and an internal attribution belief).

David, aged 14 years was referred to me. His relationship with his parents Janet and James has broken down. David refused to adhere to family rules and expectations and his frustrated father wanted him to leave the family home and go into the care of the Local Authority.

Janet and James were tired of the constant arguments that invariably led to extreme verbal abuse from David. The arguments were usually caused by David constantly staying in bed and refusing to get up and go to school. David's attendance became so poor that his parents were issued a fine for David's non attendance. David also argued with his parents when he was confronted about playing endless computer games and not leaving his computer to do anything else except to eat. Sometimes David played on his computer on line with other young people till late hours - past midnight into the early hours of the morning. David had also developed the habit of not wanting to go out of the house to do anything and refusing to carry out basic house hold chores. David had given up all the sports activity that he used to engage in and said that he is at the age at which he can do what he wants and he can't understand why his parents can't just 'chill' about it and leave him alone!

The challenges the parents were having with David were impacting on their own relationship - for Janet and James were also arguing with each other about David.

*Chapter 14*     *227*

## Stage 1 – Precontemplation (not yet thinking about change)

Prochaska, Norcross and DiClemente (1994) observe that pre-contemplators usually have no intention of changing their behaviour and will typically deny there is a problem. In the case of children and young people there may be strong factors influencing their choice to maintain behaviour that is seen by others to be problematic.

With regard to David, he was the top scorer on a particular online game and had held this position longer than anyone else had. He wanted to maintain it as long as possible. He had also made friends on line; these seemed more interesting than those at school. He also said school has nothing to offer him and that he did not have anything to get up and go out for.

Janet and James' frustration was that David is an able pupil, very talented in art and design. Janet and James felt his talent was 'wasting away' due to spending so much time on the computer.

At this initial stage asking the young person to recognise how his behaviour is impacting on the rest of the family does not normally work. Phrases such as, *"Think about how your parents feel!"* or, *"Can't you see how this makes your parents angry?"* may actually be counter productive and increase resistance from the young person towards the adult facilitator attempting to develop a supportive relationship with them.

David was not thinking about making any change in his behaviour, nor did he feel that he needed to make any changes. He said that he was doing what he wanted to do. David was not motivated by money in any way, and therefore any discussion appealing to aspirations towards good school grades and earning power was not appealing and the loss of privileges was not a deterrent.

The only factor identified that could possibly nudge David into considering the possibility of change was that he wanted the arguments to stop: he felt that arguing with his parents constantly was 'stressing him out'

Useful strategies I used at this stage included:

*Asking for a third party perspective*

This involved getting David to explore how others that have concerns might see the situation. This line of questioning addresses the issue and makes the point without coming across as critical. It also helps to avoid direct confrontation and challenge to David's behaviour.

Asking the following questions provided useful information about how David saw the situation and about the views of others.

228                          *Chapter 14*

*Someone looking at your situation might say that the reason you find it hard to get up in the morning is because you go to bed really late. What would you say to someone who thought that way about you staying in bed?*

David responded *"They may have a point, may be that is true sometimes'*

I continued by asking David *"Someone looking at your decisions might say you don't seem to be aware of how it is affecting the rest of your family? Would that be right?"*

David said *'Well it's not my fault all the time, I know I argue sometimes but that is only when my dad keeps going on at me, I know he won't believe me but I don't like arguing with them - it does my head in'.*

If the young person or the family member is able to identify concerns expressed by others, further solution-focused questions can be used to establish what they might be able to do to make a difference. In this situation with David I proceeded with the following questions and got some responses from David which facilitated movement from the pre-contemplative to contemplative stage of the stages of Change Model.

Thus the nature of the solution focused questioning at the pre contemplative stage elicited more explicit information from David about his situation and a degree of concern about it.

Movement from the pre-contemplative to contemplative phase is facilitated by achieving these two objectives (McNamara, 1992)

The solution focused conversation with David was continued as follows.

Mawuli: *What one small thing could you do differently that would convince them you want the arguments to stop?*

David: *Go to bed on time when they ask me to I guess.*

Mawuli: *What time would that be and how would you make sure you remember to take yourself to bed? Especially when you are playing and enjoying your computer games?*

David: *I can go up about 11 pm, Maybe mum can remind me 30minutes before.*

Mum: *We've tried the reminding Mawuli but it didn't work because he starts to say just another 10 minutes and so on. I would prefer 10 pm for David to go up and start winding down and go to bed for 11 pm.*

David: *10pm? I'm not a kid?! Okay I will go up at 10.30pm and settle to bed by 11pm, and I'll set my alarm on my mobile phone to remind me when it's time to come off my computer.*

Mawuli: *Who would notice first when you manage to take yourself off to bed on time?*

*Chapter 14* 229

David: *I dunno! Me? My mum and dad I guess.*

Mawuli: *What would they notice?*

David: *Well, that I am not down here playing on the computer when I'm supposed to be in bed and not arguing or getting stressed out*

Mawuli: *What difference would that make?*

David: shrugging shoulder, *Get a bit more rest*

At this stage movement towards contemplation i.e. weighing up the pros and cons of change, can be seen.

*Scaling*

Another solution-focused approach that is useful at the Pre-contemplative stage of change is to ask young people or a family member to be explicit about their motivation to change using scaling questions. The example I used with David was

On a scale of 1-10, 1 is that you <u>don't want to do anything different</u> and 10 is *that* <u>you are willing to give what we've discussed a go,</u> *Where would you put yourself on the scale?*

David put himself on 6 on the scale, I followed this up by asking David what that 6 looks like. He indicated that it meant that he was willing to give it a go and he would go to bed at the agreed time and not argue about it with his parents.

If a person's response indicated that they did not wish to change their behaviour, the following scale could be used.

*On a scale of 1-10, how confident are you that your parent/other family members would share your view that there is no problem?*

A low response to this question might represent at least some acknowledgement that there is a problem. The facilitator might want to explore this further with the young person/family member, for example by asking:

*So how come you're a 3, not a 2 or a 1?*

The facilitator can also ask follow up questions to identify what might be different if they are able to go up one point on the scale the following week: for example;

*If we come back next week, and you put yourself on a 4 instead of a 3, what would have to happen between now and next week?*

230                                 *Chapter 14*

*What would it take for that to happen?*

*Can you remember a time you did that in the past?*

## Stage 2 - Contemplation (weighing up the pros and cons of change)

At this stage, people acknowledge that they have a problem but may not be prepared to do anything about it. Prochaska et al (1994) note that although contemplators may think seriously about solving a problem they may be a long way from actually making a commitment to action. Prochaska and DiClemente (1983) suggest that contemplators should be given the opportunity to explore their beliefs about the future while McNamara (1992) suggests that at this stage they are evaluating the pros and cons of changing.

Two useful strategies for a family or a young person who may be at this stage are i) identifying exceptions and ii) looking for a preferred future.

***Exceptions*** This is a helpful way of looking at times when the problem does not exist or when the problem still exists but the family coped or managed the difficulty better. It can be used once the family has identified that a behaviour or a situation might be problematic. It is also a helpful way to engage them in looking at past solutions rather than only concentrating on the problem.

I asked Janet and James to tell me about an exception regarding David, a time they can remember when some of the difficulties they've discussed did not happen or were of less concern i.e.

- Times when the problem does not happen
- Times when the problem happens less often
- Times when the problem bothers or restricts them less
- Times when the problem is more manageable - when they are able to cope better: for example, times they were getting on as a family rather than arguing.

Identifying exceptions promotes feelings of increased self efficacy (ability to cope) : this is one of the goals of motivational interviewing aimed at promoting movement from the contemplative stage to decision-making stage (McNamara 1992).

Using this approach can also help to identify times they find things difficult as a family and when they might need further support or strategies. It can also reveal situations in which they feel confident about managing family difficulties. This highlights their strengths and past successes, however infrequently they occurred.

James, David's father, said "getting on" has been on and off, and the only time he could remember the family "getting on" was when David offered to cook a meal with a recipe he has got from school'. James turned to Janet and asked *"Do you remember that?"*

Janet replied *"yes"* and added that they took the dog out for a long walk that day in the local woodlands.

At this point David joined in the conversation and recalled how the dog was sick in the car on the way to the woodlands. At this point all the family members started to humorously point out to each other the various comical experiences they've had with the dog. I allowed this to continue for a while and even encouraged it by asking more detailed questions about the experiences they were sharing.

### *Looking for a Preferred Future*

This set of questions focuses on how life might be different in the future. If the family is able to think that life might be preferable without the problem behaviour, the likelihood of change is increased.

This set of questions thus identifies the cons of change and consequently enhances the probability of a decision to change being made, i.e. facilitates the move to the next stage of the Stages of Change Model.

Example questions include:
- How was your life before this problem?
- Lets imagine that tomorrow turns out to be a good day, how would you know that it is going well?
- When the current difficulty is no longer an issue in your life, how will life be different for you?
- When you resist the temptation to go back to the previous behaviour what will you be doing instead?

    I asked the family, *"Lets imagine that tomorrow turns out to be a good day, and you were getting on as opposed to arguing, what would be different?"*.

    Janet responded very quickly, *"We will be sitting down as a family to have a meal like we used to, instead of David eating on his own in his room while playing on his computer: and, when we plan to go out as a family David would take an interest and come with us, not all the time but just once in a while....... and to go back to having family film nights together"*.

    James said *"We won't be arguing with David to get up and get ready for school"*.

    David said *"People won't be on my back all the time about things and just Chill"*.

I decided to close the session by giving the family a task to reflect some of the discussions.

232                                    *Chapter 14*

*Task 1* David to cook a meal for the family (David can chose the recipe).

I asked who would go to the supermarket with David to buy the required food. James volunteered. I also got the family to agree the details - such as who would set the table, who would help out in the kitchen, who would wash up after the meal and so on.

David agreed to do the cooking and his parents agreed on the jobs they would do to assist.

*Task 2* I also asked the family to 'Chill' on one evening of their choice before we meet again - by watching a film together. I also asked them to decide who would organise the film, drinks, munchies and so on.

*Deciding not to change*

After having weighed up the pros and cons of changing their behaviour, it is possible that a young person/family might appear to be making an informed choice to change nothing and carry on as before. In such instances a third party perspective may again be useful, for example:

*Someone looking at your situation may say that you want to keep this problem? What would you say to them?*

This situation did not apply to David at this stage so I moved on to the next stage with David.

## Stage 3 – Preparation (getting ready for change)

This stage was previously referred to as 'Determinism' (Prochaska and DiClemente, 1982; McNamara, 1992) and represents a time at which people choose to change their behaviour or carry on as before. However, after further research into the processes of behavioural change (Prochaska, et al, 1994; Prochaska and DiClemente, 1998) a stage of 'Preparation' was proposed, in which people get ready for making behavioural changes.

With regard to David, his parents wanted David to engage in the family sessions in the hope of achieving change with regard to i) spending less time on his computer and ii) going to bed early in order to get enough rest to get up for school. They also wanted David to interact with them as a family by taking part in family activities instead of isolating himself and immersing himself in computer games. I was able to support the family through careful listening to what was important to them and nudging them towards their own solution, which then led to the tasks I gave to them.

After the session I arranged to meet the family again a week later so that we could discuss how they got on with the task.

*Chapter 14* 233

## Stage 4 – Active Change (putting the decision into practice)

The action stage is the one at which people most overtly modify their behaviour. It is a busy period and one which requires commitment in terms of time and energy from both the young person, their family and the facilitator (Prochaska et al, 1994). Once a decision has been made to change behaviour, shared contracts and targets can be negotiated with the young person/family and jointly monitored - thus, allowing them to take increased responsibility for their own situation/ behaviour management. The solution focused approach can help establish what is helpful to the young person/family at this stage.

The facilitator can help the young person/family evaluate the process of change by asking solution based questions that help them to explain and evaluate any positive impact the change is having on their life. For example

*What is better since we last met?*

It was reported that David had cooked a meal for the family and that they really enjoyed it. The parents explained how David actually went out with Dad and got the ingredients for the meal., David said he hadn't wanted his father to help as it was slowing him down in the kitchen. Dad set the table and mum cleared and washed up after the meal.

The family also reported how they had a film night together in the week. Both David and James made it a point to inform me how Janet fell asleep and snored through the film - much to their annoyance.

*What difference does the changes you have made make to you and your family?*

Janet said that she has not been arguing with James at all about David (as they did previously) and felt that they have been less stressed. Janet added that things were not quite where they would like them to be as David only went to bed at the agreed time on three occasions since we last met.

David said he has not been as tired as he used to be because he has been to bed on time for at least three nights.

I followed a line of questioning below to elicit who did what to help.

Mawuli: *David, how did you manage on the three days to take yourself off the computer and go to bed on time?*

David: *I set the alarm on my phone one day and my mum reminded me on the other two days.*

*234*                     *Chapter 14*

Mawuli: *What is it that has helped you to follow through what we agreed: , for example, when you came off the computer and went to bed on time?*

David: *I just thought it was not worth the arguments and some of my mates were not online to play with anyway.*

Mawuli: *What about the other two days when you had to be reminded by your mum?*

David: *Well I just decided to turn it off.*

Janet interrupted and said: *yes, 10 minutes later.*

David: *But I still did go up.*

Mawuli: *How confident are you about keeping this up? On a scale of 1 – 10, 1 being not at all confident you can keep it up, 10 being you are confident you will do it.*

David: *about 6 or 7.*

Mawuli: *What makes it 6 or 7 and not 5,4,3,2,or 1?*

David: *Because I prefer it when we are not arguing and I don't like being nagged at.*

Mawuli: *What would be the first clues that would tell you things are beginning to slip back a bit?*

Janet: *When David keeps saying "just another 10 minutes" and it turns to 30 minutes - and then he has to be reminded again.*

David agreed to respond to just one reminder and he said that he would do his part and come off the computer and go to bed.

I agreed with the family that they would i) continue to eat together on at least one day of the week ii) have a video night and iii) go out for a walk with the dog as a family and that I would see them the following week.

## 5. Maintenance (actively maintaining change)

Prochaska et al (1994) note that, just as at every other stage, there are great challenges associated with the maintenance of behavioural change. The family acknowledged that although they made some positive changes as a family they agreed that they needed to continue to make a conscious effort to do things as a family that were fun and positive - not drift from the positive changes they had made.

*Chapter 14* 235

Supporting the young person/family by recognising their progress and achievements can reduce the likelihood of relapse.

Questions useful to elicit responses supportive of the behaviour change include the following.

- *What is better?*
- *What helped you as a family to achieve it?*
- *How did you manage it?*
- *How did you get through that time?*
- *So what did it take to do that?*
- *How confident are you about keeping this up?*

Confidence scaling helps the individuals to assess their own ability and efficacy to be able to continue making the positive change.

The following line of questioning further highlights the skills and strengths they may possess that they are not aware of and also help them to be mindful about possible 'blips' and how they may prepare to manage it well.

- *What does this tell you about yourself/family that you did not know before?*
- *What would be the first sign that will tell you things are beginning to slip back?*

When I met with the family one week later Janet and James reported their disappoint with David slipping back into refusing to come off his computer and going to bed late. Janet became quite upset and said that they had had a disappointing week and that she was not willing to have David just 'wasting his life away under her roof'. David responded by saying *"It's my life"* and walked out of the room.

## 6. Relapse (returning to previous behavior)

Most people, when trying to change their behaviour or resolve a personal conflict, will relapse at some point. However, providing that this is anticipated and ongoing support and encouragement is provided, this can be temporary with the individuals re-achieving the previous behaviour change and returning to maintaining the positive behaviour.

I left David for about 5 minutes and then went and sat with him. I said to David, *'You seem a bit fed up'*. David said he was just fed up of his parents pecking his head about what to do. *"I just wish they would get off my back"* he observed.

Mawuli asked: *What one small thing can you do so your parents can see you are making an effort and possibly get off your back?*

David replied *"I don't know"*.

Mawuli asked: *What about what we discussed earlier?*

He reminded David about some of the things that he (David) did quite well with over the past few weeks, such as setting his phone alarm to remind him to come off the computer at the agreed time and setting the alarm to get up on time for school.

David responded by saying that he had been doing it (setting his alarm) and it was just a couple of days that he had stayed on the computer much longer than agreed. David then went on to say that he would get back to keeping to the time agreed to come off the computer and go to bed on time. He also voiced the opinion that he felt that his mum over-reacted over the two days that he slipped up.

**Anticipating Possible Relapse**

Preparing an individual or a family for possible relapse and helping them to understand that change can be a "two steps forward, one step back" process, can be done at any stage.

If a plan for relapse is drawn up before difficulties arise, the family is likely to find it easier to get back on track.

Mawuli again checked with David as to what the things were that signal that the behaviour change was being lost.

David said *I guess when I lose my temper because of mum telling me to come off the computer. Sometimes I start swearing first, and that might be a sign to me.*

David got back on track and commenced a College the following September - he liked the practical aspect of the course he enrolled on. It was a multi-skill course. His intention was to move on to a building course the following term.

**Summary**

The examples above describe ways in which techniques from MI and SFBT approach can be combined to help children, young people and their families work through the process of change. All of the approaches described here can be used flexibly. The overall aim is to create an ethos based on the principles of MI and solution focused thinking in which the responsibility for change is left with the individuals. They are treated as the expert of their own situation. The facilitator works in a non judgemental way, demonstrating understanding and empathy with the young person and their family and helping them to reflect on 'where they are'. The Model of Stages of Change helps the facilitator select the right MI and SFA strategies for supporting the young person and their family, thus enabling them to explore, challenge and change their patterns of behaviour.

## References

Amesu, M. (2004) *'Solution Focused Approaches and Motivational Interviewing'*. Paper presented at the Association of Educational Psychologists Conference, Stratford-Upon-Avon, November 25.

De Shazer, S (1985) *Keys to solutions in brief therapy.* New York : W.W. Norton

Lewis, T. F. and Osborn, C. J. (2004) 'Solution-Focused Counseling and Motivational Interviewing: A Consideration of Confluence', *Journal of Counselling and Development,* 82 (1), pp 38-49.

McNamara, E. (1992) The Theory and Practice of Eliciting Pupil Motivation: Motivational Interviewing – *A Form Teacher's Manual and Guide for Students, Parents, Psychologists, Health Visitors and Counsellors.* Ainsdale, Merseyside: Positive Behaviour Management. positivebehaviourmanagement.co.uk

Miller, W. R. and Rollnick, S. (1991) *Motivational Interviewing: Preparing People to Change Addictive Behaviour.* New York: Guildford Press.

Miller, W. R. and Rollnick, S. (2002) *Motivational Interviewing: Preparing People for Change.* New York: Guildford Press

Prochaska, J. O. and DiClemente, C. C. (1982) 'Transtheoretical Therapy: Toward a More Integrative Model of Change', *Psychotherapy: Theory Research and Practice,* 19 (3) pp 276-288.

Prochaska, J. O. and DiClemente, C.C. (1983) 'Stages and Processes of Self-Change of Smoking: Toward and Integrative Model of Change,' *Journal of Consulting and Clinical Psychology,* 51, pp 390-395

Prochaska, J. O. and DiClemente, C. C. (1998) Comments, criteria and creating better models: In response to Davidson, in Miller, W. and Heather, N. (Eds) *Treating Addictive Behaviours,* 2nd edition. New York: Plenum Press.

Prochaska, J. O., Norcross, J. C. and DiClemente, C. C. (1994) *Changing for Good: A Revolutionary Six-Stage Program for Overcoming Bad Habits and Moving Your Life Positively Forward.* New York: Quill.

*238*                    *Chapter 14*

# Chapter 15

# Concluding Observations

## Dr Eddie McNamara
### *Independent Consulting Educational Psychologist*

These concluding observations are probably best set in the context of the history of MI. Miller engaged in an extensive conversation about his career and the development of MI in a paper titled 'A Conversation with William R. Miller' which appeared on the MINT website (Motivational Interviewing Network of Trainers). An abbreviated version of this conversation appeared in the journal *Addiction* (2009, vol. 104, pages 883 - 893). In this interview, given in 2008, Miller described the origins of Motivational Interviewing. In summary, this was essentially two fold.

Firstly, Miller modelled his counselling practice with psychologists who role played the part of clients presenting as "difficult cases". Miller reported that they would "stop me and ask" what are you *thinking* at this moment in the session?', 'You asked a question there. Why did you ask *that* question, because there are other things you could have asked?', 'You reflected what the client said. Why did you reflect instead of doing something else?' and 'Of all the things that could have (been) reflected, why did you reflect that?'.

Such questions required Miller to verbalise a set of decision rules that he had been using intuitively – rules that had to do predominantly with having the client make the arguments for change and which avoided himself being the person responsible to say "you have a problem and you need to do something about it". To these decisional rules that he had made explicit he gave the working title of "motivational interviewing" - although he was drawn to the possibility of using the term "motivational conversations".

Secondly, a little after this, Miller asked himself the question 'What if you were to build a therapy intentionally around FRAMES?

240                                  *Chapter 15*

Frames is an acronym for six things that often appeared effective in brief interventions.

- •        **F**eedback about their individual status on assessment variables
- •        **R**esponsibility for change
- •        **A**dvice (clear) to change
- •        A **M**enu of options for change
- •        **E**mpathy with regard to the client
- •        **S**upport for Self-Efficacy

In the same interview, Miller goes on to observe that "……… actually you get the most enduring effects of MI when it's added on to another active treatment". He postulated that this was so because MI and the active treatment were synergistic i.e. each potentiates the other.

His concluding observation was "It's (MI) fairly compatible with other things that practitioners do, so you don't have to be converted to motivational interviewing…… It's a tool that can be used in concert with whatever else you are doing".

This ease of integration of MI into most, if not all, therapeutic interventions probably accounts for its widespread integration with diverse therapeutic intervention models focusing upon ever diverse problems - reflected in the chapters of this publication.

This publication contain chapters describing the integration of MI with anxiety management, choice theory and solution focused approaches. These are but some of the approaches which have welcomed MI as an adjunct to increase their effectiveness. Publication deadlines precluded inclusion of chapters describing the integration of MRI with Emotional Freedom Techniques (DFT) and the integration of MRI with techniques addressing self-harming behaviours, adolescent obesity, learning problems/Aspergers Syndrome difficulties and addictive behaviours – which will be included in a future publication.

The widespread and are still increasing take-up of MI necessarily generates considerations of "competency to practice (MI)" - which Gary Squires addresses in chapter 1.

My own professional career development had its origins in the Radical Behaviourist movement of the 1960's and passed through Applied Behaviour Analysis onto Client Self-Management and thence to the Cognitive Behavioural Paradigm. This last listed intervention model is based on the assumption that intervention is a collaborative exercise between client and therapist. Therefore for the collaborative intervention 'to happen' requires that the client is motivated to engage in the exercise. When this is not the case MI has a self evident part to play – although as a cognitive behaviour practitioner one has to be cautious about declaring anything to be 'self-evident'.

*Chapter 15*                                                                                    *241*

There appear to exist a continuum of views on the matter of competency to practice MI.

One pole consists of those who believe that MI should only be practised by individuals 'accredited to practice'. The alternative pole consists of those who believe that most competent professionals can incorporate the ideas and strategies of MI into their professional activities without necessarily undergoing supervised training.

While supervised training/accreditation generally enhances the effectiveness with which MI is implemented – such requirements, in the author's opinion, are best considered desirable rather than essential.

Consider the parallel of diverse professionals and others e.g. parents, incorporating behavioural principles into work with children and young people.

Teachers often incorporate the "Rules, praise, ignore paradigm" into their professional practice and sometimes utilise token economy type strategies without following the accreditation requirements to be considered "accredited Behaviour Therapists". In like manner, many parent management programs are based on behavioural psychology – yet an accreditation requirement is not demanded on the part of the parents.

This 'liberal' view has the advantage of enhancing the likelihood of access to MI theory and practice for many individuals who would benefit – individuals who probably would not able to access accredited MI practitioners because of logistical, professional and supply/demand considerations.

Nonetheless, given the importance of evidence-based practice, Wood et al's chapter is a timely reminder that rigorous evaluations of MI practice, at least in UK educational settings, are few.

The relationship between the theory and practice of MI and the TTM has been and continues to be the subject of debate. Some have sought to 'disentangle' the TTM from MI and others question the validity of the TTM.

It is only a minority of the chapters of this publication that do not make reference to the utility of the TTM when engaged in motivational interviewing. Some of the chapters emphasise the increased effectiveness with which MI can be implemented within the TTM framework. Indeed Atkinson's work, see below, is testimony as to how the TTM can act as a catalyst to enhance the effectiveness with which MI can be used to help children and young people.

Atkinson's resource package for professionals working with children and young people (Atkinson, 2005) integrated the TTM with MI and reflects the compatibility of these two models – albeit the TTM is a *descriptive model* and MI a *working model* (McNamara, page 211, 2009). The more recently produced

242                                    *Chapter 15*

resource package (Atkinson, 2013) uses the TTM in conjunction with the 'Menu of Strategies', proposed by Rollnick, Heather and Bell (1992), as a brief motivational interviewing approach and was developed following feedback from practitioners about needing greater structure when using MI. It remains arguably the best defined protocol for MI. Like the TTM, the Menu of Strategies adds structure and direction to MI making it accessible to the non-specialist. Conversely the complexity of MI in the absence of a structure such as the TTM is likely to limit its use by school-based practitioners and other none specialist professionals. In my opinion attempts to 'roll back' the integration of the TTM and MI are akin to Canute attempting to reverse the incoming movement of the tide.

Some observers on the practice of MI also raise a concern that an undue emphasis may be placed on the *techniques* of MI as apposed to the *spirit* of MRI. With regard to this it is perhaps appropriate to quote from London (1964)

"However interesting, plausible and appealing theory may be, it is technique not theories that are actually used on people. Study of the effect of psychotherapy, therefore, is always the study of effectiveness of techniques."

Both the TTM and the Menu of Strategies allow practitioners the opportunity to develop techniques and approaches which can support young people in exploring and challenging their own patterns of behaviour - and be delivered in the spirit of MI.

What then is the current position regarding the "state of the nation" vis a vis motivational interviewing theory and practice?

The answer to this question, or at least an enlightened debate about this question, can be pursued in the context of Atkinson's recent observations, namely:

"The problem is that without a theoretical underpinning e.g. TTM, SDT, or even a framework e.g. FRAMES, Menu of Strategies, which have been previously proposed by Miller and Rollnick but which now appear to be obsolete, it is hard to account for the "direction of travel" of MI. For example, in the most recent edition of *Motivational interviewing* (Miller and Rollnick, 2012), it would be helpful to understand the theoretical or empirical rationale for replacing the MI principles with processes and adding another dimension to the spirit.

Increasingly, in my view, Miller and Rollnick (2012) are trying to position MI as a complex "craft" while in parallel newcomers to MI are implementing (McNamara, 2011) and achieving success (Strait et al., 2012) with little training when engaged in short term interventions". (Atkinson, 2014, personal communication).

*Chapter 15*                                                                    *243*

## References

Atkinson, C. (2005). Facilitating Change: Using Motivational Interviewing Techniques to help young people understand their behaviour (CD: Rom). Bath: Sodapop. Available at www.facilitatingchange.org.uk

Atkinson, C. (2013). Facilitating Change 2: Using Motivational Interviewing using the Menu of Strategies (CD: Rom). Bath: Sodapop.
Available at www.facilitatingchange.org.uk

London, P. (1964). The Modes and Morals of Psychotherapy, New York: Holt, Rinehart and Winston

McNamara, C. (2011). Can Motivational Interviewing Improve the Effort and Enthusiasm Levels of Year 7 Boys within the Classroom Environment? M Ed dissertation: University College Plymouth – St Mark & St John

McNamara, E. - Editor of - (2009) The Theory and Practice of Motivational Interviewing With Children and Young People. www.positivebehaviourmanagement.co.uk

Rollnick, S., Heather, N., & Bell, A. (1992) negotiating behaviour change in medical settings: the development of brief motivational interviewing. *Journal of Mental Health,* 1, 25 – 37.

Strait, G.G., Smith, B.H., McQuillin, S., Terry, J., Swan, S. & Malone, P.S. (2012) A Randomized trial of Motivational Interviewing to improve middle school students' academic performance. *Journal of Community Psychology,* 40(8), 1032 - 1039.

---

**An Invitation**

**A third publication is planned. If you are working with children, adolescents or young adults, either directly or indirectly, using MI/TTM and would like to contribute to this publication contact:**

**gmcnam7929@aol.com**

*244*                    *Chapter 15*